THE

STATES AND TERRITORIES

OF

THE GREAT WEST;

INCLUDING

OHIO, INDIANA, ILLINOIS, MISSOURI, MICHIGAN, WISCONSIN, IOWA, MINESOTA, KANSAS, AND NEBRASKA;

THEIR

GEOGRAPHY, HISTORY, ADVANTAGES, RESOURCES, AND PROSPECTS; COMPRISING THEIR LOCAL HISTORY, INSTITUTIONS, AND LAWS.

GIVING A

TABLE OF DISTANCES,

AND THE

MOST DIRECT ROUTES AND MODES OF CONVEYANCE; ALSO, POINTING OUT THE BEST DISTRICTS FOR AGRICULTURAL, COMMERCIAL, LUMBERING, AND MINING OPERATIONS.

WITH A MAP AND NUMEROUS ILLUSTRATIONS.

BY JACOB FERRIS.

NEW YORK AND AUBURN:
MILLER, ORTON, AND MULLIGAN.
BUFFALO: E. F. BEADLE.
1856.

C. E. FELTON,
STEREOTYPER,..........BUFFALO.

PUBLISHER'S ADVERTISEMENT.

No parallel can be found in the world's history to the progress and the prospects of the Great West. Within the memory of living men, it was, for the most, an unbroken wild the abode only of wild beasts, or of wilder men; and many of its most wealthy, prosperous, and inviting sections, scarcely twenty years since were untrodden by civilized feet. Now, in population, wealth, material progress, in the means of intercommunication, in liberal and permanent provision for the general and thorough education of its rising millions, she is without a rival. Her advancement, however, has but just begun. Her real greatness is yet in the future.

The West is the common center—the grand rallying ground of the world's emigrants—of its population, its labor, and its capital.

In view of what the West now is, and what each

year is demonstrating she must become, who can estimate her future population, resources, and greatness?

The history of a region so vast, so rich, and so rapidly advancing, is one of the most interesting that can anywhere be found. In the work here offered to the public, the effort has been to give the rise, progress, and present condition of the States and Territories of the Great West.

This book also supplies a great deficiency in our literature. Most other books upon the West are confined to some limited range of country, and are filled either with adventures across the plains and over the mountains, or with details of mere local interest. But this takes a comprehensive view of the WHOLE WEST. It describes the earlier emigrations to the West, and presents a vivid picture of the modes of traveling, and of the difficulties and dangers of the way; it takes a comprehensive survey of the vast water communications which connect the West with all other portions of the continent; it contains a reliable account of the first explorations of the Mississippi valley, compiled from the original manuscripts of the explorers themselves, affording information which has never before been placed in the hands of the general reader; it brings the general history of the West down to the present time; it gives a sketch of the local history of the Western States and Territories, including Kansas and Nebraska, together with such portions of their Constitutions and Laws as possess a general interest; it traces out the great thoroughfares by which the best regions for agriculture, commerce and mining may be reached, together with tables of distances; and gives an accurate account of the mines of Lake Superior. On the whole, it is a book to be read—interesting to the general reader, and valuable to the emigrant and traveler. It is written in a style at once sprightly and elegant; its details and its facts are often relieved by romantic incidents, and exciting and interesting adventures of Western Pioneer life.

The author possesses a rare experience of the West, having visited almost every part of it this side of the Rocky Mountains, to obtain a knowledge of the country, the progress of settlements, and the manners and customs of the people.

CONTENTS.

CHAPTER I.

CHAPTER II.

EARLY HISTORY OF THE WEST.

CHAPTER III.

EXPLORATION OF THE MISSISSIPPI.

CHAPTER IV.

THE GREAT LAKES.

CHAPTER V.

FRENCH SETTLEMENTS.

CHAPTER VI.

CHAPTER VII.

PONTIAC'S WAR.

CHAPTER VIII.

CONQUEST OF THE WEST BY THE UNITED STATES.

CHAPTER IX.

THE NORTHWESTERN TERRITORY.

CHAPTER X.

OHIO.

CHAPTER XI.

MICHIGAN.

CHAPTER XII.

INDIANA.

CHAPTER XIII.

ILLINOIS.

CHAPTER XIV.

WISCONSIN.

CHAPTER XV.

IOWA.

CHAPTER XVI.

MINESOTA TERRITORY.

CHAPTER XVII.

THE SUPERIOR COUNTRY.

CHAPTER XVIII.

KANSAS AND NEBRASKA.

CHAPTER XIX.

KANSAS.

CHAPTER XX.

TABLE OF DISTANCES,

EARLY EMIGRATION TO THE WEST.

STATES AND TERRITORIES

OF

THE GREAT WEST.

CHAPTER I.

Early emigration to the West — Motives of the emigrants — Their independence and perils — The "western fever" — The substantial settler — Conveniences for traveling fifty years ago — The open-hearted frontiersman — The solitudes of the forest — Modes of conveyance — The old-fashioned Jersey-wagon — The season for emigration — The preparation — The good-by start — Progress — The wayside meal — Incidents by the way — The buried treasure.

For more than half a century public attention has been directed toward the setting sun. At the beginning of that period, the West was regarded with mingled emotions of curiosity and dread. The contemplation of a magnificent, boundless wilderness, was well calculated to excite the most sluggish imagination. But to the daring and resolute pioneer, the mystery that hung over the endless woods was continually a temptation to explore the furthest regions concealed beneath their shade. There lay, undisturbed, the hunter's paradise, with every excitement necessary to savage life, from contact with wild beasts to warfare with human beings. Other motives, however, equally powerful, influenced men of widely different characters to resort to the western country. The criminal, flying from justice, made his escape into the woods. Those who disdained conformity to the usages of civil life, who abhorred the restraints of fashion, who aspired to entire independence of all control, sought, instinctively, beyond the borders of civilization, for the wild freedom of nature. Also, the victims of misfortune looked to the West, as a proper field for renewing the struggle of life. It opened before them like another creation—rugged, unorganized; but this was charming to them. The distribution of property would have to be begun over again, in their time. There could be no aristocracy of wealth or refinement in the woods. Abject poverty and heartless affluence could not meet together there for many years. The poor man, whose limited means were insufficient for the wants of a growing family, removed to the West; contented to endure its privations, and submit to its hardships; cheered by the certainty of securing a competence to his children. But a small capital might there be made speedily to accumulate into a fortune, without having to wait upon the slow processes of industry. The speculator, eager to become rich, willing to place everything at hazard, to whom the opportunities, in populous countries, for acquiring property, were unsatisfactory, or too few, hastened impatiently into the wilderness in search of water-power, and sites for future cities, delighting himself in the solitudes, with the prospect of public streets, whose lines were blazed trees.

And, at the close of the Revolution, many of the heroes of that war, having become impoverished, sought in the western plantations a restoration of their fortunes; carrying with them into the woods the patient endurance and discipline acquired in the army, and manifesting a most courageous diligence in subduing alike the wilderness and its savage inhabitants. Rocky New England, also, sent forth its hardy sons, inured to toil, laborious, calculating, frugal, and resolute, to plant in the new country the system of schools and churches that had been the blessing of their earlier days, and the pride of their fathers; rejoicing, moreover, to exchange the stubborn hill-sides, where they had been born, for the productive plains and fertile valleys of the West.

To the young man, energetic, hopeful, ambitious, the new country was a theater for noble aspirations. He could grow with its growth. Nothing seemed to be impossible to him there. He could mingle with the brave, and participate in the glory of their achievements. He could associate with the wise, and share their renown.

But another interesting class of men took part in the formation of the early settlements. The European emigrant might well avail himself of the opportunities presented to him by a new territory. He had heard the story of its fabulous advantages. Adventurous hunters, and soldiers returned from the Indian wars, had spoken of the marvels which their own eyes had seen. The men of the woods, seated at the hospitable firesides of the older states, and partaking of the good cheer of the long winter evenings, while the cider, and the apples, and the nuts were passing around, had recited to tingling ears the story of their long trails, and had stirred up afresh their smouldering camp-fires. The reports which had reached New York, New England, Pennsylvania, and Virginia, of the unexampled fertility of the West, of its early springs and lingering autumns, its forests of valuable timber, its sea-like lakes and majestic rivers, its prairies of waving grass, its abounding mineral wealth, had flown also across the Atlantic, and had awakened, universally, a desire to participate in the fortunes of so magnificent a country. But often the European emigrant was acted upon by sterner necessities. A political outcast, whose only crime consisted in his loving his native country too well, he looked for shelter to a foreign land. The interest with which he contemplated Republican institutions had strengthened his attachment to a government whose sway he had never felt, and whose flag he had never seen. The sturdy peasants of France and Germany, the mountaineers of Switzerland, the yeomanry of England, the patriotic Irishmen fleeing from unnatural oppression, found an asylum in the wilds of America.

It was to have been expected that, with these streams of population flowing in upon the West from unfailing sources, the center of political power in the Union would become removed beyond the Alleghanies. The founders of the Republic seem, indeed, to have contemplated the formation of states to the north-west of the river Ohio; and they made ample provision for the integrity of them. It may well be doubted, however, if any of the framers of the American system of government could have foreseen the splendors of that reality which has been unfolded before our eyes.

But the West had its perils as well as its advantages; and the settler had to brave the former, in order to the enjoyment of the latter. A homestead he could there have, at little expense beyond that of taking possession of the land, and reducing it into cultivation; but it would have to be obtained at the risks incident to a howling wilderness. The soil might be fertile; but it was covered over with dense forests. The exuberant vegetation of the prairies might furnish pastures for innumerable herds of buffalo; but the Indian war-paths intersected these prairies in all directions. Life in the wilderness, evidently, was one of rugged independence; free from officious neighbors, free from meddlesome impertinence of every sort;

free from the wholesome restraints, also, of established customs and laws. But such a life was clearly deficient in many things necessary to civilized man. It could furnish no security to person or property, beyond the exercise of mere brute force in self-defense. It could not surround itself with those genial influences of civilization which call into play the finer qualities of human nature. The school was wanting. The church was wanting. Society was wanting. The majority of those, however, who contemplated removing to the West, looked habitually on the brighter side of the picture. Visions of sunlit woods, of glittering streams and silvery lakes, of tables groaning with venison, of barns filled with grain, of days spent in wild, boisterous enjoyment, kept the mind feverish and impatient. If a dark shadow did occasionally flit over the view, it was but for a moment only, and then the reaction carried the mind to a still higher degree of excitement. This was the "Western fever," a disease that has carried many a one off—West. But the man of a cool head and clear judgment, not unmindful of the difficulties of the undertaking, could see his way opening gradually before him to solid and enduring results. Brawny arms and a muscular frame could contend successfully with the trees of the forest that had swayed to the winds for centuries. In skillful hands, the American ax is a masterly weapon of warfare upon wood. The burning to ashes of great slashings of timber and underbrush would prepare the ground as well for seed as it could be done with the plow. A bountiful harvest would allay all anxiety respecting a scarcity of provisions. Incessant toil, in a few years, would turn the hunting-grounds into farms. Orchards could be planted. Buildings could be erected. Each isolated house, in the new country, would be a point of attraction to future emigrants; it would soon become the center of a growing neighborhood; and a society would be steadily forming, which, for a time, at least, would remain free from those odious contrasts which deform and corrupt more populous communities.

Such was the prospect which was pleasing to the substantial settler. But it is human to magnify anticipated results, and to diminish anticipated obstacles. The most difficult thing in this world is, to forecast so wisely that our calculations shall correspond to the rigid severity of experience. Before a single blow could be struck in the wilderness, before a place could be selected where to put up a temporary cabin, a long and dangerous journey had to be accomplished. And traveling, fifty years ago, to any considerable distance, was not an affair of trifling moment. The era of steamboats and railroads had not then dawned on the world. The canal which connects the Hudson River with the lakes, existed only as a dream in the mind of an enthusiastic statesman. The highways leading westward were little more than wheel-ruts cut deep in the soil. Bridges were rarely seen. The struggling teams were plunged into the waters at the fording-places. On approaching the remote frontier, the traces of a road had become more and more faint and indistinct; a little further on, the road itself had dwindled into a horse-path, then a blind trail, and then, as a facetious traveler has said, "it turned into a squirrel track, and ran up a tree."

New roadways and wagon-tracks are thrust forward by civilization, in advance of its great, general movements. When, therefore, the emigrant had passed all those, he had got beyond the border — he had come into the midst of the great western woods. And there the difficulties of the way began to thicken around him. His perilous journey was but just beginning. For, although he may have been traveling for weeks, since he had left the eastern shore of Virginia, or the river counties of New York, or the hills of New England, his course thus far had taken him along the line of the settlements, where he had been sure of a cordial reception at every farm-house. The inhabitants of a country which has been brought recently into occupation, dwelling far apart from each other, are keenly alive to every opportunity for social intercourse. They live with an open door to strangers. The choicest fare is brought out, the best accommodations made ready which the house affords, to promote the traveler's comfort, so long as he shall choose to remain with them. The stranger is always welcome. The settler feels a manly pride in extending to all a free invitation to take shelter beneath his roof. To pass him by without so much as halting, or apologizing for such an apparent slight, is looked upon as an exceedingly shabby proceeding. It is contrary to all his notions of propriety. Instances have occurred of grave offense being given, by refusing to stop to dinner, or to stay all night with the rude, open-hearted frontiersman; who, actuated by a generous instinct, acknowledges that all new-comers have claims upon him, which he is anxious to make good; and who feels that he, in his turn, has demands upon them, for conversation, for news from down-country, for friction of mind upon mind, which they ought to satisfy. Indeed, a capital story is received as lawful tender for victuals and lodging, eyerywhere along the border.

The unstinted hospitality of the settlers scattered along the ways leading toward the West greatly facilitated the progress of emigration, by softening its hardships and lessening its expenses. But between the settlements lay wide reaches of forest, and, further on, the unbroken wilderness. When, therefore, the emigrant had pressed forward beyond the established dwelling-places of men, his journey began to assume an entirely different character. Cultivated fields no longer opened before him, with the grateful assurance of plenty and welcome good cheer near at hand. No longer the smoke curled upward invitingly from the house by the roadside. Surrounded now by the grand old forms of nature, the emigrant felt isolated, cut off from all human associations. In the midst of savage sights and savage sounds, he was moving onward through perpetual shade. His present situation would be apt to make the stoutest heart feel its weakness and dependence. Alone in the wilderness, the trees must be his companions by day and his shelter by night. The woods were before him, the woods were round about him. They interposed their huge trunks between him and the world. They lifted on high their umbrageous tops, and shut out the heavens. Many have turned back from their awful presence. But the solitude of the forest was far from being repulsive; it was simply overpowering. Its terrors were softened by many peculiar beauties. There was the witchery of its swinging shadows. There was the sunshine glancing from innumerable leaves. And on every hand, opening down into the distant gloom, were long avenues of trees, arched over with waving branches and foliage, through which the struggling light penetrated below, and danced to the music of the winds. At night, the stars hung out upon the tree-tops. If no human voice was responsive to the emigrant's voice, yet the birds, morning and evening, poured their songs into his ear. And in the repose of midday, and in the silence of night, all was not hushed; for the very stillness of the woods was audible. The trees were continually sighing and moaning in the breathing air. But when storms swept down upon them, they writhed, and shrieked, and clashed their rude arms, and roared upon a thousand trumpets.

Day after day, amid scenes of solitary grandeur, the emigrant had to grope about in the woods with no other guides than the sun and stars, the courses of the hills and streams, hewing for himself a passage through interminable windfalls of timber, winding around swamps, rafting over rivers—toward that distant point where he was hoping to be able to ascertain and secure his claim. In this present age of rapid and easy transition from place to place, it is difficult to form a just conception of the length, the tediousness, the hardships of those earlier emigrations to the West.

When men, alone, undertook to penetrate into the depths of the wilderness, they usually went forward on horseback, or on foot, as was best suited to their circumstances or convenience. Quite frequently, however, a whole family was to be removed at once, together with the household goods, farming implements, tools, and cattle. It must have required great resolution to break up the old attachments which bind men to the places of their birth. It must have required an heroic courage to do this for the purpose of seeking a new home, not only among strangers, but among wild beasts and savages. But the fathers and mothers, fifty years ago, seem to have possessed a spirit which rose above the perils of their times. They went forward, unhesitatingly, in their long and toilsome journeys westward, driving their slow-footed oxen and lumbering-wagons hundreds of miles over ground where no road was, through woods infested with bears, and wolves, and panthers, and warlike tribes of Indians, settling in the midst of those dangerous enemies, and conquering them all.

After it had been decided upon to remove with the family to the West, a mode of conveyance had to be provided, suited to the feebleness of women and children, and to the carrying of supplies for man and beast. A few were so fortunately situated on the banks of rivers that they could float down with the current in flat-boats, while their cattle were being driven along the shore; or if it was necessary to ascend toward the head-waters of a river, they could work their way up stream with setting-poles. But very many of the emigrants traveled wholly with teams. Some of those who went part of the way in boats had to begin or end their journeys on wagons. The vehicles which they provided on such occasions, for land-carriage, were curiosities of wheelcraft.

The old-fashioned Jersey-wagon has long since given place to more showy and flexible vehicles. Before open buggies, or buggies with tops, had a being; before light farm-wagons or democrat market-wagons were ever thought of; before the miscreant was born that invented those airy nothings, consisting of thills and wheels, on which fools ride astraddle, with a horse's tail switching between their legs — the old-fashioned Jersey-wagon was an established institution. It once rolled deep in the sands between the Delaware and the Hudson. It once rumbled among the mountains of Pennsylvania. It once toted corn and tobacco on the eastern shore of Virginia. It once toiled heavily up and down the Mohawk. Where is it now? It used to descend with the family name, from father to son, without injury and without repair. But it has mysteriously disappeared. The old-fashioned Jersey-wagon, its broad fellies heavily tired, its solid-running gearing, its liberal allowance of tongue, its high end-boards and curving side-boards, ribbed, and barred, and riveted, glaring in red paint, was not gotten up for show.

It made no pretensions to beauty. It was altogether a substantial piece of work. What has become of the old-fashioned Jersey-wagon, with the four horses sweating along before it, the driver on the near wheel-horse, twitching at a single rein? The old-fashioned Jersey-wagon was the great original of the emigrant wagon of the West.

The spring of the year was the season usually selected for moving. Much preparation had to be made before entering upon a journey which would require months for its completion. During many weeks previous to the appointed time, the emigrant had been anxiously providing against the possible accidents and probable discomforts of the road. The wagon-box had been fitted up with flat, iron staples, about eighteen inches apart, along its sides, and in those had been placed, upright, ashen hoops, that stood some five feet above the bottom-boards, the forward hoops projecting considerably over the hounds, and the back ones over the end of the reach, which stuck out behind. Over this frame-work had been drawn a covering of canvas or cotton, puckered up a little around the edges in front, but drawn together, like a bag, behind, and tied with a string. Upon one side of the wagon-box had been fastened cleats, to secure the axes, spades, chisels, and augers; and on the other side, a rack, for pots, kettles, and pans. Beneath the hinder axletree, from a staple driven into the firm wood, swung the tar-bucket. Across the back end of the wagon-box, extending outward, its ends even with the wheels, was suspended the feeding-trough for the team, strongly secured in its place by iron straps. An extra log-chain had been coiled around the reach, underneath the wagon. The crowbar was flung into the feeding-trough.

Having made sale of his surplus goods at an old-fashioned vendue, where his neighbors had bought many articles as keepsakes; having had one more friendly gathering beneath his roof, to bid all good-by, the emigrant loaded his wagon, and was ready to start. Now, when the teams had been brought up, the women and children took their places on the chests, and boxes, and bundles of bedding. The little baby-girl sat on its mother's lap, sucking its thumb, wondering. The youngest boy crouched at his grandmother's feet; and he inquired of her, as soon as they were fairly out of the gate, if they were not most there now. Slowly trudged the oxen along with the huge, high, awkward, rattling load. The biggest boy walked alongside the team, the post of honor, driving. Now he would pat "Old Buck" affectionately on the neck, at which the patient brute would keep lolling out his tongue, and flapping his ears; then he would look round, and ask father some question, who walked thoughtfully midway between the wheels; or speak gently to mother, who could barely smile through her tears. The other boys drove the cows, and "Bose" jogged along under the feeding-trough, his nose just clear of the tar-bucket.

I do not intend to follow the emigrants throughout their long journeyings toward the West. Captivating as a tramp into the woods may seem to be to those who are living within the glare of brick walls, it is, in reality, a laborious, wearisome undertaking. Sweating through the brush, climbing over logs, slumping into marshes, tumbling over roots, in fair weather, is downright hard work, to say nothing of those nuisances, the musquitoes and gnats. There is poetry, it is true, in standing under trees during a shower, listening to the pattering drops, and seeing the leaves lift themselves up to drink the rain. But poetry was never intended to keep the skin dry. And the interest gives way to terror, when the trees, bending and swinging in the wind, knock off their branches overhead, or the lightning shivers down their huge trunks. The daily experiences of those who penetrate into the woods of a country fit to become the future abiding-place of men are, indeed, quite uniform. And the incidents, therefore, that befell the emigrants were characterized by a tedious sameness, which, after a while, began to blunt the senses, and weigh down upon the spirits. The most attractive scenery, if perpetually before the eyes, will lose its power to please, by losing its power to fix the attention. This effect was hastened by the constant recurrence of vexations, cares, and annoyances, which, although they did not strip from the road through the wilderness its grand and beautiful objects, indisposed the mind to the perception and enjoyment of them. When man is placed under unfavorable circumstances, deprived of those beneficent influences that flow from intelligence and refinement, he will assume an insensibility which makes him blind to the most beautiful creations, and his spiritual activity will become greatly irregular, flashing forth, on some sudden emergence, with terrific power, and then subsiding as quickly into habitual, uniform stolidity. Life, in proportion as it deteriorates from civilization toward the conditions of the savage state, may sometimes, indeed, be intensely pleasurable in its excitements; but it will have lost the elasticity of its spring, and be incapable of vibrating, except when some opposing force is hurled violently against it.

The emigrants, ere long, found that the wilderness had lost the charm of novelty. Sights and sounds that were at first pleasing, and had lessened the sense of discomfort, soon ceased to attract attention. Their minds, solely occupied with obstacles, inconveniences, and obstructions, at every step of the way, became sullen, or, at the least,

2

indifferent. For the first few days in the woods, they had had a wild satisfaction in the wayside meal, beneath the high, o'erarching canopy of foliage. "Buck" and "Bright," at the feeding-trough, were up to their eyes in bran and shorts. The cows straightened out their jaws in a line with their throats, and chewed awkwardly upon the hard nubbins of corn. The flames were crackling. The pork sputtered in the frying-pan. The children, among the wild violets, were playing at fighting roosters. With the wreathing smoke went up the grateful incense of tea. How they cracked jokes over their victuals, seated around on the carpet of leaves, and laughed, and shouted, and poked fun at each other. Altogether, it was a delightful picnic. But picnics, three times a day for a month or two, will become odious.

In this manner the earlier emigrants went forward. Driving before them their heavy teams and cattle by day, they slept around the camp-fire at night. There was little variety in the work that had to be done during the journey. Old, moss-covered logs, rotting on the ground, had to be cut away. Rude bridges had to be built over the creeks. Sometimes the wagons would sink to the hub in a slough-hole, and would have to be pried out; and then, the "haw"-ing, and "gee"-ing, and shouting, and the curses, rough enough to take the bark off the trees, would give full play to the lungs and throat. But when they had come to a deep river, they could resort only to the raft.

The casualties of life clustered thickly around the emigrants upon the road. They were exposed to great personal risks. An unlucky step might wrench an ankle. The ax might glance from a twig, and split a foot open. A broken leg, or a severed artery, is a frightful thing, where no surgeon can be had. Exposure to all the changes of the weather — sleeping upon the damp ground, frequently brought on fevers; and sickness is a great calamity, always, to the traveler. It must have been appalling in the woods. Many a mother has carried her wailing, languishing child in her arms, to lessen the jolting of the wagon, without being able to render it the necessary assistance. Many a family has paused on the way to gather a leafy couch for a dying brother or sister. Many a parent has laid in the grave, in the lonely wilderness, the child he shall meet no more till the morning of the resurrection; and then has gone on sorrowing. Many a heart, at the West, has yearned at the thought of the buried, treasured beneath the spreading tree. After-comers have stopped over the little mound, and pondered upon the rude memorial carved in the bark above it; and those who had sustained a similar loss, have wrung their hands and wept over it, for their own wounds were opened afresh.

But in spite of every obstacle, in the face of every consideration of personal ease and convenience, in defiance of every peril, known and unknown, the earlier emigrants pressed forward — the pioneers of civilization in the West. This view of their hardships, and difficulties, and sufferings, tends to show what a noble race of men they were. A heroism was displayed by them, as grand, as exalted, as that of an army marching and conquering through a hostile land. Among the benefactors of mankind, a place should be given to those who led the way in reducing a howling wilderness into a flourishing empire.

CHAPTER II.

EARLY HISTORY OF THE WEST.

Territory included in the Great West — Water-shed, or divide — The rivers and their tributaries — The fur-hunter's canoe-passage to the Gulf of Mexico — River system — Progress of the French missionaries, as early as 1632 — Nicolet — His influence over the Indians — The journey of his life — His reception at Green Bay — Council with the chiefs — Iroquois war — Its effects on the missions — The great river west of the lakes — Claude Allouez, the first explorer of Lake Michigan — Frozen in on Lake Michigan — Sailing on the ice in a canoe — Pitch Rock — Visit to the villages of the Illinois — M. Joliet and James Marquette, explorers of the Mississippi — Their birth, education, and character — Marquette among the missions — Visited by the Illinois Indians — Contemplates exploring the Mississippi alone — Is stationed at Michilimackinac — Arrival of Joliet with orders to explore the Mississippi — Prayers and thanksgiving for the favors conferred on them — Preparation and outfit — The Canadian canoe.

The region of country denominated the West has been constantly decreasing in extent of surface on the eastern side, although the land still lies just where it was fashioned by the hand of God. It once spread out from ocean to ocean. But it first began to recede when an opening was made in the woods at Plymouth and at Jamestown. Since then, the growth of population has steadily driven the wilderness before it, over the mountains, and beyond the great lakes. And the progress of civilization will continue to sweep away westward, narrowing the limits of wild beasts and Indians, until the sound of the woodman's ax shall mingle with the roar of the waves along the coast of the Pacific. But that time has not yet come. The West may still be found, without following the apocryphal directions of an old hunter, who said, that it was situated "about half a mile this side of sundown." The eastern slope of the Rocky Mountains descends, gradually, through a distance of five hundred miles, to the Mississippi River. That elevated table-land, channeled by rivers, dotted and belted with forests, its openings undulating as the sea, with the exceptions of Iowa, Missouri, Arkansas, and the settlements of Minesota, Nebraska, and Kansas, is the hunting-ground of savage tribes. And all around the southern shore of Lake Superior, and in the lower peninsula of Michigan north of the Grand River, in the north-western portions of Wisconsin, and the western part of Iowa, is the great wilderness of woods, still standing in the solitary magnificence of Nature. The West properly includes, also, the states of Illinois, Indiana, and Ohio.

There is not another region on the face of the earth, comparing with this in size, that is so abundantly supplied with running water. It is laced all over with a vast net-work of rivers. The streams, flowing toward all the points of the compass, converge, at last, and pour their accumulated floods far out into the gulfs of Mexico and St. Lawrence. Between the Alleghanies and the Rocky Mountains is an extensive water-shed, or divide, more than two thousand miles in length, which gives rise to three distinct river systems, of incalculable advantage to the West. Commencing in the county of Cattaraugus, in the state of New York, the general direction of this water-shed is south-west, through a part of Pennsylvania, and west, through Ohio and Indiana; thence passing up, in a north-westerly direction, through Illinois, within sixty miles of Chicago, through Wisconsin, and the north-eastern part of Minesota, it turns away westward. It consists of a ridge of land so slightly elevated that it can scarcely be perceived to be either ascending or descending. It separates the western waters, which flow into the Red River of the north, and into the St. Lawrence, and into the Mississippi. Through these great natural channels of water communication, the West may draw to itself the manufactures of the East, and the tropical productions of the South, and the furs of the North. Through them, also, it may send its inexhaustible supplies of grain, and beef, and pork, to all the world. And when a connection shall have been established between the Missouri and the Columbia rivers, it may hold commercial intercourse with the four quarters of the globe. Distinguished from all other water-sheds, which, like the Andes, the Pyrenées, and the Alps, are mountainous and uninhabitable, this is surpassingly fertile. Those seem to have been formed with a design to divide and separate nations; this, to bind a whole continent into one.

Far away, in the interior of North America, between the forty-sixth and the forty-seventh parallels of latitude, where they are intersected by the sixteenth degree of longitude, west from Washington, is a sandy plain, six miles wide, which alone separates the head-waters of the St. Lawrence from the waters of the Mississippi. And in the central portions of Minesota there are two streams of water, flowing within three miles of each other, through an open prairie,—the one, a branch of the St. Peter's running southward to the Gulf of Mexico; the other, a branch of the Red River of the north, emptying into Hudson's Bay.

The St. Lawrence, including also the great lakes—which are but vast expansions of its stream—is the most remarkable river of which we have any knowledge. Rising in the center of the great American plain, it runs east and north-east, through a fertile and beautiful country, for more than three thousand miles, to the Atlantic Ocean. Other rivers there are, which expand in picturesque basins, and which have been celebrated in story and in song. The Hudson has its lake at Saratoga, and its Tappan Zee; the Rhone has its Lake Geneva; the Oswego has its broader lakelets, Oneida, Owasco, Skeneateles, Cayuga, and Seneca. But the St. Lawrence spreads out into five principal seas, whose waves, roused up by tempests, dash and roar like the billows of the ocean; whose harbors, also, thronged with shipping, present their forests of masts in rivalry with seaport towns. It is worthy of notice, that the largest of those lakes, Huron, Superior, and Michigan, are placed furthest inland, as if to invite a display of commercial enterprise, on a grand scale, in the heart of the continent.

The Mississippi is not so long, following its main channel, as the St. Lawrence; but it takes hold on a much wider reach of country, by reason of its larger tributaries. Upon the eastern side, the Tennessee, rising in the mountains of North Carolina and Virginia, bends round through the states of Alabama, Tennessee, and Kentucky, and sends its branches down into Georgia and Mississippi. The Ohio comes flowing from Carolina and Virginia, from the confines of Maryland and New York, through Pennsylvania, and forms the boundary of five great states. From the north-east come the Wabash, Kaskaskia, Illinois, Rock, and Wisconsin rivers. And on the western side, the Red River of Louisiana, and the Arkansas, pour through northern Texas the waters accumulating among the mountains of New Mexico and Utah. While the Missouri, and its branches, the Kansas, the Platte, and the Yellow Stone, are swelling with the floods of the Rocky Mountains.

The imagination can not grasp the extent of the inland

water communication of the West with all the other portions of North America. The very fur-hunter himself, on the frozen shores of the Arctic Ocean, by paddling his canoe along Hudson's Bay, and up the Red River of the north, and by drifting down with the current of the Mississippi, may float, at last, in the Gulf of Mexico, having traversed the entire length of the continent from sea to sea, by water alone, with the single exception of a portage of only three miles. The warm, sunny South, and the cold, icy North, meet together in the West. The land of perpetual summer, where the orange-tree blooms in the fragrant air, where the cotton-plant flowers, and the sugar-cane yields its sweetness, is bound fast, by a continuous chain of rivers, with the dreary regions of everlasting snows. But the water communications across the continent are no less wonderful. These, also, open through the West. A traveler embarking at Pittsburg, on board a steamboat, may pass down the river Ohio, and up the Missouri, so far, that the asthmatic coughing of the escape-pipe will frighten the buffaloes feeding at the foot of the Rocky Mountains. And the most astonishing feature of this latter voyage of three thousand miles would be, that, throughout its whole length, in its beginning, and in its continuance, and in its ending, it is everywhere hundreds of miles inland from the ocean.

The fertility and beauty of the western country, supplied with those magnificent river systems, make it, indeed, the garden of the world. But whoever has stood at Niagara, and contemplated the mighty volume of the waters of the St. Lawrence, forever pouring into the abyss; or on the levee, at New Orleans, and watched the turbulent flood of the Mississippi, seething and rolling along at his feet, may well have wondered whence comes the supply of these exhaustless rivers. The problem would seem to have been solved. The trade-winds, sweeping across the broad surface of the Pacific Ocean, reach the American shore, heavily laden with moisture; condensing into clouds in the cooler air, they hang for a while on the pinnacles of the mountains; then, sailing away to the eastward, they discharge their contents over the West.

We are in the habit of thinking and speaking of the region beyond the lakes, and upon the upper tributaries of the Mississippi, as a new country. It is new in the sense that it has only lately been opened and occupied by permanent settlements. Notwithstanding that, it has a history which extends through a period of two hundred years. In 1632, Canada, which had previously fallen into the hands of the English, was restored to the possession again of the French. The colonies of France seem to have rivaled those of Spain, in the energy with which they prosecuted their discoveries in the New World. But they adopted a widely different system of exploration. The Spaniards sent forth armed bands of marauders, with the pomp and splendor of war, through an unknown territory, to reduce all before them into submission. They precipitated themselves with crushing force upon the illy-prepared and unsuspecting people. In this manner, under the lead of Cortez, the Spaniards achieved the conquest of Mexico; and under the lead of Pizarro, the conquest of Peru. But their violence aroused the vindictive hatred of the native population, and that has been kept alive against them to the present day. The French, on the contrary, sent forward, in advance, the olive-branch, instead of the sword. With a wiser policy, they humanely sought to win over the people among whom they had come to dwell, and to attach them to the crown of France. With great flexibility of character, they readily adapted themselves to the languages, manners, and customs of the Indian tribes, treating their chiefs with the consideration due to their rank, and awakening personal attachments. They also intermarried with the tawny maidens, and strengthened the ties of friendship with those stronger ties of kindred and family. Great consequences followed from this prudent course. Instead of being hemmed in, like most other colonists, by a barrier of exasperated savages, the French were invited into the interior of the continent.

It was the missionaries of France, not her soldiers, that first penetrated into the depths of the wilderness. And now, since the province was restored, the work of exploring the country and Christainizing the Indians, which had been abandoned upon the conquest by the English, was prosecuted with uncommon vigor. The indefatigable Jesuits struck boldly into the woods in all directions. From the St. Lawrence, they crossed over to the coast of Maine, where they had established a settlement. The North was not so terrible but that they could lead the way, overland, from Quebec to Hudson's Bay, and commence the exploration of its waters. Curious to know more of their own great river, they had followed up the St. Lawrence into Lake Ontario; and had there struck off to the south, into New York. They were the first to discover the celebrated salt-springs of Onondaga. But the country to the westward had more powerful attractions for them. Their eyes had seen the astonishing vision of an ocean of fresh water, high above the level of the sea, far inland, spreading out from its wooded shores beyond the horizon. From an unknown region, the waves came rolling toward them, and broke in thunder along the beach. Indian rumors had told them of greater waters, also, still beyond. A world of wonders was about opening before them in the wilderness. The love of the marvelous was combining with national pride and religious enthusiasm in urging them onward toward the West.

As early as 1640, the missionaries had followed up the chain of the lakes as far as Lake Superior. Within twenty years after the Pilgrims of New England had landed at Plymouth, and at the very time when the Dutch at New York were regarding the Hudson River as a terror, the French missionaries were at home in the center of North America. It may be painful to contrast their activity with the sluggishness of the Dutch, and with the indifference of the English colonists. While the Dutch were yet swapping tobacco-pipes and trinkets for peltry, with the Indians around their forts, and several years before Elliot, the Puritan missionary, had spoken to the Indians in the vicinity of Boston harbor, the Jesuits had planted the Cross at Sault Ste. Marie, and were preparing to descend into the valley of the Mississippi. But no great river from the far interior came flowing through New York or New England, inviting the adventurous to enter upon a career of exploration.

Canada, in this respect, had a superiority over the other colonies of the Atlantic. Yet Canada was not a flourishing colony. Its climate was not favorable. Its soil was not the most productive. Its government was military, and despotic. The simple, credulous colonists were deficient in energy, and had rather dream away existence, after the fashion of the Indians in their wigwams, than endure additional hardships in extending the boundaries of knowledge, that had conferred so few of its favors on them. But the missionaries, indeed, were noble exceptions, possessing rare attainments for that age, and an enthusiasm which sustained them under the severest trials. Fortunately for them, the colony had an able officer in the person of its interpreter and commissary, who encouraged the thorough exploration of the country, and bravely led the way himself.

The gallant Nicolet had come out to Canada, in 1618. His great abilities had placed him, at once, in active service. From the time of his arrival to the conquest by the English, he had been kept employed among the Indians; and he had become a great favorite with them. He spoke their languages. He understood the Indian character better than any other man of his times. Indeed, so constantly had he been with the Indians, that he had almost become an Indian himself; but without losing that stubborn integrity which makes good faith possible among men in the savage state. Nicolet was the negotiator for the colony at all the Indian councils. His character for probity had sent its influence far out into the wilderness. When he spoke, chiefs listened and believed; and they called him the Straight Tongue of the French. He had been dispatched on the hazardous undertaking of treating for peace with the Iroquois, after their terrible war upon Canada, and he had succeeded in inducing them to bury the hatchet. As a reward for his services, upon the restoration of the colony, he had been appointed interpreter and commissary. Seven years afterward, he undertook the great journey of his life.

In the spring of 1639, as soon as the accumulated ice of a long winter had been broken up, and the St. Lawrence set free, Nicolet took his departure from Quebec, for the purpose of completing the explorations of the lake region. He had previously been as far as Lake Huron; and along its shores, and the shores of Ontario, the Cross was already planted. But the journey which he was now entering upon must have possessed peculiar attractions to him. For, two seasons before that, when treating with the Indians that had come down from the regions around Lake Superior, he had learned that the Great Waters existed, also, to the southward, and to the westward of their country. But the Men of the Sea, as the Indians of the Mississippi Valley were called, had been represented to be powerful, and engaged in frequent wars with the Indians of Lake Superior.

After having assisted in establishing a mission at Sault Ste. Marie, and taken a survey of that interesting river, Nicolet passed through the Straits of Michilimackinac. Following along the shore, he entered an opening to the west, and reached the head of Green Bay. The season was advancing. But a council had to be called. So runners were dispatched to the hunting-grounds, giving notice of the arrival of strange white men. After awhile, the Men of the Sea gathered, at Green Bay, four or five thousand warriors. It was a sublime spectacle of savage life, even to Nicolet, who had spent twenty years in the wilderness. Never before had he seen such gigantic trees as there darkened the woods at noonday. Never, since the great council with the Iroquois, had he been among so powerful and warlike a people. At Green Bay, Nicolet's capacity as a negotiator shone forth most conspicuously. He not only accomplished a treaty of everlasting amity between the Men of the Sea and the French, but he made peace, also, between them and the tribes of Lake Superior.

During that council, the chiefs, in speaking of the Great Water, had stretched forth their arms toward the West. It would seem, however, that Nicolet did not understand them to mean a river. He was not sufficiently well acquainted with the language of the Men of the Sea, and he thought they applied the term Great Water to the ocean, for thė lakes, surely, were great waters; and each of those had a distinctive name. He was confident that the western ocean was not far distant; and he left that impression upon his return to Quebec. The season was drawing to its close. But Nicolet was too adventurous not to make an attempt to reach the Great Water, before retracing his steps. Accordingly, paddling up the Fox River, and crossing the portage, he launched his canoe on the Wisconsin. And he was soon floating down with the current that helps to swell the mighty volume of the Mississippi. He, however, did not reach the main channel of that river, though he was the first to explore one of its head streams. For some reason which has never transpired, he was obliged to go back to Green Bay, and from thence to Quebec. Nicolet had, indeed, been within three days' sail of the mysterious Great Water; but it was not his destiny ever to lift the veil which hung over it. The exigency of affairs detained him, during the two succeeding years, in the vicinity of Quebec. And in 1642, having been sent on an errand of mercy, to rescue a poor Christian prisoner from the hands of the Pagan Indians, his boat, on the last day of October, at sunset, was capsized in a gale, near Sillery, and Nicolet was drowned. The little that is known concerning him deserves to be remembered, for he was the first white man to reach the valley of the Mississippi by the way of the great lakes.

The road to the Mississippi could now seem to have been fairly opened. Fifteen missions dotted the shores of the lakes, and brought the distant St. Mary's into communication with Quebec. But a greater calamity than the loss of Nicolet was impending over the feeble colony. No sooner had the waves closed over the late interpreter and commissary, than the Iroquois war broke out with ten-fold fury, and raged for more than fifteen years. All the province was drenched in blood. The Indian allies of the French were driven with fearful slaughter beyond the great lakes. Montreal itself was besieged. And in 1650, all Upper Canada was a desert. Not a single mission—not an Indian village remained. The pastor and his flock had been butchered together. Six of the fifteen missionaries had been slain, and another had been put to the most frightful tortures. Bressani was beaten, mangled, mutilated; driven barefoot over rough paths, and naked through briars and thickets; scourged by a whole village; burned, tortured, and scarred; he was an eye-witness of the fate of one of his companions, who was boiled and eaten. And, although the knowledge of the interior country survived until the return of peace, yet the work of establishing missions and military-posts had all to be gone over again. But danger continued a great while lingering along the shores of the St. Lawrence. In 1656, Garreau set out for Lake Superior, in search of his scattered flock; but he was waylaid and tomahawked before reaching Lake Ontario. Groseillas, with a single companion, more fortunate in their undertaking, escaped the lurking enemy, and wintered two years later at St. Mary's. There they met with the returning bands of the fugitive Indians, who, more than ten years before, had been swept away from their hunting-grounds and the graves of their fathers, by the tempests of war. And from them they obtained a clear idea of the Great River, which flows toward the south. A vivid impression may be had of the terrible sway of the Iroquois over the continent, by contemplating this feeble remnant of their enemies, creeping back, broken and dispirited, from the plains beyond the Mississippi.

The evidences of the existence of a great river to the west of the lakes had begun to multiply rapidly. The missionaries in New York saw Iroquois war-parties set out, by the way of the Ohio River, which, they said, flowed into another river, and led to the sea. And in 1660, Menard, for many years a missionary among the Hurons, now an old man, his hair white, his frame shrunken, but with the soul of a hero, skirted along Lake Superior, and founded a mission on the southern shore. He, too, heard frequently of the Great River, and he had resolved to reach it in his old age, undeterred by the difficulties before him. But he was called away in another direction, and soon after perished, at a lonely place in the wilderness, on the banks of the Menominee.

The mantle of Menard would seem to have fallen, with his office, to his successor. Claude Allouez, the first explorer of Lake Michigan, has imperishably connected his name with the progress of discovery in the West. He left Quebec on the fourteenth day of May, 1665, and reached St. Mary's in the September following. Without any delay, he launched his frail canoe on Lake Superior, and surveyed the whole southern shore. How impressive to him must have been the views upon that vast inland sea, whose waters contrast so strangely with the fantastic scenery on the land; for the shores still bear the marks of the volcanic fires, which shivered the crags into ten thousand capricious forms, and poured the molten copper over them, as if in sport. He spent the winter in erecting and dedicating his chapel. After that, crossing the lake to the north, he visited in their distress the remnant of a once powerful tribe of Indians, who had been driven halfway to the frozen ocean, by the fierce and vengeful Iroquois. Allouez passed the winter of 1669 at Green Bay, and early in April of the next year, ascending the Fox River to Lake Winnebago, he explored that river beyond the lake, following up its three principal streams. Then crossing over to the Wisconsin, and searching out its head in the lakes and marshes, he, upon returning, floated down with the waters which reach the Mississippi, as Nicolet had done thirty years before. Neither did Allouez reach that river. His missionary duties recalled him to Green Bay. And soon after, the presence of all the missionaries was required at the great council, at St. Mary's, in 1671, of the French commander with the Indians, to assist as interpreters. After that, the missionaries turned their attention toward the more southern tribes.

Near the close of October, 1676, having completed his preparations for founding a mission in the Illinois country, Allouez, and two others, embarked in a canoe upon the waters of Lake Michigan. The winter set in much earlier than common, and the forming ice prevented their further progress up the lake. But the indomitable spirit of the brave missionary would not yield even to the fearful elements. A return to St. Mary's was not to be thought of. Boldly pushing to the unknown shore, a camp was established, where, through falling snows and howling tempests, Allouez waited till in the month of February, for the ice to become sufficiently solid to support them securely on its surface. Then setting forth again, he adopted a novel method of lake navigation. The canoe was drawn upon the ice, the sails spread, and away they glided before the wind. Their curiosity, one day, was very much excited by a rock standing seven or eight feet out of the water, and about three fathoms in circumference, which they called Pitch Rock. Indeed, they saw the pitch running down it, in little drops, on the side which was warmed by the sun. It was found to be good to pitch the canoe, and Allouez used it to seal his letters. Allouez, at last, entered the river which leads to the Illinois. That must have been at Chicago. The Indians received him handsomely. "The chief," he said, "advanced about thirty steps to meet me, holding in one hand a firebrand, and in the other a feathered calumet. As he drew near, he raised it to my mouth, and himself lit the tobacco, which obliged me to pretend to smoke." The Reverend Father, it would seem, was not accomplished in the use of the weed.

A few days afterward, in company with these Indians, Allouez proceeded inland to the principal village of the Illinois, which was found to be situated on the rising ground, a little way back from the river, and upon the edge of a prairie of vast extent. It was composed of several hundred cabins, made of double mats of flat rushes sewed together, scattered along in a single street, and all of them fronting toward a marsh which skirted the river. The Illinois Indians are described as having been tall of stature, strong, and robust; in character, proud and valiant. The richness and fertility of the country gave them fields everywhere. They ordinarily carried the war-club, bow, and a quiver full of arrows, which they could discharge so adroitly and quickly that men armed with guns had hardly time to raise them to the shoulder. They had bucklers, also, made of the skins of wild cattle, which were arrow-proof, and covered the whole body. The warriors had as many wives as they might choose to have, often selecting several sisters, that they might better agree together. The men had no great reputation for gallantry; they made jealous husbands, and would cut off their wives' noses on the slightest suspicion. The women are represented to have dressed modestly, and behaved well; while their lords, in the summer-time, strutted about in all the dignity of painted faces, and well-greased skins, without a particle of covering, except a few feathers stuck on the top of the head.

The time for Allouez' departure having arrived, he went back to the North, intending to return the next season to the Illinois. But others were sent there in his stead. And in 1680, that tribe was scattered, and the mission broken up, by an inroad of the Iroquois and Miamis, from the eastern shore of Lake Michigan. In the meanwhile, the information which the missionaries possessed of the country to the westward of them had been enlarging. The traders, who had shared with them all the dangers of the wilderness, had felt an interested curiosity as to the courses and directions of the streams that might open to them new avenues for trafficking. The Great River had become known to them by its name—the Mississippi. They had learned from the Indians its general features, and the nature of the country through which it was flowing. It seemed to them to encircle all the lakes, rising in the north, and running to the south, till it emptied into a sea, which they supposed to be the Gulf of California, or the Gulf of Mexico; and some even imagined that it wound around to the east as far as Chesapeake Bay. Rumor always runs far in advance of our knowledge of a new country, and keeps the mind perplexed between curiosity and doubt. But the time had, at length, arrived, when all those uncertainties respecting the river were about to be dispelled. The men to whom belongs the honor of subjecting the Mississippi to the dominion of the white man, were already preparing for their memorable voyage.

Of M. Joliet but little is now known, beyond the circumstances which cluster more immediately around his celebrated adventure down the Mississippi. He was a native of Canada. But the remembrance of the particular place of his birth has quite faded away from among men. Joliet owed his education to the Jesuit college of Quebec, where he is said to have been a classmate of the first Canadian that was advanced to the priesthood. After quitting the college, he had proceeded to the West, to seek his fortune in the fur-trade. And during that period of his life, he is known to have acquired the knowledge and experience which induced the government to select him as the explorer of the Mississippi. This choice was most agreeable to the western missionaries, for Joliet had always been on terms of close intimacy with them. His equally illustrious companion of the voyage, James Marquette, has given us a sketch of M. Joliet's character, which shows him to have been eminently fitted for the arduous and perilous undertaking. Marquette says: "The Sieur Joliet was a young man, born in this country, and endowed with every quality that could be desired in such an enterprise. He possessed experience, and a knowledge of the languages of the Ottawa country, where he had spent several years. He had the tact and prudence so necessary for the success of a voyage equally dangerous and difficult. And lastly, he had the courage to fear nothing, where all is to be feared." A noble tribute, indeed, as honorable to the heart of Marquette as it is advantageous to the character of M. Joliet.

James Marquette was born in the year 1637, at the city of Laon, in the mountainous department of Aisne, in France. He accordingly was thirty-six years old when he set out on his great voyage upon the Mississippi. The family of the Marquettes is the most ancient family of Laon; and it has always been characterized by a martial spirit, which drove its members into the armies of France, in pursuit after distinction. And the United States, also, are under obligations to cherish the memory of that distinguished family, for three of its sons accompanied the French army to our own shores, and perished on the battle-fields of the American Revolution. James Marquette was as ardent and enthusiastic in following the Cross as the others of the name have been in following the sword. At his own request, he was removed from the province of Champaigne, which contained no foreign mission, and was transferred to the province of France, which contained the missions in the far West. Having, at the earliest opportunity, sailed for that new field of labor, he had arrived at Quebec on the 20th day of September, 1666. That was a period of deep interest in the history of the colony, and in the progress of discovery in the interior of the continent. The long war of extermination waged by the Iroquois upon the French and their Indian allies had been brought to a conclusion; and, with the return of peace, the prospects of the missionaries had begun to brighten. The region of the western missions, so long laid waste and neglected, had been reöpened, and was then being enlarged. All New York, from Onondaga to the Niagara River, had been explored. The deserted missions had been revived along Lake Huron, and at St. Mary's at Keweenaw Bay, on Lake Superior, and at Green Bay.

Marquette was stationed, at first, for two years, at the mouth of the Saguenay — a most strange river that pours nearly a fathomless tide into the shallower St. Lawrence. That was not more important as a mission than as a place of traffic with the Indians; who, since the war was over, yearly flocked to it from Nova Scotia, from Hudson's Bay, and from Lake Superior. During the season for trading, religious instruction alternated with sharp bargains. The twists which conscience received in the daytime could hardly be taken out by a few hours' devotion in the evening. The missionaries, however, managed their affairs with great prudence, mollifying the irritated feelings of the Indians, and rebuking the rapacity of the traders. Much of human nature in its wildest aspects was to have been learned there, as well as the Indian languages, and a general knowledge of the surrounding country.

At the conclusion of that period, Marquette had been ordered to Lake Superior. In going there, he followed up the usual route of the western missionaries, ascending the Ottawa River, thence down the French River to Lake Huron, and across that lake to St. Mary's. It was both a toilsome and a dangerous journey. At St. Mary's, Marquette built his cabin on the American side, just at the foot of the rapids, where he continued instructing the Indians that were returning from their long flight from the Iroquois, until after Allouez' departure for Green Bay, and the Fox and Wisconsin Rivers.

Marquette had been dispatched, next after that, to Lapointe, the most distant mission on Lake Superior, and also the most dangerous. There he added considerably to the information which he had already obtained respecting the Mississippi. The occasion of a visit from some Illinois Indians, who had come a thirty-days' journey from the south, by land, and some part of the way along that river, afforded him an excellent opportunity for prosecuting his inquiries. They told him that that river ran so far to the south that they did not know where it might terminate. They described a portion of the Missouri also, and named over various tribes on both those rivers, even so far down as those that raised two crops of corn in a single summer. All these things Marquette had carefully written down, and he had begun digesting a plan for exploring the whole course of the Mississippi, and would have set out alone. But the mission at Lapointe was a disastrous one, and had to be abandoned, soon after that, in consequence of a threatened inroad of the Dacotahs, a fierce race, with long, black, streaming hair, and who wore stone knives in their belts. The poor Christian Indians, who had been driven, years before, across the Mississippi by the Iroquois, were now driven back again across Lake Superior by the Dacotahs. Making their escape in a fleet of canoes, they reached the foot of the lake, and from thence went down to Michilimackinac, and established themselves on the northern shore of those straits.

A mission had been attempted the previous year on the neighboring island of that name, but it had become deserted. The spot which Marquette had there selected as a new home for his flock was, indeed, bleak and sterile, surrounded by tempestuous lakes; but the waters were teeming with fish, and would afford them an easy communication with all the other missions. A rude chapel of logs was speedily erected, its roof covered over with bark. The Indians built, near by, a palisade fort, as an additional security against the danger of being again dislodged by their enemies. There they have remained to this day. The mission of St. Ignatius, at Michilimackinac, was founded in the summer of 1672. And it was while engaged in laying the foundation of that mission that Marquette received the joyful intelligence that the government was preparing an expedition to the Mississippi, and that he had been appointed to accompany it.

Joliet, however, did not arrive there, on his way from Quebec, until late in the fall, when the navigation of the lakes was about closing; but he brought with him the commissions, and the instructions to proceed, as soon as it should become practicable, to the Mississippi, and explore its waters. He was received at Michilimackinac with rejoicings, and much prayer and thanksgiving, for the great favor conferred on them of being sent to open the way into a new region, reputed to be filled with marvels and wonders. The succeeding winter was spent in making preparations for the great journey, which was to immortalize their names, and by its results affect the destiny of nations. All that before then had become known concerning the Mississippi, and the country and nations along its banks, was carefully reviewed. The various rumors that had reached the different missions, from Lapointe to the Illinois, were rigidly scrutinized, and compared with the reports of the Christian Indians, many of whom had crossed over the plains as far as the Missouri. Those wanderers were gathered into Marquette's cabin, and questioned as to what they had seen and heard in that distant country. The figurative language of the Indians had to be stripped of its exuberant metaphors, and reduced into harmony with well-known facts respecting other rivers and other countries. And there, in that gloomy abode in the center of the North American wilderness, in midwinter, Marquette and Joliet drew upon the ground, for want of a table, the first rude map of the Mississippi River, and the water-courses that might lead to it. The spectacle must have been sublime, of those two solitary white men, kneeling within a tawny circle of wondering Indians, and planning out the most important discovery of that age.

When at length the dissolving snows indicated the near approach of the season for lake and river navigation, they set about providing the more material and substantial parts of their outfit. The Canadian canoe is constructed very differently from those canoes which were in use on the Hudson and the Delaware, and which may now occasionally be seen on our western and southern waters. The latter is more properly called a "dug-out"—the name by which it is known throughout the south-west. The Canadian canoe consists of a frame-work of slender cedar splints, running lengthwise from stem to stern, supported upon ribs of spruce, and encased in a covering of birch bark, which is securely fastened with fibrous roots, and smeared along the seams with pitch. It possesses sufficient strength, and, at the same time, is so light that it may easily be carried across portages on the shoulders of two men; and it may be paddled through smooth water at the rate of four or five miles an hour. The Canadian canoe sits gracefully on the water, and, at a little distance off, seems scarcely to touch the surface; but it is a lively craft, and has the reputation of being tricky with strangers. A novice stepping into it might find himself suddenly plumped into the water.

CHAPTER III.

EXPLORATION OF THE MISSISSIPPI.

Departure from Michilimackinac — Wild oats — The tide at Green Bay — Ascending the Fox River — Indian village on the shore of Lake Winnebago — Wisconsin River — Its peculiarities — Joy at reaching the Mississippi — Strange fish — The abundance of game — Foot-prints on the shore — Discover an Indian village — Council — Feast of corn meal, fish, and boiled dog — Presented with a calumet — A strange plant — Monsters painted on a rock — Frightful appearance of the water at the junction of the Missouri — Clay paint — Indian method of dealing with musquitoes — "Snags" and "Sawyers" — Arkansas Indians — Return up the Mississippi and Illinois — Portage to Chicago — Arrival at Green Bay — James Marquette sets out on a return to Chicago, to instruct the Illinois Indians — Is detained all winter at the portage by sickness — Reaches the Illinois country in April, and founds a mission — His malady increasing, he sets out on his return to Michilimackinac — Driven by westerly winds to the mouth of the St. Joseph's — Becomes too weak to proceed — Expires on a bed of boughs, on the shore of Lake Michigan.

On the seventeenth day of May, 1673, M. Joliet and James Marquette set out from Michilimackinac in two bark canoes, to explore the Mississippi River. They were accompanied from that place by five men. The whole stock of provisions for the voyage consisted of Indian corn and some dried meat. But they were firmly resolved to do all and suffer all for so glorious an enterprise. Marquette says, in his narrative, "Our joy at being chosen for this expedition roused our courage, and sweetened the labor of rowing from morning till night."

They made their paddles play merrily along the straits, and across Lake Michigan and Green Bay, to the mouth of the Menominee River, then called the Wild Oats, from the quantities of that grass growing in its vicinity; where they remained several days with the Indians, who had taken their name, also, from the river.

The wild oats, or wild rice, as it is now called, is the principal food of the north-western Indians, and might be raised in all parts of the country where there are rivers that annually overflow the rich bottom-lands. The experiment was tried in the state of Connecticut, a few years ago, and proved to be successful. The wild oats are a kind of grass which grows spontaneously, at the West, in little rivers with slimy bottoms, and in marshy places. They resemble the wild oats that grow up among our wheat. In the month of June, the stalks, which are jointed at intervals, begin to shoot up through the water, and continue growing till they float about two feet above it. The grains are not thicker than our oats, but are as long again, so that the meal is much more abundant. The wild oats ripen in September. The Indians boil the grains in water with meat or grease, and in this way they make a dish about as palatable as rice would be when not better seasoned.

The voyagers then proceeded up to the head of Green Bay, where, Marquette says, "It is easy to remark the tide, which has its regular flow and ebb, almost like that of the sea." This tidal movement has been frequently observed at that place, and it may be accounted for by the pressure of the winds upon the distant parts of Lake Michigan, making the waters to rise and fall along the shores of Green Bay. From thence they ascended the Fox River to Lake Winnebago, and in doing so, their feet were very much cut by the sharp stones, while dragging their canoes up through the rapids of that river. They stopped some time at the Indian village, which was built on a hill, overlooking the lake and a beautiful and picturesque country. On every side, the prairies spread out as far as they could see, and were dotted with groves of lofty trees.

On the tenth day of June, they again embarked, with two Miamis for guides to the portage between the Fox and the Wisconsin rivers, and set out, in sight of a great crowd of Indians, who were wondering and amazed to see the Frenchmen daring to undertake so strange and so hazardous an expedition. The distance to the Wisconsin was already known from the explorations of Nicolet and Allouez. The course bore by compass west-south-west; but the river branched off through so many marshes and little lakes, and the channel was so concealed by the wild oats, that it was easy to have gone astray. But the guides led them safely to a portage, twenty-seven hundred paces across, helped them over with the canoes, and then returned to Lake Winnebago, leaving the voyagers alone in an unknown country, in the hands of Providence.

Marquette and Joliet were soon afloat upon the waters of the Wisconsin River. They had got to the westward of the streams which flow into the St. Lawrence, and were passing quietly down with a current that was bearing them still further into the wilderness. They found the Wisconsin to be a broad river, its sandy bottom having formed into shallows, which rendered navigation difficult. It was filled with little islands, that were grown up to shrubbery and covered with vines; and the long branches bent over from the shores, and trailed in the water. Along the banks were, sometimes, woodland and hills, but more generally prairies. They saw no fish in that river. The timber consisted of oak, walnut, whitewood, and another kind of tree whose branches were armed with long thorns. Deer were plenty, and they would frequently spring out of the island covers, and dash and splurge through the water to the shore, and then bound away, their white stub-tails teetering up and down in the air, as far as the eye could follow them.

On the seventeenth day of June, just one month after they had left Michilimackinac, the voyagers passed out of the mouth of the Wisconsin into the long-looked-for Mississippi. Great was their joy at beholding the broad sweep of its waters. They immediately cast their nets, and took some sturgeon, and a very extraordinary fish, which Marquette describes as follows: "It resembles a trout with this difference, that it has a larger mouth, but smaller eyes and snout. Near the latter is a large bone, like a woman's busk, three fingers wide, and a cubit long; the end is circular, and as wide as the hand. In leaping out of the water, the weight of this often throws it back." This was the *polyodon spatula*,—a very rare fish, and but seldom found in the Mississippi.

Following down the river, for a day or two, the land appeared to have undergone an entire change. There was almost no wood to be seen anywhere. Deer were to be met with, and moose, bustards and wingless swans; for those latter are said to shed their plumes in that country. They saw a great many enormous fish, with black, broad, ugly heads; and one of these struck against the canoe so violently that Marquette took it for a large tree about to knock them to pieces. It was undoubtedly a huge catfish on which they were so nearly snagged. The voyagers soon came into the region of wild turkeys and buffaloes. All other game had disappeared. The turkeys would sometimes fly in vast flocks across the river, when those that became weary with the flight would tumble into the water. A number were obtained in that way. With the buffaloes the Frenchmen were very much interested. They saw immense droves of them every day, trampling and bellowing along the banks.

The voyagers had floated down with the current several hundred miles, without discovering anything more dangerous than beasts and birds. Yet, they kept well on their guard; making only a little fire on the shore at night, to cook their meal; and then, anchoring the canoes far out in the river, they took turns watching and sleeping on the water. At length, on the twenty-fifth day of June, they perceived some foot-prints of men by the water-side, and a beaten path entering a beautiful prairie. Following along that path four or five miles, they came to a large village of the Illinois Indians, and were there received by them in a very friendly manner. A council had to be held, as is usual upon the arrival of strangers into a country occupied by a particular tribe of Indians. Speeches were then made and replied to, presents given, and presents received. The council was succeeded by a feast; and the Indians, being the hosts, got it up and conducted it after their own fashion. The Frenchmen were the passive recipients of the savage favors. The first course consisted of a great wooden dish, full of corn-meal, boiled in water, and seasoned with grease. The master of the ceremonies, with a spoonful of that greasy pudding, presented it three or four times in succession to the mouths of the guests, as we would do with little children. For the second course, he brought in a second dish, containing three fish, and took some pains to remove the bones with his fingers; and having blown upon it to cool it, he put it into their mouths, as we would do in feeding young birds. The third course was boiled dog; but that was going beyond even French capacity to eat, of all living creatures, and had to be withdrawn, as M. Joliet had discovered an entrail dangling from the kettle. The fourth, and last course, was a piece of buffalo-beef, the fattest portions of which were put into their mouths on the end of a stick. After the feast came the process of lionizing; which, also, was conducted after the Indian mode. The guests had to march slowly through the whole length of the village, and back again, an orator stepping along just before them, constantly haranguing and gesticulating, to oblige all to come out and see them, without being troublesome.

These Indians gave to the Frenchmen an additional evidence of their kindly disposition, in presenting them with a beautiful calumet, or pipe, to carry with them, as a means of security against Indian violence. The calumet is said to have been highly reverenced by the aborigines of America. Whoever carried it might have walked fearlessly amid enemies, and they would have lain down their arms so soon as it had been shown to them. Marquette gives a description of it: "It is made of polished red stone, like marble; so pierced, that one end serves to hold the tobacco, while the other is fastened on the stem, which is a stick two feet long, as thick as a common cane, and pierced in the middle. It is ornamented with the head and neck of different birds of beautiful plumage. They also add large feathers of red, green, and other colors, with which it is all covered. They esteem it particularly, because they regard it as the calumet of the sun; and, in fact, they present it to him to smoke, when they wish to obtain a calm, or rain, or fair weather."

The voyagers took leave of the Illinois Indians about the end of June, some six hundred accompanying them to the river-bank, and very much admiring the canoes, having never before seen the like of them. Marquette promised these Indians to return the next year, and stop at their village and instruct them. Soon after shoving off from the shore, the canoes began to float down along some pretty high rocks which lined the river; and there the company paused to examine a plant which seemed to them to be very remarkable. Its root was like small turnips, linked together by little fibers, and it had the taste of carrots. This root put forth a leaf as wide as the hand, half the thickness of one's finger, and spotted along the middle. From that leaf sprung other leaves, shaped like the sockets of the old-fashioned chandeliers; and each leaf bore five or six bell-shaped yellow flowers. That was, probably, the *cactus opuntia*, several species of which are known to grow in the western states. They also found an abundance of mulberries and persimmons; and they were quite disgusted with the latter tree, on account of its shocking bad smell. The prairies there abounded with the chincapin, a fruit resembling filberts, but more tender; the leaves were larger, and sprung from a stalk crowned at the top with a head like a sunflower, in which all those nuts were neatly arranged.

A little further down the river, as they were coasting along rocks frightful for their hight and length, they saw two monsters painted on one of those rocks, which startled them at first, and made the boldest Indian cover his head with his blanket. These monsters were each as large as a calf, with horns on the head like a deer: they had a fearful look, red eyes, and were bearded like a tiger; the face was like a man's face, the body covered with scales, and the tail so long that it wound twice around the body, passed over the head and down between the legs, and ended like a fish. These monsters were well painted; and they were so high up on the face of the rock that it is difficult to conceive how anybody could have got at them to paint them. The pictured rock is still a noted feature of the Mississippi.

As the voyagers were discoursing of these painted

monsters, and sailing gently down a beautiful, still, clear water, they heard a roaring noise, as of a great rapid, into which they were about to fall. Marquette says of it: "I have seen nothing more frightful. A mass of trees, entire, with branches, came rushing from the mouth of a great river so impetuously that we could not, without great danger, expose ourselves to pass across. The agitation was so great that the water was all muddy, and could not get clear." They, at length, by hugging the shore, got by the horrible tumult occasioned by the commingling of the turbulent floods of the Missouri with the waters of the Mississippi. The junction of these rivers continues to present pretty much the same appearance and the same dangers as were then, for the first time, seen by white men. Acres of drifting timber, supplied by rafts from above, keep on clashing, and roaring, and spinning round in the whirlpool formed by the rushing waters.

Before reaching the mouth of the Ohio, the explorers came upon a place in the river that was much dreaded by the Indians, because they thought a demon was living there, that would devour all who should attempt to pass that way. At that place there was a bay full of rocks, some of which were twenty feet high; and the whole current, striking against them, was whirled back, and driven over against a neighboring island, along which the mass of water was forced, tumbling and roaring, through a narrow channel. That was what struck terror into the Indians, "who," as Marquette says, "fear everything." Just above the Ohio River, they found in great quantities a kind of unctuous earth, of different colors, purple, violet, and red. That spot has always been a favorite resort of the Indians, to obtain the clay with which they paint themselves. There, also, they found a heavy red sand, and Marquette put some of it on his paddle, which took the color so well that it was not effaced after fifteen days' rowing in the water. About this time they began to enter the region of canes or large reeds lining the banks of the river. These were of a beautiful green — the knots or joints crowned with long, narrow, pointed leaves. The canes were set so thickly that the buffaloes could, with difficulty, force their way through them. And in that vicinity they, one morning, saw a strange animal swimming across. It had the head of a tiger, and a snout pointed like a wildcat, with a beard, and ears that were erect. Its head was grayish, and the neck black. On approaching nearer, and slapping the water with the paddles, the creature sprang briskly forward, spitting furiously like a scared cat.

So far, down the river, the voyagers had gone, without meeting with any very serious annoyance to distract them, and withdraw their attention from the beautiful and varied scenery of the country. But now the air was alive with musquitoes; so that it was scarcely possible to handle the paddles, because of the continued slapping and brushing away the pestiferous swarms. The more that were killed the more there seemed to come. The musquitoes got into the ears, and around the neck; dashed into the eyes, and hair, and mouth; crawled up the shirt sleeves, bit through the breeches. Indeed, it was quite impossible to look, or talk, or eat, or sleep, with any degree of comfort. A prayerful state of mind was out of the question. So, to escape the tormentors, they rolled themselves up in thick blankets, legs, bodies, heads, and faces, till nearly suffocated; then, as a change, took to fresh air and bites; and when the stings became intolerable, went back again to sweltering blankets.

Marquette gives a minute description of the Indian method, in that country, of dealing with the musquitoes:

"They raise a scaffolding, the floor of which is made of simple poles, and consequently a mere grate-work, to give passage to the smoke of a fire which they build underneath. This drives off the little animals, as they can not bear it. The Indians sleep on the poles, having pieces of bark stretched above them to keep off the rain. This scaffolding shelters them, too, from the excessive and insupportable heat of the country; for they lie in the shade in the lower story, and enjoy the cool air, which passes freely through the scaffold." After the same plan the voyagers lashed their canoes together, and made a rude cabin of the sails to keep off the musquitoes, and shelter themselves from the sun. In this manner, shut in from the light and from the view around them, they floated down the river blindfolded; peering out once in awhile, to see what might be ahead.

Sailing along thus at the mercy of the current, they one day came upon some Indians, and learned from them that it was not more than ten days' journey further to the sea. This news aroused their courage again, and they took up their paddles with renewed ardor, and passed swiftly down the river. They soon began to see less prairie-land, because both the banks were lined with lofty woods. The cotton-wood, elm, and whitewood, were of enormous hight and size. But the numbers of buffaloes they heard bellowing made them believe the prairies were not far off. They heard the quails whistling along the water's edge; and they killed a little parrot, with half the head red, the rest, with the neck, yellow, and the body green.

The greatest danger, however, which was constantly present to the minds of the voyagers, in this part of the river, was occasioned by the snags and sawyers. Vast tracts of fertile land along the banks of the Mississippi and Missouri annually cave into those streams, unloosing thousands of forest trees, which are by this means set adrift. Some of these gigantic trees, swept along down with the floods, become fastened in the deep channel, with their trunks pointing up stream; and then, shedding their lesser branches, they present the long, formidable shafts, known as "snags," in river navigation at the West. Other trees, again, become fixed in the current, with their trunks pointing down stream. The rolling flood forces them under, until the bending roots overcome the unequal pressure, and then the huge top slowly rises above the surface, shakes its dripping limbs, to disappear again for awhile in the depths below. Those latter are the much-dreaded "sawyers," the terror of the early navigators of the Mississippi; for the large swaying trunks might rise directly beneath the canoe or skiff, and give it an uncomfortable elevation into the air.

At last the voyagers had gone down stream as far as the mouth of the Arkansas River. They were received in a friendly manner, and entertained by the Indians that lived along its banks, who had corn in abundance, but little meat; not daring to hunt buffaloes on account of the large war-parties of their enemies scouring the prairies. These Indians were raising, in that warm climate, three crops of corn a year. Marquette says: "We saw some ripe, more just sprouting, and more still in the milk." The Arkansas Indians used large, well-made earthen pots, for cooking; and they had plates also made of baked earth. The men were entirely naked, wore their hair cut short, their noses and ears pierced and strung with beads. The women were dressed in wretched skins, and without ornaments to adorn their persons. They had about their cabins, which were built of rush mats, enormous gourds, as large as half barrels, for storing corn. The Arkansas Indians were in possession of fire-arms, having obtained them from the Spaniards at the mouth of the river, which was but eight days' journey, by water, below them.

Joliet and Marquette had then ascertained where the Mississippi emptied. They had explored it from the Wisconsin to the Arkansas. The general course of the river was due south, and they were far below the latitude of Chesapeake Bay, and to the east of the Gulf of California. By going further down they would have risked losing the fruits of their voyage, of which they could have given no information; for the Spaniards, claiming the whole country along the Gulf of Mexico, were excessively jealous of strangers, and would undoubtedly have detained them close prisoners. It was deemed advisable, therefore, to return to Quebec. Having been nearly one month upon the river, they left the Arkansas, for the north, on the seventeenth day of July. It is of no consequence, but, after all, a little curious, that they should have taken their departure from Michilimackinac on the seventeenth day of May, and from the mouth of the Wisconsin on the seventeenth day of June, and set out upon their return on the seventeenth day of July.

Now, in going up stream, the explorers had to contend against the current of the Mississippi, which ran at the rate of from three to five miles per hour. Every inch of progress had to be made by incessant rowing. At length they succeeded in getting as high up as the Illinois River, which, perceiving that it came from the north-east, they entered, and followed it to the portage which led to Chicago. Crossing over to Lake Michigan, they arrived at Green Bay in the September following. In all their travels, they had seen nothing to compare with the Illinois country, for the fertility of its lands, its prairies, woods, buffaloes, deer, swans, and ducks. The river had many little lakes and branches, and was navigable its whole length. During the spring of the year, the only portage was one of one and a half miles.

Thus the greater part of the Mississippi was already explored. For De Soto, crossing it from the east through the country of the Choctaws, and wandering for a year in Louisiana, Texas, and New Mexico, had returned to it in 1542, by the Arkansas River; and there dying, his body had been committed to its waters. A hundred and thirty-one years later, Joliet and Marquette had completed their memorable voyage. All, therefore, below the Wisconsin was known. In 1680, Louis Hennepin, a prisoner among the Sioux, was taken up the Mississippi to the Falls of St. Anthony; and upon his release, he returned by the way of the Wisconsin River. One hundred and fifty years after Hennepin's captivity, the United States government commissioned Henry R. Schoolcraft to put an end to the war then raging between the Chippewas and Sioux. In the performance of that mission, he crossed over from Lake Superior and the St. Louis River; and, following up the Mississippi, discovered its source in Itasca Lake. Three different nations participated in the exploration of that great river, and their attempts extended through a period of three centuries.

But it will be interesting a little longer to follow the fortunes of M. Joliet and James Marquette. Both of them had written complete narratives of their expeditions, and prepared maps of the countries they had visited. But the former, on his way to Quebec, in October, 1673, was capsized among the Rapids of the St. Lawrence, losing all his papers, and only himself escaping, as by a miracle, swimming, and reaching the bank in a state of insensibility. He made a verbal report, which he wrote out for the government, and dispatched it to France, together with a map, drawn from recollection, and was waiting in hopes of receiving a suitable reward for his distinguished services.

Doomed to disappointment, he was put off, as if in mockery, with the barren island of Anticosti, in the Gulf of St. Lawrence; and that was captured and taken from him by the English. His subsequent career is lost in obscurity, and even the place of his death is unknown.

James Marquette was detained at Green Bay the whole season of 1674, by a dysentery, brought on by the hardships which he had suffered during the voyage. Recovering a little toward the close of the succeeding summer, he proceeded up Lake Michigan to Chicago, intending to fulfill his promise to the Illinois Indians, to return and instruct them. But tempestuous weather kept him a month along the lake; and his malady returning, he was obliged to remain all winter at the portage, prostrate with sickness, and without medical attendance. It was not until in April that he was able to reach the Illinois country; and, although in feeble health, he laid the foundation of the mission at Kaskaskia. His malady, however, increasing in violence, made it indispensable that he should return to Michilimackinac. He set out in a canoe with two companions. But westerly winds drove them over to the eastern shore, near the mouth of the St. Joseph's River, where Marquette became so much weaker as to require lifting to and from the canoe. He was still anxious to be carried forward. His companions, seeing him sinking fast, moved with gentle strokes along near the shore. But his hour was come. Pausing at the entrance of a little river of Michigan, a cabin was hastily erected, and there, on a bed of boughs, the great explorer of the Mississippi breathed his last, in the gloom and solitude of the wilderness. His companions buried him reverently, and marked the place of his grave. Two years later, the Illinois Indians, who had loved him as a father, exhumed his remains, and carried them with solemn pomp to Michilimackinac, where they deposited them in their final resting-place.

CHAPTER IV.

THE GREAT LAKES.

Ottawa and French rivers — Robert Cavalier de La Salle, first navigator upon the lakes — His patent for the monopoly of the trade of the West — "The Griffin," the first sail-vessel built on the Lakes — Her first and only trip — La Salle's misfortune — Descends the Mississippi — Loses one of his hunters in the woods — Takes formal possession of the country at the mouth of the Mississippi — Plate engraved, and deposited in the earth — La Salle goes to France — Returns with three ships — The store-ship dashed in pieces on the coast of Texas — One hundred men lost by sickness — La Salle and sixteen men set out overland for the Illinois — La Salle murdered by two of his companions.

NEXT after the discoveries in the Valley of the Mississippi, our attention is attracted to the exploration of the great lakes, from the Falls of Niagara to Green Bay. The lower lakes had all along been so infested by war parties of the Iroquois, that safety, as well as directness, had led to the adoption of another route. The earlier adventurers, leaving the St. Lawrence at Montreal, followed the courses of the Ottawa and French rivers to Lake Huron. But those streams were interrupted by frequent and toilsome portages. It led through a region horrible with forests. All day long, they had to wade or handle the oar. Around thirty-five water-falls their canoes had to be carried on the shoulders, through tangled woods, and over rough stones; and be dragged by hand up through fifty rapids. The new route, by the way of the lakes, made more accessible the whole interior of the continent; and, sweeping further south, along Lake Erie, opened at once into the beautiful and fertile regions of the Ohio. The missionaries had heretofore taken the lead in the progress of discovery at the West. A merchant was now about to enter the field. Religious enthusiasm was to be superseded by commercial enterprise.

Robert Cavalier de La Salle, the first navigator upon the lakes, was a native of Rouen, in the north of France. His intellectual endowments were of a high order. He had been brought up exclusively for literary pursuits. Accomplished in all the sciences, especially the mathematics, he had spent ten years of his life teaching and studying in the Jesuit colleges. But all his plans for the promotion of learning were broken up by the loss of his inheritance, which had been stripped from him by the unjust provisions of the French law; and he had been compelled to seek, in a new employment, and in a new country, the means of restoring his fortunes. The precise time of his coming out to Canada can not now be ascertained; but it must have been as early as 1670; for, two years later, we find him in command at Frontenac — a military post at the foot of Lake Ontario, near the site of the city of Kingston. He obtained a grant of the lake and its dependencies, together with a monopoly of its trade; but upon the condition that he should maintain a fort upon its shores, and a sufficient garrison, at his own expense. In compliance with this condition, La Salle, in 1675, built a regular stone fort, with four bastions, inclosing the old fort, and commanding a bay, in which a considerable fleet of vessels might have ridden with safety. The governor of Canada went up to Frontenac each year, at the assembling of the chiefs of the Iroquois nations; and, by distributing among them flattering presents, secured the alliance and commerce of that powerful confederacy.

Although La Salle had met with M. Joliet, at Frontenac,

when that distinguished adventurer was returning from the West, and had inspected the journals and maps which, soon after that, were lost in the Rapids of the St. Lawrence, yet he was so much occupied with his own plans of making a fortune out of his monopoly of the trade of the lake that he does not seem to have been desirous of participating then in securing the traffic upon the Mississippi. Three years later, however, finding that his monopoly had aroused the jealousy of all the other traders, who, scattered throughout the wilderness, were thwarting him in every possible manner, he conceived the vast enterprise of shipping the furs of the Mississippi and its tributaries direct to France, by the way of the Gulf of Mexico. The Indians would have to be conciliated, the Spaniards expelled, forts and trading stations established; but La Salle had a genius for commerce, and a courage that was equal to any hazard. In 1677, he made a voyage to France, to press his new application; and upon receiving his patent for the monopoly of the trade of the West, he returned in September, bringing with him Tonti, an Italian soldier, as his lieutenant, and a body of mechanics and sailors, together with all things necessary for his expedition.

Such was the speed with which this extraordinary man perfected his arrangements, that, on the eighteenth day of November, he embarked, at Frontenac, in a brigantine, with his company, and set sail for the Niagara River. But contrary winds prevented him from reaching the place of destination until the sixth day of December. A site for a fort was immediately selected, where the yawning chasm opened toward the lake, to obtain the control of the outlet of the upper lakes, and give additional security to the commerce of Ontario. Above the cataract, near the present village of Schlosser, La Salle caused the ways to be laid down, and commenced the construction of a vessel, for the purpose of going round by water to the Illinois country. Soon, the ringing sound of axes and of hammers was heard in the grand old woods, mingling with the deep booming of Niagara. At the same time that the Dutch were paddling about on the Mohawk in broad-bottomed skiffs, between Schenectady and Albany, and just as the Puritans were beginning the precious war upon witches in Massachusetts, the brave French merchant was building ships in the profoundest depths of the American wilderness.

Meanwhile, the enemies of La Salle were busy raising clamors against him, and throwing obstacles in his way; and they succeeded so far as to awaken distrust among the Senecas; so that the building of the fort had to be abandoned, for a time, and in its place substituted a house surrounded by palisades. Misfortunes, also, seem to have pressed heavily upon him. One of his vessels, on Lake Ontario, loaded with materials, provisions, and merchandise, was cast away in a gale, and became a total wreck.

But La Salle was not a man to be disheartened by ordinary losses. He vigorously prosecuted the building of his vessel at Niagara; and at the close of July, 1679, he had the pleasure of seeing it glide into the water. He gave it the name of "The Griffin," in honor of the arms of the Count de Frontenac, then governor of Canada, to whose friendly assistance he was greatly indebted for the early completion of his preparations. On the seventh day of August, La Salle embarked with the greater part of his company, and set about stemming the swift current of the river. And just as the sun was going down behind the dark Canadian forests, The Griffin began plowing her way through the waters of Lake Erie, on the route to the West.

La Salle had with him during the voyage Tonti, his lieutenant, several friars, and sixty sailors, boatmen, hunters, and soldiers. After a quick passage — considering that it was, in part, upon unknown waters — they arrived at Green Bay in twenty days, and cast anchor at its head, having traced out a channel which has already become one of the great highways of commerce. The Griffin was sent back with a rich lading of furs, under orders to return with provisions and merchandise, to be conveyed to the head of Lake Michigan; whither La Salle was preparing to go, forthwith, with a fleet of bark canoes. Traversing the whole length of that lake in those frail vessels, he spent the autumn in erecting a fort at the mouth of the St. Joseph's River, in sounding the channel, and establishing a depot for supplies and goods. Impatiently awaiting the return of The Griffin until the snows began to fall, he crossed over to Chicago, and remained there some weeks, in hopes that she still might arrive. But upon returning he got no tidings of her. Misfortune seems to have followed upon misfortune. The Griffin was wrecked on her homeward voyage. Hearing nothing more of her, La Salle proceeded south to the Kankakee, a branch of the Illinois, and, descending the latter river, below Peoria, he passed the winter in building another fort, which he called *Crevecœur*, (Heart-break,) to signify how great was his disappointment. But he spent no time in lamenting his losses. His resolution appears to have risen in proportion with his disasters. He laid the foundations of a new vessel at the foot of Lake Peoria, but was obliged to abandon it for want of materials.

In March, 1680, La Salle determined upon a plan to hasten or replace the necessary supplies; and for that purpose he set off, with only three attendants, and following along the water-shed, or divide, which separates the streams that flow into the Ohio River from those which flow into Lake Erie, he traveled the entire length of the wilderness on foot, and reached Frontenac in safety. There, however, new difficulties awaited him. He found his affairs in the utmost confusion. With the loss of the Griffin had come the report of La Salle's death, which had been eagerly circulated by his enemies. His property had been seized upon by his creditors. That would seem to have been sufficient to have made his cup of bitterness run over. But the invincible man was not to be made to be dead before his time. The waste of waters, the howling wilderness, malicious enemies, and hungry creditors, had all to yield to his iron will. Applying once more to the governor for aid, he made arrangements to continue the prosecution of his enterprise.

While thus conquering his embarrassments in Canada, other disasters had befallen him in Michigan and in Illinois. No sooner had La Salle set his face toward the east than most of his men deserted their posts. That at St. Josephs was completely abandoned. Tonti, with a few brave companions, continued to hold out at Peoria. But while his master was yet traversing the wilderness, some roving bands of Iroquois attacked the Illinois villages, drove Tonti from his post, which, together with timber for the vessel, they burned with fire. Tonti fled to Green Bay, and from thence proceeded by the northern route to seek after La Salle. Long before Tonti had reached Frontenac, La Salle was again on his way, with recruits and supplies, overland, through Michigan to the St. Josephs, and down that river to the lake. He arrived at Peoria late in October, and found his fort a blackened ruin. He resolutely began building still another fort on the Illinois, sufficiently strong to bid defiance to the warfare of savages. . It was situated upon a cliff that rose two hundred feet above the river, in the center of a lovely country of verdant prairies, bordered by distant slopes, richly tufted with oak and black-walnut, and the noblest trees of the American forest. And when that was well-nigh completed, he set out again, in 1681, to return to Frontenac for more recruits. But on his way he met the faithful Tonti, at Michilimackinac, with a company of men, hastening westward to his assistance. With these, La Salle went back to his new fort, which he named St. Louis.

He found it necessary to change the plan of his expedition. He had not time to build a ship. He would explore the river to the Gulf of Mexico, take formal possession of the country; and then, going from Quebec to France, he would return and enter the Mississippi from the sea. La Salle proceeded to organize the expedition according to that plan. He broke his followers up into three companies, and appointed Dautray, also, to act as lieutenant. Hastening his preparations, with his usual celerity, he caused three large boats to be constructed, during the winter, complete; and was ready, with the opening of the Illinois, to embark.

On the sixth day of February, 1682, the expedition, conducted by La Salle in person, and his lieutenants, Tonti and Dautray, with Zenobius Membré as chaplain, and Indians as hunters and guides, entered the wide waters of the Mississippi. They waited at the mouth of the Illinois till the thirteenth, to get clear of the floating ice; and then proceeded down the river. They passed the mouth of the muddy Missouri, and the rapids which the Indians had so much dreaded; then the Ohio, and the region of canes. The expedition was obliged to send out hunting and fishing parties daily, not having been able to lay in a stock of provisions, except Indian corn. On the twenty-fourth, all the hunters came in, but one; the rest reported having seen an Indian trail; and that led to the supposition that the Frenchman had been killed or taken captive. With characteristic humanity, La Salle directed the boats to anchor near a high bluff, on the top of which he threw up intrenchments, determined to rescue the man, or chastise his murderers. The most skillful hunters were dispatched along the trail. None were allowed to relax their efforts, until, on the ninth day, the missing hunter, who had got bewildered and lost, was found.

As the expedition proceeded down the river, La Salle took formal possession of the country at the mouth of the Arkansas, and at Natchez. On the sixth of April, it arrived at a place where the Mississippi divided into three channels, and the boats separated so as to explore them all. The water soon became brackish as they advanced; and on the ninth, they reached the open sea. An authentic act was then drawn up, and signed by all the party; and, amid a volley of musketry, a leaden plate, inscribed with the arms of France and the names of those who had made the discovery, was deposited in the earth. The expedition then ascended the river to Illinois; and La Salle dispatched Membré to France, to lay an account of his voyage before the government.

The next year La Salle himself reached France, and meeting with much favor, procured a fleet of four ships— two of them, the Joly and the Belle, ships of war; the Amaible, a store-ship; and the St. Francis, a ketch. The St. Francis was captured by the Spaniards soon after sailing. About the first of December, 1684, the three ships, having stopped at St. Domingo, arrived off the island of Cuba; and, steering to the north-west, sought the mouths of the Mississippi. But all on board were ignorant of the coast, and the fleet went too far westward, which was perceived, at last, by the land setting off south. In attempting to enter the mouth of a river, on the coast of Texas, the store-ship got fast aground, and was soon after broken to pieces by the waves. The goods were saved; and La Salle determined upon planting his colony in that country. The ships of war returned to France. Sickness, within a year, carried off an hundred men, and the survivors were reduced to great distress. La Salle, having made an ineffectual attempt to reach the Mississippi, through the swamps along the gulf, resolved to cross the continent to Illinois, by land. He set out on that desperate undertaking in January, 1687, with sixteen men; and after interminable wanderings through the wilderness, he was murdered, on the nineteenth day of March, by two mutinous companions. The murderers themselves were afterward murdered. Only five of the company succeeded in reaching the Arkansas River, and returning to Canada. In the meanwhile, Tonti had been twice down the Mississippi to meet his master; but failing in that, he left a letter for him with the Indians nearest the gulf, which was religiously kept by them for fourteen years, and delivered to the first white man that afterward arrived in their country.

CHAPTER V.

FRENCH SETTLEMENTS.

Destruction of Montreal by the Iroquois — Iroquois conquered — Treaty of peace — French emigration — Fort Chartres — Manufacture of flour in the Wabash country — The adaptation of the Indian manners, etc., by the French — Its effects — Description of the French settlements — Dress of the settlers — Inroads upon the French — Attempts of the Spaniards to dispossess the French — Their defeat, and overthrow of the Santa Fé expedition — Progress of English settlements toward the West — An English trader among the French — His fate — The Ohio Company's grant — Gov. Dinwiddie dispatches Geo. Washington with a message to the French — Beginning of the French war — The West open to English emigration — Taking possession of the military posts — Robert Rogers — Rogers' Rangers — Character of the Rangers — The Rangers at Cleveland — Visit from Pontiac — The forts delivered to the English.

Although La Salle had miserably perished, and Marquette had died in the wilderness, and Joliet been shamefully neglected, yet their glowing descriptions of the western country had filled the imaginations of adventurous men with visions of a terrestrial paradise in the delightful regions of the Illinois and the Mississippi. Many of the inhabitants along the Lower St. Lawrence were becoming dissatisfied with its sterile shores and rigorous winters, and were preparing to seek new homes in the great valley of the West, where the summer extended through more than half the year; where the rich soils produced, spontaneously, the choicest grains, the most delicious fruits. But, for a time, the progress of the French settlements was checked by the breaking out of another Iroquois war. Bitterly had the Canadians rued the day on which Champlain, the founder of the colony, had joined the Huron war-parties in an irruption into the Mohawk country. The hatred of the fierce Mohawk warriors had scarcely slumbered during a period of eighty years. It again broke out afresh.

On the twenty-fifth day of August, 1689, fifteen hundred Iroquois warriors, horrible with paint, and thirsty for blood, made a sudden and terrible inroad into Canada. They ravaged the island of Montreal with fire and sword; destroyed all the settlements, captured the town and fort, and butchered, with frightful cruelties, the victims that fell into their hands. After having spread desolation, and woe, and death, in every direction, they only retired at the approach of winter. The war continued to rage for more than five years. In the meanwhile, Frontenac, then upward of seventy years old, concentrated the whole military force of the colony upon the shore of Lake Ontario. The fields around the fort at the foot of the lake became white with tents; in the bay floated two schooners, armed, and a fleet of canoes. Soon afterward, he made a descent, with four thousand men, upon the Iroquois country. Crossing the lake, and ascending the Oswego, he destroyed the villages and cornfields of the Onondagas and Oneidas, cut down their orchards, burnt up their canoes, and laid waste their country. This great invasion taught the Iroquois an important lesson: the French were too numerous for extermination. The chiefs consented to treat at a council to be held at Montreal. In the summer of the year 1700, the Ottawas and Hurons, from Lake Superior; the Sioux, from the Upper Mississippi; and four of the Iroquois nations, entered into negotiations for an everlasting peace. A treaty was drawn up with great formality, and signed by all the parties, each Indian nation placing for itself a symbol: the Senecas and Onondagas, a spider; the Oneidas, a forked stick; and the Mohawks, a bear. It declared that war should cease along the whole frontier; that peace should reach beyond the Mississippi.

The way of French emigration to the West had then, at last, become safe. Missionary stations soon began to grow into regular parishes. At Peoria a settlement was rapidly forming. Kaskaskia became a happy and prosperous village. Other places were rapidly rising into note. In June, 1701, De la Motte Cadillac, and one hundred men, took possession of Detroit River and Lake St. Clair, then deemed the loveliest part of country; and the French began the assertion of their claim to the country south and west of the lakes, and upon the streams occupied by their Indian allies, comprising all the territory drained by the St. Lawrence and the Mississippi. This extensive region, the best watered, the most fertile of any on the face of the earth, was called New France. Five years later, extensive settlements had been formed in the valley of the Wabash, from which fifteen thousand hides and skins were annually sent south to Mobile, for the European market.

Great efforts were made to secure the possession of the vast inland territory which opened, through such magnificent water communications, to the east and to the south. The Spaniards were creeping up the Rio Grande into New Mexico. The English were yet spread out along the sea-coast, and were hemmed in by the mountains. For that purpose, strong military posts were built on the western and interior waters. In 1720, the construction of a stronghold was commenced in the Illinois country, to serve as the head-quarters of Upper Louisiana. This was Fort Chartres, on the east side of the Mississippi, and sixty-five miles below the mouth of the Missouri. Having been designed for one of the strongest fortresses in America, its walls were built of solid masonry, which required eighteen months for their completion. But, one hundred years afterward, its massive ruins were so overgrown with vines and forest-trees as to be almost impenetrable to the traveler. Previous to 1735, the fort which had previously been abandoned by La Salle, had been rebuilt at Niagara, near the mouth of the river; another frowned at Vincennes over the Wabash valley, one hundred and fifty miles above the Ohio River; another at Presque Isle overlooked the waters of Lake Erie; that at Detroit commanded the passage to the upper lakes; and, soon after, Fort Du Quesne, now Pittsburgh, controlled the navigation of the Ohio, Monongahela, and Alleghany rivers.

As early as 1746, six hundred barrels of flour were manufactured in the Wabash country, in a single year, and transported to New Orleans, beside large quantities of hides, tallow, and beeswax. The Upper Wabash was the seat of a quiet, industrious, and agricultural people. A few years later, the Illinois country was found to contain six distinct settlements, with their respective villages. Cahokia, at the mouth of a creek of the same name, five miles below the present site of St. Louis; St. Philips, forty-five miles further down the river; Fort Chartres, twelve miles above Kaskaskia; Kaskaskia, on the river of that name, upon a peninsula, and within two miles of the Mississippi; Prairie du Rocker, near Fort Chartres; St. Genevibve, upon Gabarre creek. These were among the oldest villages of the West. And Kaskaskia, before the country passed into the hands of the English, was quite a large town, containing between three and four thousand inhabitants. These villages were secure, though in the midst of an Indian country, and surrounded by many warlike tribes.

Throughout all their efforts at planting settlements in the western country, the French had steadily adhered to the policy of conciliating the Indians. They, indeed, seem to have been peculiarly adapted to harmonize, in their habits and feelings, with the wild denizens of the forest and the prairie. In their explorations of the remotest rivers, in their long journeys overland, in the wigwams, in the cabins, at the forts, they associated with their red brethren on terms of entire equality. The French temper, so pliant, so plastic, so strongly in contrast with the stubborn spirit of Englishmen, was readily moulded to Indian customs and Indian forms. The wandering Frenchman, with his free and easy manners, his merry laughter, his fondness for display, mingling in the dusky crowd, was cordially welcomed at all the Indian villages of the West. He might choose himself a wife among his Indian friends, and live there with them, and be one of them. In fact, amalgamation existed to a very considerable extent, and in a few generations scarcely a tribe was free from an infusion of Celtic blood.

The ready adoption of the Indian manners and mode of living, and more than that, the frequent intermarriages between the two races, had a tendency to bind the native tribes more closely to the French, who seemed to be bone of their bone, and flesh of their flesh. In all the West, the Indian villages were thronged with Frenchmen, who joined in the dances, went forth with the hunting-parties, and along the war-paths. But while this policy of intimate association with the different tribes had strengthened the hold of the government upon the country, it also had tended to sink the Frenchman into a barbarian. Casting off the habits of civilization, he soon imbibed the notions, whims, and prejudices of his wild associates. He loved to decorate his hair with the feathers of eagles, and adorn his hunting-shirt with hairy fringes, and his moccasins with a web-work of porcupine quills. He came to have faith in the magic drum of the Indian conjuror. He believed in omens and in dreams. He would whistle away vigorously through the hollow wing-bone of a bird, to dispel the approaching thunder-storm. He would carry the horny tails of rattlesnakes in his bullet-pouch, as charms, to give certainty to his aim. But only a small portion of the French population was thus easily degenerated. It was the ignorant, who, everywhere, and among all people, sink rather to the level below them than climb to the level above them.

Beside the missionaries, other intelligent Frenchmen were scattered throughout the West, studying the languages of their Indian allies, complying with their usages, flattering their prejudices, and assisting them in acquiring the arts of white men. These agents were careful not to ruffle the self-complacent dignity of the Indian nature. They never shocked the religious notions, nor ridiculed the ancient customs of their savage friends. They attended at all public ceremonies, and took part in them, and strove to manifest a disposition to meet their companions of the wilderness half-way. Count Frontenac, himself, plumed and painted like a chief, danced the war-dance, and yelled the war-song, at the camp-fires of his delighted allies. And whenever a party of sachems paid a visit to a French fort, they were received with military honors; the troops presented arms, the drums rolled, the cannons belched forth their thundering welcomes. Indian vanity was delighted with such pompous and showy friendship. The chiefs were regaled at the officers' tables; and when they took their departure, were loaded with presents, and adorned with medals and decorations, and brilliant uniforms, and flags. Their treatment was always respectful. None smiled at the strange fancies, or stared at the ridiculous appearance of the daubed and greasy warriors. The shirtless savage, in cocked-hat and plume, his scarlet coat-tails flapping behind his naked legs, might stalk all over the parade-ground, and never suspect that he was not an object of intense admiration to all. The hatred of the Iroquois, even, was not toward the Frenchmen as men, but toward them as the allies of the Hurons, the hereditary enemies of their confederacy.

The French settlements at the West, therefore, were safe from Indian depredations. They, indeed, were situated in the midst of a wilderness, but it was a wilderness of beauty, and inhabited by friendly races. The tribes around them were but so many outposts to repel enemies, and give timely warning of danger. The French settlements were compact villages, isolated from each other, and a thousand miles distant through woods and waters from Canada. The settlers were sociable, as well as vagrant, and loved to congregate together. No farm-houses were scattered, as with the English, along highways cut through the woods. The French settlements were on the bank of some pleasant stream; a single narrow street ran along in front; each lot, a few rods in width, extended back as far again, fenced in with rude pickets; each house contiguous to the houses right and left. The merry villagers could pour out their volubility at the windows or on the stoops. The young men and maidens could readily pass from door to door. The houses were uniform, one story high, surrounded by galleries. The houses were constructed of corner-posts, and studs, connected by numerous cross-ties, to hold the mud mixed up with cut straw into a stiff mortar, and plastered on with the hand. The whole outside was shingled over with bark to shed off the rains. The outside chimney was a rude stack of dried mud, supported by a pyramid of poles and slats.

The French settlements had each a "commons," in the rear of their houses, inclosing hundreds of acres within one continuous fence, for the benefit of all. Each villager had assigned him a certain portion of it, as a field or garden, graduated to the size of his family. Each one cultivated and reaped his own allotment, to his own use, and kept up the fence where it adjoined on him. The times for plowing, planting, and reaping in the "commons" were regulated by special enactments. Around the common field was left a vast tract of vacant land, open to all as a pasture-ground. In the French settlements, poverty was unknown, for the fields and pastures were free to all that would work. The newly-married received an outfit from the whole village, and had their place on the street, and in the field, assigned to them. The pasture-grounds of the French settlements were well stocked with cattle, horses, and hogs, wandering at large, the property of all. Care was a stranger to the villager, and was rarely entertained as a guest. Amusements, festivals, and holidays, came with frequency, to sweeten toil, and stimulate cheerfulness.

In addition to the villages, there were scattered throughout the West, on the smaller prairies, and the rich bottom-lands of rivers, country settlements of a patriarchal character. These, also, were uniform in appearance. In the middle of an inclosure of about two acres, stood the homestead, occupied by the parent family. Around the inclosure, and fronting on it, were placed, one after another, the houses of children and grandchildren. So that, in time, the aged father became surrounded by many growing families of his own lineage, all of them having a community of interest and feeling, each occupying its own cottage contiguous to the paternal roof. Scenes of this kind were frequent in the Illinois country, and on the Wabash, among the French, before the English had extended their sway over that beautiful region. Scenes of this kind may yet be found upon the coast above and below New Orleans. While the Anglo-Saxons along the Atlantic were struggling with a rugged soil, and fighting with the savages among the mountains, the French settlers at the West, far removed from civilization, surrounded by everything in nature which could please the eye or delight the fancy, were living at peace with the Indians, contented, prosperous, and happy, in the full enjoyment of the terrestrial paradise of America.

In the French settlements, the lands were held in common, and the vacant lands were free to all. The system of landlord and tenant had no existence among them. Hospitality was not so much esteemed a virtue, as a duty, which all cheerfully performed. Taverns were unknown; each house supplied the deficiency. They had no statute books, no courts of law, no prisons, no instruments of public punishment. Learning and science were terms beyond the comprehension of the simple villagers. In all matters appertaining to learning or religion, the priest was their oracle. On politics, and the affairs of the nation, they never suffered a moment's anxiety, believing, implicitly, that France ruled the world, and ruled it right. They had no trades or professions in their villages. The business of all was agriculture, and the care of flocks and herds. Each man was his own mechanic.

The winter dress of the men was a coarse blanket *capote*, drawn over the shirt and long red vest, and serving the double purpose of cloak and hat; for the hood, hanging down from the collar, upon the shoulders and back, could be drawn up over the head, to keep off the cold. On festive occasions, the blooming damsels wound around their foreheads fancy-colored handkerchiefs, streaming with gay ribbons, or plumed with flowers. The matrons wore the short jacket and petticoat. The foot was left uncovered and free; but, on the holidays it was adorned with the light moccasin, brilliant with porcupine quills, shells, beads, and lace.

The peculiar manners and customs of these French settlements, isolated at first—isolated for a century afterward—separated by more than a thousand miles from any other civilized communities, became characteristic and hereditary with the people, and have been perpetuated to the present time. In their ordinary deportment the villagers were grave and saturnine, from habit acquired from their Indian neighbors. In their amusements, however, they exhibited all the gayety of the original Frenchmen. The remnants of that peculiar population stand out now, among the bustling Yankees at the West, as distinct, as unbending, as the Indian races.

The French settlements, extending from Lake Ontario to the Mississippi, from Lake Superior to the Gulf of Mexico, though unmolested by the Indians, were, nevertheless, exposed to greater dangers upon the eastern and upon the western sides. The English were chopping their way up the Mohawk. The English were forcing passages through the Alleghany Mountains at the point of the bayonet. The English were clambering over the Blue Ridge, and hunting along the southern bank of the Ohio. And the Spaniards, in Florida and Mexico, laid claim to a large portion of the territory occupied by the French. As early as 1719, the Spaniards, alarmed at the rapid encroachments of the French in the upper and lower Mississippi valleys, made strenuous exertions to dispossess them. The war raged in Florida, and along the delta of the Mississippi, and among the swamps and uplands of the Red River of Louisiana. Nor was it confined alone to those regions. A grand scheme of conquest, worthy the days of Cortez and De Soto, was formed in Mexico. The hunters and traders of the Rio Grande had explored the great American desert, and had led the way overland to the borders of the Illinois country. Detachments of cavalry had penetrated the dreary waste, crossed from the branches of the Arkansas to the Missouri, and, following down the river, had witnessed the advance of the French in that quarter. The Spaniards planned the extermination of the French, along the Upper Mississippi, together with the Missouri Indians, their allies, and the establishment, in their place, of a colony from Mexico, to hold possession of the country, and perpetuate their claim to the interior of the continent.

As the spring of 1720 was advancing, all Santa Fé was in a state of unusual excitement. Armed troops of horsemen were galloping along the streets; foot soldiers were parading in the public square; the flat-roofed houses were covered with a gaping crowd; the wild Indians of the plains were there dancing the war-dance. Soon the horsemen, and the footmen, and the Indians filed off toward the mountains—a long and motley train, with waving banners, and swords gleaming in the sun, and strains of martial music sweetly floating in the air. As the head of the column approached the pass which led to the Canadian River, and the cavalry bugles were ringing and echoing from jagged rocks and precipices, there followed, in the rear, the body of the colonists struggling along the rugged and winding pathway — armed men; women and children on horseback; mules loaded with goods; priests in their robes; and mixed up with them, immense droves of cattle and swine, to be slaughtered for food, and to stock the plantations of the new colony.

After many days spent in the desert, wandering over arid plains, and crossing the numerous tributaries of the Upper Arkansas, the guides became bewildered. It was their design to reach the Osage country, and stir up those Indians to war upon the Missouris and French. But the guides lost the proper route, and led the way unconsciously into the heart of the Missouri tribes. The Spaniards did not discover the mistake, for the Missouris spoke the same language with the Osages. Believing themselves, therefore, among friends, they revealed their plans without reserve, and supplied the Missouris with arms and ammunition to aid in their own extermination. The wily savage perceived the fatal mistake, but encouraged the error. They requested two days to assemble the warriors for the contemplated expedition, in which they professed to engage with pleasure. The appointed time had nearly elapsed. The days were spent in feasting. The Spaniards, completely deceived, had fixed upon the next morning for renewing the march. But before the dawn of day, the Missouris fell upon their treacherous enemies, and dispatched them, every one, with indiscriminate slaughter. The tents were all spattered with the brains and blood of men, and women, and children. One priest alone was spared, and sent to bear the disastrous tidings to Mexico. That terrible defeat, together with the fall of Pensacola, about the same time, broke the spirit of the Spaniards, who, during two centuries, have been degenerating in the soft and balmy regions of Mexico and Florida.

The news of the terrible overthrow of the Santa Fé expedition soon reached the French, and apprised them of the designs of the Spaniards upon the Illinois country. To arrest any further attempt from the same quarter, a military post was established on an island in the Missouri River, above the mouth of the Osage. The late attempted invasion was the immediate cause, also, of the erection of Fort Chartres. About the same time, a detachment of ninety men was sent up the Mississippi and St. Peter's, and they built a fort and trading station at the mouth of the Blue Earth River, among the Sioux Indians. Fort Chartres was originally one mile and a half from the river bank. It was built in the form of a square. Each side was three hundred and forty feet in length. The walls were of stone, and were three feet thick, and fifteen feet high. It was a place of great strength for the Indian country. Fifty years afterward, the river broke through its banks, and, forming a new channel, undermined two of the bastions, and Fort Chartres had to be abandoned. The French, however, were never again threatened with Spanish expeditions across the plains. The fate of the first one had filled all Mexico with horror.

But the great danger to the French possessions in the interior of America frowned along the eastern mountains. The progress of the English settlements, from the first, had been exceedingly slow. Differing as widely from the French in policy as in character — stern, unyielding, unflinching — the English had, for a long time, been engaged in almost incessant war with the tribes of the Atlantic coast. The French had assimilated to the Indians; the English had exterminated them. In the populous parts of Canada were many flourishing native villages, cherished by the government; among the older provinces of the English, scarcely an Indian was to be seen. He was only to be found on the distant border.

The English policy was to subjugate the wilderness, to sweep away the forests, to cover the ground with an intelligent, hardy, thrifty population. Before them the crashing trees, the huge gaps in the woods, the dark, ascending smoke of the autumnal fires, heralded the advance of Anglo-Saxon civilization, from which the Indians fled as from a pestilence. It was the destiny of the French to overrun the great West. It was the destiny of the English to subdue it.

Their modes of effecting settlements contrasted as strongly as the policies which dictated them. The French penetrated into remote parts of the country, without any fixed plan of occupation; scattered over a boundless region; located hundreds of miles apart—on the Muskingum, the Wabash, Kaskaskia, Missouri, and Blue Earth rivers; at Niagara, at Detroit, Michilimackinac, and Green Bay. These distant settlements, feeble, isolated, scarcely made an impression on the wilderness. The English began within the sound of the sea, and established themselves firmly on the ground. They progressed slowly; but they cut everything clean as they went along. At each step they left behind them cultivated fields, flourishing towns, cities, institutions of learning, commerce, and the arts. The English settlements were generally close upon the borders, within reach of populous neighborhoods that connected directly with the strongholds of civilization and power. But this was the mode of the progress of English civilization between the sea-coast and the mountains. When those huge barriers had to be crossed, the pioneers had to go forward in detachments, and were separated, necessarily, at wide intervals from each other and from the older settlements. Thus disadvantageously situated, the English colonists at the West had to contend with confederated enemies;

they had to combat the hatred of the Indians and of the French combined.

Both the English and the French laid claim to the western country. But the French were in possession; which is nine points in law—with nations, the tenth point is the point of the bayonet. The French, from the beginning, were exceedingly jealous of English encroachments on the Ohio and along the lakes. They seem to have had a presentiment of the mighty force that would one day pour over the Alleghanies, and sweep them before it. They seem to have striven to keep the knowledge of the beautiful region of lakes and rivers, of forest and prairie, wholly to themselves. They seized all the Englishmen west of the mountains that they could lay their hands on, and detained them as prisoners of war. The French settlers were hospitable toward each other, kindly with the Indians, but murderous toward the English.

As early as 1687, Major McGregory, favored by the friendship of the Iroquois, had ascended with a boat-load of goods to Lake Huron, for the purpose of trafficking with the Indians along its shores. The appearance of an Englishman on those waters excited great commotion. He was promptly seized and imprisoned, and his goods distributed among the Hurons as presents from the French. English trade in that quarter was repressed for a time; the example of plundering Englishmen was distinctly set before the Indians; and the plunder distributed as bribes to follow the example. In 1749, La Jonquiere, governor of Canada, sent clear down to the mouth of the Muskingum River, in Ohio, to capture four English traders, and had them conveyed to Quebec. But English curiosity, resolution, and enterprise, were soon to break through all the restrictions imposed on them by the French.

Even as far back as 1716, Governor Spotswood, of Virginia, had recommended the establishment of a chain of forts along the Ohio River, to secure the possession of the western country. His proposition, however, had not been acted upon. The time had not then arrived for the English population to seek an outlet beyond the mountains. But, thirty years afterward, the region around the head-waters of that river had attracted considerable attention in Pennsylvania and in Virginia. Rumors of the advance of the French trading-posts, south of the lakes, had begun to disturb the English provincial statesmen. It was to have been feared, that their determined rivals upon the St. Lawrence would succeed in getting the entire possession of the interior, and in confining the English to the Atlantic coast. In order to counteract the plans of the French, and neutralize their influence over the western tribes, and obtain also a footing in the valley of the Ohio, a company had been formed in Virginia, with Gov. Dinwiddie at its head, known as the Ohio Company. The grant originally made by the British crown to that company, in 1748, for six hundred thousand acres of land, had afterward been transferred, in greater part, to the Washington family; and in such enterprising hands, measures speedily were taken to ascertain the precise positions of the French, and establish a fortress on the Ohio River. Gist, the company's surveyor, soon carried the compass and chain as far down as the falls at Louisville, to the great disgust of the Indians.

The summer of 1753 brought with it, to the middle provinces, the startling intelligence that the French troops, having crossed Lake Erie and fortified Presque Isle, had also erected military posts on the northern tributaries of the Ohio. Dinwiddie immediately dispatched George Washington with a message to the intruders, requiring their removal from the English territory. The distance through the wilderness to the French posts was six hundred miles. It was late in the season before the messenger was ready to depart. Washington took with him a company of eight men. He traveled to the border with horses, carrying tents, baggage, and provisions. The little cavalcade attracted much attention as it passed slowly through the remote settlements, scattered at the foot of the mountains. Toward the close of November—a month dreary with storms of rain and snow—the company plunged through the forest, and wound along beneath the dripping branches. The snow already lay on the mountains. Reaching the Monongahela, Washington passed down it in canoes to its junction with the Alleghany, and then up the latter river to Venango. There he saw the French flag flying over the captured dwelling of an English trader. He was referred to the commanding officer at Fort Le Bœuf, on French creek, a few miles south of Presque Isle. Repairing thither to deliver his message, the officer replied, that he would forward it to Canada; but that, in the meanwhile, he should hold possession of the country for the French. Washington's journey, going and returning, occupied four months. This mission confirmed the truthfulness of the rumors of the preceding summer. It became evident that the time for immediate action had arrived. The French had then to be forestalled in their progress toward the other parts of the territory, and driven out of their present fastnesses, or the whole West would have to be abandoned to them.

Early, therefore, in the following spring, Captain Trent, and a company of backwoodsmen, crossed over the mountains, from Virginia to the Ohio, with instructions to fortify the point at the confluence of the Monongahela and Alleghany rivers. The Virginians had begun the erection of a fort, and the woods were resounding to the axes, when, suddenly, they were attacked by a host of French and Indians, who, with sixty boats and three hundred bark-canoes, had descended from Venango to expel them from the territory. Captain Trent was obliged to withdraw in great discomfiture toward Virginia. At the same time, Washington himself was advancing in considerable force beyond the border; but, hearing of Captain Trent's disaster, he, also, fell back; after having captured a large detachment of the enemy, and after fighting all day long against fearful odds, at the Great Meadows. The disputed territory still remained in the possession of the French. This was the beginning of the old French war. Thus, in the forest, on the western slope of the Alleghany Mountains, was kindled a war between England and France, which involved in its struggles half the kingdoms of Europe. The contending parties were also on the Ganges as well as on the Ohio. America, Europe, and Asia, furnished each the great theaters for military display. Battles were being fought at one and the same time on the opposite sides of the globe. But in America the war assumed a new and striking aspect. A wilderness concealed the combatants. Army met army under the shadows of primeval forests: and when they did come together, the ax of the pioneer had to hew a passage for the bayonet of the soldier.

Upon the retreat of Captain Trent, the French proceeded with the fortifications which he had abandoned. They named the new fort Fort Du Quesne. The war thus begun continued for five years. That whole period was one of great suffering to the English colonists, who, perceiving the extent of their danger, spared no pains to avert it. General Braddock had been defeated and slain on the banks of the Monongahela; —but Nova Scotia and

New Brunswick had fallen to the English. The expeditions against Niagara and Crown Point had failed; —but a French army had been put to utter rout on the headwaters of the Hudson; and their general, Dieskau, taken prisoner. The tide of war had at last fully turned in favor of the English. General Amherst had captured Fort Du Quesne; Colonel Bradstreet had destroyed Fort Frontenac; and General Wolfe had taken Quebec. On the eighth day of September, 1760, the Marquis de Vaudreuil surrendered Canada, with all its dependencies, to the British crown.

The Great West at last was open to English emigration; the French no longer were standing in the way. But the western Indians were not included in the peace; and though deserted by the surrender of their white allies, the Indians were not dismayed. During the war, they had been taught by the French to believe that the sole object of the English was to get possession of all the fine lands in the country. They, therefore, became desperate in their determination to resist the advance of the settlements, and were preparing, under Pontiac, to renew the war, for the security of their ancient hunting-grounds between the Alleghanies and the Mississippi.

The West in the main was then a howling wilderness, promising, indeed, for the future; but for the present grandly desolate, and dangerous to English emigration. Over the vast tract of the Indian country was spread out one continuous forest, covering all the land, sweeping over hill and hollow in endless undulation, burying mountains in masses of verdure, and darkening the streams from the light of day. Green intervals dotted with deer, and broad plains blackened by herds of buffaloes, alone broke the sameness of the woodland scenery. And to these natural openings must be added the sparse and widely-scattered settlements of the French. Throughout that vast wilderness of woods were roaming Indian hunting-parties, and war-parties, hostile to each other; but, under French influence, grown more hostile toward the English. Taking advantage of this feeling, common to all the western and northern Indians, Pontiac, a great chieftain, began combining all the tribes in one savage confederation to surprise and exterminate the hated race. His arrangements were being made, over a territory of a thousand miles in width, among hundreds of different chiefs and warriors, with the characteristic secresy of the Indian nature. Not one single solitary indication of the approaching danger reached an English eye, while all the horrid elements of war in its most savage form were gathering along the whole frontier.

But, immediately upon the fall of Canada, while the Indians were yet concocting their scheme of indiscriminate slaughter, it remained to the English to complete the work of French subjugation, by taking possession of the military posts upon the Ohio and the Wabash, at Detroit, Michilimackinac, and Green Bay. The execution of that task was both difficult and dangerous. The nearest of these ports was six hundred miles from any English colony, and they also were hundreds of miles apart from each other. The route to them led through the midst of the exasperated allies of the French; but, fortunately, these allies, for the time, were bewildered and confounded. The perilous expedition to these distant parts of the Indian country was committed to the charge of Major Rogers — a man eminently qualified to perform that duty with speed and success.

Robert Rogers was born in New Hampshire. He was tall, broad-shouldered, athletic. His features were stern, almost rugged. His constitution and temper were as tough as the granite of his native hills. With a mind remarkably active, and leading a roving life, he was by no means uncultivated. His letters show that he was in the habit of thinking closely, quickly, and to the point; and they are written in a pithy, forcible style. Having been kept engaged, for many years, in frontier warfare with the savage hordes that poured into New England from the north, he had become versed in all the arts of woodcraft—in all the wiles of Indian cunning. He was sagacious, prompt, decisive, fearless; yet so cautious and so prudent that he has sometimes been charged, most unjustly, with cowardice. He never acted from impulse. Constitutionally wary, he had grown more so by experience. Neither passion nor the surprise of sudden danger could start him one jot. All his movements, even the most critical, were dictated by cool, deliberate calculation.

Major Rogers stood high as a partisan officer. He was in command of a body of provincial rangers, who, like their chief, had become inured to the hardships and perils of the border. Rogers' Rangers were equally hunters, woodsmen, and soldiers. Armed, like the Indians, with rifles, tomahawks, and knives, they were trained in tactics of their own, peculiarly adapted to wild bush-fighting. The principal theater of their action had been among the mountains around lakes George and Champlain, between the hostile fortresses at Ticonderoga and Crown Point. These solitudes had often been awakened by the frightful warwhoop, and the answering shout of the fearless rangers. In summer time, they had passed up and down those eastern lakes in whale-boats and canoes, or threaded their way over the shores in single file, creeping around rocks, peering out from behind trees, with all the caution of experienced Indian warriors.

Dressed in gray homespun, with close-fitting caps, and soft moccasins, they moved along like shadows. In winter time, they had tramped through the woods and swamps on snow-shoes; or, putting on skates, they had flown over the glary ice with the speed of the wind; at night they had slept in the drifting snows. The rangers had become a terror to the Canadian Indians. The savages did not feel safe for a single moment while passing through that region. Their white foemen had become as subtle as themselves, and ten-fold more persistent. Storms of rain or driving sleet afforded no security, for the rangers had become accustomed to face everything and endure everything, and would hunt a Canadian Indian to death in the track of a thunderbolt. The rangers were not naturally blood-thirsty; but some of them had been present when their own brothers and sisters had been butchered and scalped; others had seen from a distance the paternal dwelling wrapped in flames, and the father, and the mother, the guileless child, the helpless infant, all consumed; others had themselves been taken captive, their flesh stuck full of burning splinters, scourged, shot at, mocked at, in their agony. All of them had wrongs like these, of their own, or of their kindred, to avenge, the very remembrance of which made their sinews like triple steel. The achievements of the rangers, their rapid marches and counter-marches, their determined fighting, their midwinter battles, had made them famous throughout America.

On the evening of the twelfth of September, 1760, Major Rogers received orders to ascend the lakes with a detachment of rangers, and take possession of the forts included in the late capitulation. The troops were then encamped at Montreal. He embarked with two hundred rangers, in whale-boats, and swept along with steady strokes up the St. Lawrence. Winding through the channels among the Thousand Islands into Lake Ontario, they skirted the northern shore. The weather was rough, and their progress slow. They did not reach Niagara before the first day of October. Then their boats had to be carried over the difficult portage around the falls. Having seen his expedition safely afloat above the cataract, Rogers, with a small company, hastened on foot to Pittsburgh, with dispatches for General Markton. He rejoined his command at Presque Isle about the close of the month. The prospect, as they hugged along the shore, was dreary enough. The chilly winds came sweeping across the lake. The yellow-leaved beeches and maples were shedding their foliage. Dark clumps of hemlock and pine frowned gloomily over the shores. On the seventh day of November, the little fleet swept into Cuyahoga River. The British flag had never before been carried so far westward. The fall rains having set in, the rangers encamped on the bank until the twelfth.

Soon after the landing of the rangers, a party of Indians entered the camp, proclaiming themselves an embassy from Pontiac, ruler of all that country, and requiring the English to proceed no further without his permission. Before the close of the day Pontiac himself approached, with a number of chiefs, and demanded to know Rogers' business in that country. This was explained to him. Pontiac replied that he should stand in the way of the English until morning. He withdrew at dusk. The rangers, suspecting treachery, stood well on their guard throughout the night. In the morning Pontiac returned, and made a more formal reply, in substance, that he was willing to live at peace with the English, and suffer them to remain in his country, so long as they should treat him with deference.

That wily chief had been a fast ally of the French. The American forest never produced a man more shrewd, politic, ambitious. He saw the French power waning, and he would no longer openly prop a falling cause. By appearing friendly with the English, he would gain time to bring about concert of action among the disjointed tribes. He would seek to lull the English into fatal security. A blow too soon, though successful, would be ruinous. It would thwart the scheme of combining the whole Indian race in one universal war of extermination. It would bring the hated English upon the tribes separately, to destroy them by piecemeal. These may have been the reasons why Pontiac should dissemble, and assume the offices of friendship, and offer Rogers any supplies which he might have stood in need of.

The whale-boats of the rangers, toward the close of November, began moving up slowly between the low banks of the Detroit River. At last, the uniformity of marsh and wood-lands was relieved by the appearance of Canadian houses, on either side,—the outskirts of the secluded settlement. Before them, in the distance, was seen the French flag, flying above the bark roofs and weather-stained palisades of the fortified town. In obedience to the English summons, the garrison laid down their arms, and the red cross of England rose to the peak of the flag-staff. This was on the twenty-ninth day of November, 1760. The garrison were sent prisoners down the lake. The inhabitants were disarmed. An officer was dispatched southward to take possession of the forts Miami and Ouatanon, which guarded the communications with the Ohio River. The gathering storms of winter, and the drifting ice from Lake Huron, prevented Rogers proceeding further. Besides, his company had been weakened by the detachments sent off to the south, and seven hundred Indians were reported to be in the immediate vicinity of Detroit. Upon the return of spring, Michilimackinac, St. Mary's, Green Bay, and St. Josephs were delivered up to the English. Nothing was left to the power of the French, except their posts on the Mississippi, not included in the capitulation of Montreal. The conquest appeared to have been consummated.

The English, having gone into possession of the territory yielded up to them after five years of incessant war, succeeded to all the rights of the French. The English flag was waving over the fortresses along the Ohio and around the great lakes. But the West was an immense region, accessible only to the most fearless and hardy adventurers. The forts were altogether insignificant, when compared with the extent of country to be awed into submission by them. A few hundred men, broken up into small detachments, stationed at prodigious distances from each other, were charged with the keeping of nearly half the continent. The hands of the French were, indeed, tied by the treaty. It was supposed that the Indians, now their civilized allies had been conquered, would offer but little resistance to English power. Peace, it was hoped, would continue pretty much unbroken. All the wars with the Indians—all the savage inroads into English territory—had, for more than a generation, been ascribed to the machinations of the French in Canada. In every hostile war-party that, within the remembrance of the living, had brought conflagration and slaughter into the English homes, the sword and the tomahawk had been seen to gleam together. The fall of Canada had, indeed, been a terrible blow to the western Indians. They, for a while, were staggering from the effects of it. They were agitated for a season by conflicting emotions and passions. Surprise at the overthrow of their great ally, wonder at the sudden growth of their enemy bewildered them, and held their hatred of the English in suspense. The woods appeared to be all quiet. The Indians appeared submissive. But before two years had elapsed, the delusion of the English was dispelled, and the whole West was wrapped in flame.

CHAPTER VI.

Manner of trading with the Indians — Early routes to the West — The Albany route — The Philadelphia route — The Indian trader — His dress — Trading stations — The Indian's notion of the surveyor's compass and chain — The Acadians — Destruction of their property — Transported to the sea-coast — They gather, and emigrate in a body to the French settlements — Received with great hospitality — The Indian character.

At the close of the old French war, the English settlements extended from Georgia to Maine, along the Atlantic, and reached in from the coast about one hundred and fifty miles, to the mountains — a narrow border of civilization upon the edge of the dark back-ground of wilderness. Hostile military posts no longer frowned upon the western waters. Bold, adventurous men were eager to penetrate the wilds. Ever since Major McGregory had been plundered on Lake Huron, English traders had been impatient to secure to themselves the traffic with the Indians. The rich furs could be bought for a song. A few strings of beads, gaudy ribbons, hatchets, knives, gunpowder, and lead, and a little poor whisky, was all the stock required for the trade. In the distant forest, far beyond the reach of the law, dealing with ignorant savages, a system of cheating could be carried on with impunity, and enormous profits could be realized. The trader's goods were disposed of in packages, or by the piece, at prices regulated by his own greediness. Competition would seem to have been impossible. Whatever was bought of the Indians was bought by weight; a white man's hand placed on the scale was allowed to weigh a pound, and his foot five pounds. It is needless to say, that the weights grew heavier in proportion to the value of the furs that swung at the other end of the beam. Even though the bargaining may have been conducted honestly throughout, the trader's goods were unconscionably dear, while the Indian's goods were rated at merely nominal prices. With such golden opportunities before them, on the return of peace the greedy traders hastened into the West.

The American forest, in 1761, may be compared with the sea, in this respect: the sea had its ports, and the forest had its places of rendezvous and outfit. While the former were thronged with merchants and seamen, the latter were swarming with traders and borderers. The ocean and the woods were alike lawless and perilous. In the northern provinces there were two important places for fitting out for the wilderness. Albany and Philadelphia were competing with each other for the monopoly of the trade of the West. Both held communications immediately with the sea; and they had each a peculiar mode of inland transportation. Their advantages and disadvantages were about equally balanced. Albany had intercourse with the interior by means of rivers and the great lakes; Philadelphia, overland, and through the head-waters of the Ohio. The route from Albany was interrupted by frequent carrying-places; that from Philadelphia by a double chain of mountains.

Availing themselves of the opportunity for developing the western trade, which the surrender of Canada had, for the first time, afforded them, large swarms of traders set out from Albany and from Philadelphia with such kinds of goods as were thought most likely to please their savage customers. Those who went by the more northern route, passed up the Mohawk in boats or canoes, paddling where the current was not too swift, and at other times working their way against the stream with setting-poles. The latter process was called "punting." Passing by Fort Hunter, at the mouth of the Schoharie creek, and Fort Herkimer, at German Flats, they would make a halt for a while at Fort Stanwix, now Rome, at the head of river navigation. Thence crossing through the swamp to Wood creek, they would again embark. The channel of that creek was so crooked, that it is said to have run through in the night and got lost. Taking to the oars once more, on Oneida Lake, they would pass Fort Brewerton by the outlet to the Oswego River, which was once a broad, deep, clear stream, before the canal was dug along its banks; but, on account of that, the river is said to have been running swamp water, from sheer mortification, ever since. Shooting the falls, they would soon arrive at Lake Ontario. The rest of the way was plain sailing, except the long portage at Niagara.

The troops often followed this route. Lieutenant Gorrell, in 1763, passed over it with a detachment of soldiers. His diary shows some of the inconveniences which attended upon him: "July 2d. Dined with Sir William, at Johnson Hall. The office of superintendent very troublesome. Sir William continually plagued with Indians about him—generally from three hundred to nine hundred in number—spoil his garden, and keep his house always dirty.

"10th. Punted and rowed up the Mohawk River against the stream, which, on account of the rapidity of the current, is very hard work for the poor soldiers. Encamped on the banks of the river. Musquitoes. The inconveniences attending a married subaltern strongly appear in this tour. What with the sickness of their wives, the squealing of their children, and the smallness of their pay, I think the gentlemen discover no common share of philosophy in keeping themselves from running mad.

"Monday, 14th. Went on horseback by the side of Wood creek, twenty miles, to the Royal Block-house, a kind of wooden castle, proof against any Indian attacks. It is now abandoned by the troops, and a sutler lives there, who keeps rum, milk, raccoons, etc., which, though none of the most elegant, is comfortable to strangers passing that way."

When the Albany traders had arrived at Presque Isle, they could either continue on up the lakes, and spread out through Michigan and the north, or crossing to French creek, and down the Alleghany River, penetrate into southern Ohio and Indiana.

From Philadelphia, the route led over to the Susquehanna, at Harrisburgh; thence up the valley of the lovely Juniata, winding for an hundred miles through scenes of romantic beauty; and then across the mountains to Pittsburgh. Thence following down the Ohio, the traders could ascend its tributaries into the heart of the northwest. More commonly, the journeys by the southern route were made with brigades of pack-horses, loaded with goods, and led along the rugged pathways of the mountains, and urged on through thickets, and swimming the rivers, under the guidance of drivers who had been trained to their calling in the midst of the perils of the borders.

That class of frontiersmen who were engaged in the Indian trade have long since disappeared from the regions of their former renown. They were rough, bold men, intractable and fierce. During their seasons of repose among the homes of civilization, they kept the sober and steady people in constant alarm with their wild pranks. They loved to drink. They loved to dance with an earnestness and noise that sounded like the stamping of horses. They loved to fight, as they said, to keep from "spilin'." After sleeping a half a day on a hard bench in a bar-room, they would rouse up, "licker," go out of doors, and give a yell that would scare half a township. They wore coon-skin caps; huge blanket-coats, or hunting-shirts of smoked deer-skin; carried a rifle, knife, and tomahawk; made use of enormous powder-horns; and smoked, and swore, and drank, from morning till night. In the employ of a principal trader, these tough, fearless men would push ahead into the depths of the wilderness, shooting, as they went along, at a deer or at an Indian, just as the one or the other happened to come first within range. When the trains of horses had penetrated far enough into the Indian country, the owner of the goods would fix his head-quarters at some village, whence he would dispatch his subordinates in every direction, with supplies of red cloth, tobacco, paint, beads, and trinkets. This wild kind of traffic was liable to every species of disorder. And the overreaching and cheating of the traders, in the end, increased the exasperation of the Indians against the English.

In a very short period of time, regular trading-stations had been established at Pittsburgh, on the Muskingum and the Miami, at Sandusky, at Detroit, on the Maumee and St. Joseph's, at Michilimackinac and Green Bay; while numerous other places, on the branches of the great rivers, were visited, periodically, for the purpose of traffic. When the traders and hunters had fairly broken pathways through the wilderness, another class of men speedily followed after them. The agents of land companies, and surveyors, began looking up valuable tracts of land, running lines and blazing trees. Now nothing disgusted the Indians so much as this. They regarded the surveyor, squinting over his compass, and making marks on trees and in his books, as the white man's devil. He seemed to them to exercise some sort of enchantment over their lands,by means of which the English got into the possession of them. Squatting on their haunches around the wigwam-fires, they would talk it all over to one another, how the magical instruments stuck on the top of a stick would turn toward all the best lands, and how the chain would bind all fast to the white man.

These rude notions respecting the power of the surveyor's compass and chain were confirmed by the stories of the Delawares, and other tribes that had been defrauded of their lands in the older provinces. The miserable remnants, driven from their hunting-grounds, had sought a refuge beyond the Alleghanies, and, mingling with the Indians there, had taught them to regard these instruments with astonishment and fear. Wherever the chain had been drawn, settlements would surely follow, the woods would be cut down, and the Indians expelled. The French, also, had encouraged the notion, and had founded an argument upon it to induce the Indians to take sides against the English. And although Canada had fallen, Upper Louisiana was still a colony of France, and included the forts and settlements on the Mississippi, and Fort Massac on the Ohio, forty miles above its mouth. From these, agents and traders were going forth among the tribes with whom they had held friendly intercourse for nearly a century, and perceiving the cause of the dissatisfaction, they strove to promote it, in the hope of regaining their lost territory in the event of a general Indian war.

About this same time an event occurred which greatly strengthened the charge of rapacity brought against the English, and served to convince the Indians that there could be no safety in permitting the hated race to exist on the continent. It seems that during the late war, England had committed one of those acts of oppression which can only be justified, if at all, by appealing to the terrible emergencies of military strife. Acadia adjoined Canada. The inhabitants of both colonies had sprung from the same stock, spoke the same language, professed the same faith. They had been united in their history. They had entertained the same prejudices. They had cherished the same hopes; and both had participated in a common hatred of the English. Upon the breaking out of the war, which had raged clear round the globe, and had involved the most civilized as well as the most savage nations, it was feared that the Acadians might do more than sympathize with their kindred; and that, by joining with the other French and the Indians, they would make the burden of the war in America too great for England and the English provinces to bear. The situation of the English on this continent was then far more critical than at any other period since the first settlements at Plymouth and at Jamestown. A powerful enemy was in all the north, with fortresses and troops extending half way from ocean to ocean. The savages of a boundless wilderness, also, were in arms against them. The dwellings of Englishmen, along the borders, were blazing in midnight conflagrations, and the inhabitants, without regard to age or sex, were butchered with horrible barbarity. The frightened multitudes, fleeing from the ghastly terror, were crowding into the Atlantic cities.

England, therefore, had resolved to put it forever out of the power of the Acadians to take part with her numerous enemies. A fleet was dispatched to the suspected colony, commissioned to seize the inhabitants, destroy their property, and transport them to the coasts of New Jersey,

Delaware, Maryland, and Virginia. Thousands of those unfortunate people were torn from their homes, and cast upon the cold charity of the world. Strangers to our language, strangers to our manners, penniless, helpless, their mute sorrow had touched the humanity of the Anglo-Americans, who, by private subscription and legislative bounty, had endeavored to soften the hardships of their terrible lot. The work of despoiling the Acadians had been accomplished with a zeal bordering on ferocity. To prevent any lingering desire of home prompting them to return, they were not only stripped of their money and available property, but they had been compelled to look on while their fields were being wasted, while their houses and barns were burning, and their flocks and herds slaughtered.

The treatment of the Acadians could not have had a tendency to lessen their dislike of British rule. The inhumanity of tearing them from their homes, destroying all their possessions, and converting the places of their birth into a desert, had been too great to be atoned for by any subsequent acts of sympathy and kindness. At length the peace had come. Then, with a spirit honorable to them, and honorable to human nature, they determined no longer to eat the bread of charity at the hands of a race which had been guilty of so atrocious an offense against the rights of mankind. Gathering at last into one of the middle provinces, a band of desolate outcasts, they set their faces toward the West. A thousand miles of wilderness lay between them and the French settlements on the Mississippi; and they resolved to brave its perils. The aged grandsire, tottering on his staff; the slender child; men once rich, now beggared forever; women with infants at their breasts; all, all undertook the journey. The wilderness never beheld a more melancholy spectacle than when that company of fugitives passed into its shadows. Some died by the way. Some, from exposure, became hopelessly decrepit.

After a while, the wanderers, weary and foot-sore, reached the Ohio, and floated down in canoes and on rafts. They were received at the French settlements with great hospitality. Every house was flung open to them. Everything, in fact, was done to promote their comfort. Lands were allotted to them. Tools and seeds were given to them. Rations were furnished them from the public stores. But the iron had entered too deeply into their souls. Many pined away and died broken-hearted. Those who survived perpetuated their hatred of the English name. The wrongs of the Acadians were related from village to village. The dancers stopped in the midst of their graceful movements; the herdsman forsook his flocks; the hunters and voyagers delayed their departure, to listen to the terrible story. Anger was kindled anew in every Frenchman's bosom. Then they carried abroad with them what they had heard. Whereever a Frenchman could go in the wilderness, the story flew. Chiefs in council listened to it, and saw in the fate of the Acadians the fate of their tribes. The story was repeated in all the dialects of the West, and helped to bind the Indians still more closely with the French. From that time forward, their common enmity to the English was directed to the development of a great plan of extermination.

Another cause which also tended to hasten the catastrophe arose from the impolitic conduct of the English toward the tribes around them. The Indian nature is peculiarly constituted. It is tough, rugged, and inflexible. Its strongest element is inordinate pride. However ignorant he may be, or poverty-stricken, or whimsical, the

Indian, uncontaminated with the vices of civilization, has a most exalted sense of character. He is every whit a man; and, in his own opinion, a great man. An insult seems to leave a scar on his very heart. The remembrance of a wrong done him clings to him through life. His hatred is the most bitter of all hatreds; it may be smothered for a time, but never quenched. Though bare and breechless, he walks the earth with all the dignity of a born lord. It is his pride that makes the Indian so stoical as he is. He will not manifest his feelings. He may suffer keenly; but he will repress every expression of pain. It would be unmanly in him to give evidence of distress. His pride enables him to endure the most frightful torments at the hands of his enemies without flinching. When tied at the stake, in a position of utter helplessness, he will not move a muscle, though the explosion of fire-arms in his face should singe off his eyebrows. He will not so much as wink, though the tomahawk, hurled whistling through the air, should chip the top-knot from his head within an ace of the skin. But the Indian's pride is fully equaled by his vanity.

The French had understood the Indian character far better than their rivals, and they had adapted their policy to it. They had taken advantage of his overweening self-importance, and had won him to their cause. They had treated the Indian throughout, with the most flattering attentions; and had made him feel as though they thought about as much of him as he thought of himself. He could withstand the most awful tortures, but he could not resist the crafty appeals to his vanity. This was the secret of the French success in creating and maintaining alliances with the Indian tribes. But the English, on the contrary, had been altogether unaccommodating in their treatment of the Indian. They regarded him as an intruder on the soil, and he regarded them in the same light. They could not harmonize in any respect whatever. An Englishman, upon meeting with an Indian for the first time, would stand and stare at him as at a wild beast. That was offensive. But, grown more familiar with the sight, the Englishman would not notice him at all. That was more offensive still. Soon the Indian had become a nuisance, to be rudely jostled from the path; and that was a mortal offense. When the chiefs visited the forts, they were no longer received, as before, with every mark of honor and distinction, but were met with coldness and suspicion, or with utter indifference. The soldiers would make fun of them, mimic the tones of their voices and their pompous airs, and ridicule their appearance generally. The very boys were allowed to tease them with impertinent questions, call them nicknames, make faces at them. The officers would not invite them to the tables; but, after dinner, would send out crusts and bones to them in the yards with the dogs.

The pride of the Indians was constantly wounded by the conduct of the English. Repeated insults had been superadded to repeated injuries. The sagacious chiefs had seen the surveyors tramping about in search of the choicest lands, and they believed that a crowd of Englishmen would soon follow after them to destroy all the hunting-grounds. They had seen the unprincipled traders cheating their people out of their property, exchanging the most worthless goods for the richest furs, and making them foolish with strong drink. And these offensive things were not accidental, but intentional. Outrage had been reduced to a system. And the English forts and military posts had become like so many springs of bitter water, overflowing, and sending out their poisonous streams further and further through the wilderness. Such a state of things could not last much longer. A rupture had become inevitable.

CHAPTER VII.

PONTIAC'S WAR.

Pontiac — Indian method of drilling their warriors — Pontiac assembles a council — Pontiac's speech — His dream — The fort at Detroit — Pontiac inspects the fort during a calumet dance — Pontiac's conspiracy on the fort at Detroit defeated — A general destruction of the forts and settlements by the Indians — Stratagems of the game of ball, between the Ojibways and Sacs, and destruction of Michilimackinac — Fall of Venango — Condition of the frontier settlements — Colonel Henry Bouquet — His victory near Fort Pitt — A council with the chiefs — Their apology for the war — Bouquet's reply — Orders the Indians to bring in all their prisoners before giving them the hand of friendship — Meeting of long-lost friends — Conclusion of the Indian war — Assassination of Pontiac.

THE English colonies were illy prepared to meet the impending war. Those armies which had conquered Canada, had been broken up and dispersed. The rangers had been disbanded. The regulars had been sent home to England. There remained barely troops sufficient to garrison the posts in the Indian country. In the meanwhile, the deeply-rooted hatred of their oppressors was urging the Indians on precipitately to action, which would have much weakened the effect of the meditated blow, and have given the English time for preparation. But a master mind was busy restraining the impetuosity of the Indian character, and wielding a moral influence over the wild, discordant elements, to reduce them into a species of military order. An Indian chieftain, ruling over a large confederacy, with broad, comprehensive views of policy, is, indeed, an anomaly in the history of the wilderness.

Pontiac, the great leader of the Indian confederacy, is reported to have been not above the average hight of men. But his muscular form is said to have been remarkable for its symmetry and vigor. His features were irregular. His complexion was darker than is common with the Indian. The expression of his face was bold, stern, determined. His whole bearing was imperious. At the commencement of the war, he is said to have been about fifty years old. Ordinarily, his dress consisted of a scanty cloth, girt about his loins. His hair was not shaven, but hung flowing over his shoulders. Upon great occasions, he appeared before his warriors, plumed and painted, and in a robe, and leggins, and moccasins richly ornamented, in the most impressive style of savage art. He was resolute, wise, and eloquent. His capacious intellect grasped everything within the range of Indian vision. He possessed uncommon force of character; and in subtlety, he was more than a match for the wiliest chieftains of his race. With all those qualities which distinguish great men, it was his misfortune to have been born an Indian. He was passionate, treacherous, and cruel. One of Nature's noblemen by birth, he had been reduced by circumstances and position to a savage. His splendid genius blazed for a while in the wilderness like a fallen star.

During the summer of 1762 the conspiracy against the English had ripened to perfection. The hour of vengeance was drawing near. The danger extended the whole length of the western border, and was imminent to all the middle provinces. Early in the fall, Pontiac had dispatched his ambassadors to the Indian tribes. He had his head-quarters in a small, secluded island, at the opening of Lake St. Clair. From that place he had sent his messages throughout the country of the Ohio and its tributaries;

through the vast region of the upper lakes; through the wild fastnesses of the Ottawa River; through the entire length of the Valley of the Mississippi. And all the tribes north of the Cherokee country, between the Alleghanies and the great plains on the Missouri, had joined in the conspiracy, including even the Senecas, one of the Iroquois nations.

Pontiac had directed that the blow should be struck in the month of May following. The precise time had been indicated by reference to the changes of the moon. The tribes had been counseled to make a general and an instantaneous rising. Each tribe had been charged with the destruction of the English garrison in its own neighborhood. Then they were to fling themselves in a mass on the defenseless colonists. Throughout the recesses of the forest the preparations for war had already been begun. The Indians, indeed, had no armies to drill in complicated tactics, no military stores to provide; but a deep personal interest in the approaching contest had to be awakened in every warrior. The success of an Indian campaign would be dependent on the intensity of the passion which should urge each one on to heroic deeds. Concert of action could be secured in no other way than by bringing similar influences to bear with nearly equal force on them all. That was the scope of the Indian tactics.

For that purpose, the Indian war-songs and the Indian war-dances had long ago been devised. These were peculiarly adapted to stimulate savage natures to the highest pitch of excitement. Mere animal courage always will kindle quickly, by contact with its like, into a fierce and furious flame. Could the English, in 1762, have pierced the gloom of the wilderness, they would have beheld the enacting of scenes of demoniac grandeur that would have startled them from their fancied security. Throughout the vast region of lakes and rivers, in all the valleys, along the mountains, and the heavily-timbered plains, from north to south, from east to west, wherever the blood-stained hatchets of Pontiac had been accepted, the English would have beheld the gathering of the tribes for the rude discipline of savage warfare. In the night-time, fires would have been seen blazing beneath the leafy canopies, and sending out mingling streams of light and shadow into the woods around. And near each crackling heap of knots and brushwood, they would have seen a post, driven firmly in the earth, and so painted as to designate the enemy, against whom the direst of passions were to be wrought up to frenzy. Within the gaping circle of women and children, the warriors would have been seen, all painted and plumed, swaying with fierce exultation at the expected display of hatred toward the white men. Soon they would have beheld a savage, leaping and bounding impulsively within the ring, with brandished tomahawk, as if in the act of rushing on a foe, and the crowd, pressing and jostling each other, in the intensity of excitement more nearly about him; while he, loudly chanting the exploits of himself and his ancestors, with furious gesticulations, enacting the deeds he was reciting, becoming wholly frantic with passion, would strike at the post as he would strike an enemy, and tear the scalp from his imaginary victim. Then the swarms of warriors, unable longer to refrain from bursting into the arena, would have been seen jumping, and stamping, and rushing and leaping, their tomahawks gleaming, and their knives flashing, hacking, and stabbing the air in the fury of battle, exciting themselves and each other to madness.

That was the Indian method of drilling their troops for war. Each warrior knew how to use his weapons well. But the midnight pantomimes of murder gave him the spirit to use them on the designated foe. When all his excitable nature had been concentrated into one single burning point, he was ready for the war-path. From that little island in Lake St. Clair had gone forth an influence that had kindled hundreds of those baleful night-fires; and from that same island had gone forth another influence, also, that had restrained the fiercest passions of an excitable people, until the hour for action had fully come. Under so accomplished a leader as Pontiac, and following implicitly his directions, the Indians, though on the eve of an outbreak, effectually concealed their design. With the deep dissimulation of the race, they had become more friendly in their intercourse with the English, in proportion as the spring was advancing. When the troops had first taken possession of the forts, the Indians had come thronging within the inclosures, to gratify their curiosity, and observe the ways of the enemy, against whom they had been so long at war. In a little while, however, having become disgusted with the treatment which they had received, they had withdrawn altogether to the woods. And the soldiers had been congratulating themselves at being well rid of the nuisances. But while the winter of 1762–3 was passing away, the Indians had begun to come back again, in a most desultory manner and from different quarters, straggling into the vicinities of the forts, and pitching their tents a little way off. The warriors, as before, would hang listlessly around near the sentries, or squat in groups in the corners of the parade-grounds, smoking and grunting, apparently undisturbed by the rude taunts and jeers of the soldiers, and would endure to be poked about with the butt-ends of muskets without even a show of displeasure. They would beg, importunately as ever, for tobacco, gunpowder, and whisky. Observing this humility of the Indians, the English officers had flattered themselves that the wilderness was becoming entirely quiet. Major Gladwyn, at Detroit, had written in March, to General Amherst, that, in the neighborhood of his own post, the savages were perfectly tranquil. While, within cannon-shot from where that deluded officer was writing, lay the secluded island in the Lake St. Clair, where Pontiac, who had completed his preparations for the general rising, was planning a surprise of the very fortress of which the major was in command.

On the twenty-seventh day of April, 1763, the chiefs and warriors of the three great north-western tribes, in obedience to a summons from Pontiac, assembled in council on the banks of the River Ecorces. The spot which had been selected was a natural meadow, about eight miles below Detroit. As the bands came in and set up their lodges, the field became dotted with wigwams. There were the Ojibways, tall and naked, with their quivers slung, and war-clubs resting in the hollows of their arms. There were the Ottawas, close wrapped in blankets. There were the Wyandots, flaunting in shirts of painted skins, their hair adorned with feathers, and their leggins with bells. The assembly were seated in circles, row within row. Around were the women and the young men; further off, the groups of children and ponies; and beyond all, the woods.

Rising in the midst, Pontiac addressed them. He railed against the English, dwelling upon their rapacity, their arrogance, their injustice. He said the English had expelled the French, and were only waiting for some pretext to turn upon the Indians, also, and destroy them. He told them that the French king, at last, had awakened from his long sleep, and had heard the voices of his red children crying to him from the woods; that he was coming in his big war-canoes to wreak vengeance on their enemies. He told them that the Indians and the French together should again strike down the English, as they had done before, on the field of Braddock's defeat.

Pontiac then strove to enlist their superstitious feelings. He told them that the Great Spirit was angry with them for permitting the English to live among them, and adopting the English weapons and tools. He told them that a great prophet had been mourning over the destruction of the Indians, and had become desirous of learning wisdom from the Master of Life, but he was ignorant where to find him. Then he had fasted, and dreamed dreams; and it had been revealed to him, that, by moving forward in a straight line, he should reach the abode of the Great Spirit. The prophet had provided him a gun and powder-horn, ammunition, and a kettle, and had set out on his journey. On the evening of the eighth day, he had stopped in the edge of a prairie, and was cooking his meal, when he saw three openings into the woods, and three beaten paths entering them. Great was his wonder, for the paths grew plainer as the darkness was increasing. He had entered the largest opening a short way into the woods, when bright flames had leaped out of the ground, blazing before him. He had tried a second path with the like result. But he had followed the third path a whole day, when he came to a mountain of dazzling whiteness. It was steep, and the prophet had despaired of going further. Then a beautiful woman had arisen, as he was looking upon her, and she said to him, "How can you hope to see the Master of Life! with your gun, and powder-horn, ammunition, and kettle. Go! throw them away, and your meal, and your blanket, and wash you in yon stream. Then you will be prepared to see the Master of Life." The prophet had done as the woman had bidden him. And he had climbed to the top of the mountain. There a beautiful plain was spread out before him, and the wildest animals were tame; and the fiercest, gentle. And he saw there three large villages, the wigwams made of the most beautiful timber, far superior to the timber used by the Indians. While the prophet was standing, hesitating to enter, a man had come forth, dressed in gorgeous apparel, and had taken him by the hand, and bade him welcome. Then he conducted him into the presence of the Great Spirit, and left him confronting the dazzling splendors. And the Great Spirit said to him: "I am the Maker of the heaven and earth, the trees, lakes, rivers, and all things else. I am the Maker of mankind. And because I love you, you must do as I bid you. The land you live on, I have made it for you, and not for others. Why do you suffer the white men to dwell among you? My children, you have forgotten the customs and traditions of your forefathers. Why do you not clothe yourselves in skins, as they did, and use the bows and arrows, and the stone-pointed lances, which they used? You have bought your guns, knives, kettles, and blankets from the white men, until you can no longer do without them. You have drank their fire-water, which turns you to fools. Fling away all these things. Live as your wise forefathers lived before you. And as for those English—those dogs dressed in red, who have come to rob you of your hunting-grounds, and scare away the game—you must lift the hatchet against them. Go! wipe them off the face of the earth. Then you shall win back my favor; and I will make you prosperous and happy once more." Then the prophet had departed, and had reported the wonders which he had seen and heard.

Such is the meager sketch of a part of Pontiac's speech, which has been preserved to us by the Canadian French, a few of whom had been permitted to be present, and had heard him that day. Coming through two translations, and reported from recollection, it must fall far short of displaying the eloquence and beauty of the original. It is quite probable that other chiefs, also, may have spoken; but, with us, the interest of that occasion attaches to Pontiac alone. The encampment was broken up the next morning, so early that when the sun had risen and lifted the mists from the river the meadow was bare.

The western forts were situated as follows, namely: Presque Isle, now Erie; Venango, on the Alleghany River, at the mouth of French creek; Fort Pitt; Sandusky, on Sandusky Bay; Detroit; Miamis, on the Maumee River, one hundred miles above its mouth; Michilimackinac; Green Bay; Ouatanon, on the Upper Wabash, one hundred miles south of Lake Michigan; and St. Josephs, on the shore of that lake. Into the neighborhoods of all these forts the Indians were seen gathering early in the month of May.

Detroit was one of the strongest of the English posts. Some of them were merely block-houses. At the close of the French war, Detroit had contained twenty-five hundred inhabitants. On the western bank of the river, midway the settlement, stood the fortified town or fort, surrounded by a palisade twenty feet high, inclosing about one hundred houses, thatched, some with bark and some with straw, and a council-house, and a little church. The village straggled along the river, above and below. At each corner of the fort was a wooden bastion, which brought the sides within range of a cross-fire. The gateways opened beneath block-houses. The fort was nearly square, and it had two principal entrances, one from the river, the other from a large field, that had been cleared of trees, stumps, hillocks — everything that could shelter an enemy. Within, the streets were extremely narrow, except a broad passage, running entirely around between the houses and the palisade. Two small schooners, armed, the Beaver and the Gladwyn, lay at anchor in the river. And several light pieces of artillery showed their black, open throats over the bastions. The garrison consisted of one hundred and twenty soldiers, under the command of Major Gladwyn, and about forty fur traders, their clerks and attendants. Across the river, the bank was lined for five miles with French houses, terminating toward Lake St. Clair at the village of the Ottawas, and below at the Wyandots, opposite the Pottawatamies. The Canadian dwellings had each its garden and orchard, fenced in with rounded pickets, and extending back in narrow lines to the woods. Detroit, in 1763, was a lonely place to Englishmen.

The nearest English settlements lay along the Mohawk River. The nearest English post was the mere blockhouse at Sandusky. In the woods around Detroit, the Indians had been slowly gathering, all the spring, to the number of about two thousand warriors. But those who had appeared in the village and at the fort seemed docile, submissive, and friendly. Their apparent purpose was to trade, and have a good time, smoking and drinking, after the tedium of winter.

On the first day of May, Pontiac came to the gateway, and asked permission to enter, and dance the calumet dance before the officers of the garrison. He had brought with him forty Ottawa warriors. Upon being admitted they had proceeded to the corner of the street in front of the house of the commandant, and began the dance, in the presence of Major Gladwyn and several of his subordinates. The Indians first spread upon the ground a large mat, made from rushes of divers colors, and placed on it the calumet, and their bows, quivers, and tomahawks. Then they began a monotonous chant, during which, each, in turn, advanced to the calumet, taking a whiff and puffing out the smoke, as if offering incense. After that, they repeated their advances, tossing the calumet with their hands in time with the song, and displaying it to the spectators from side to side. When that had been gone through with, the dance properly began. Each singly, as before, moved over the mat with a shuffling gait, keeping step to the music, pluming the feathers of the calumet, and waving its wings, as in the act of flying from mouth to mouth. Next came the mimic combats to the thumping of a drum, the singing having ceased. Two warriors at a time advanced together, one with the calumet, the other with his weapons; and they went through a mock battle, keeping step as before, thrusting, parrying, flying, pursuing — the calumet always being victorious. Then the victor had to make a speech, bragging of what he had done, and of his ancestors, and tribe, and the Indians generally. All of them went through with the performance with spirit and effect; and before it had been concluded, the novel spectacle had attracted to the spot every officer, soldier, trader, and clerk, not on duty. The doors and windows around had been flung open, and women and children were gazing. It was remembered afterward that ten of the Indians had slipped away early in the dance, and were found prying about in different parts of the fort; but nothing had been thought of it at the time. That was the method which Pontiac had resorted to, in procuring an inspection of the condition of the fortress.

Modern experiments have demonstrated that the proper length of the rifle-barrel is about twenty-eight inches; but the hunters an hundred years ago prized that weapon for the length of its barrel, which usually was from three to four feet. On the fifth of May, Mrs. St. Aubin, a

Canadian woman, went over to the Ottawa village for maple-sugar and venison, and she there saw several warriors filing off their rifle-barrels about the middle. She mentioned this fact in surprise among her neighbors, when the village blacksmith remarked, that the Indians had been coming to him lately to borrow files and saws, and would not tell him what they wanted them for.

The next day a beautiful Pottawatamie girl, who had become much attached to one of the officers, revealed to her lover the grand plot for the destruction of the fort and garrison. Her affection had prevailed over her duty to her tribe. "To-morrow," she said, "Pontiac will come to the fort with sixty chiefs, each armed with a gun, cut short, and hidden under his blanket. He will demand a council; and, after making his speech, he will offer a peace-belt of wampum, holding it in a reversed position. That will be the signal of attack."

Major Gladwyn was possessed of rare courage and address. Calling his officers together, and communicating the plot to them, he set about the defense. Greatly fearing that the Indians might precipitate matters, and attempt carrying the fort by assault before morning, he kept half the garrison under arms; and, with his officers, spent the night watching. Early the next morning, a fleet of canoes was seen through the mists, coming over, with two or three Indians in each, moving slowly, and deeply laden. It turned out that the canoes were filled with warriors, lying flat on their faces, to escape observation. Soon, the field behind the fort became thronged with Indians, seemingly preparing for a game of ball. Warriors, wrapped in blankets, dropped in among them from time to time. Some approached the gate. Gladwyn had them admitted; determined to convince them, that, while he had discovered their plot, he also despised their hostility.

The whole garrison was under arms. The English traders had closed their houses and armed their men. Meanwhile, Pontiac was seen coming up the river road, with his sixty chiefs. Beaufait, a Canadian, says that he was standing on the bridge over Parent's creek, when they filed past him; and that the chief in the rear was an old friend, who, loosening the folds of his blanket, for an instant, displayed his shortened gun, with a significant gesture toward the fort.

At ten o'clock, Pontiac passed into the inclosure between the lines of soldiers; and though he must have seen that his plan was discovered, he did not alter his bearing in the least, but led the way directly across to the council-house. The officers were there to receive him, fully armed. "Why," asked Pontiac, "do I see so many of my father's young men standing in the street with their guns?" Gladwyn replied, that they had been out for review. The chiefs were seated, and, after the customary pause, Pontiac rose to speak, holding in his hand a wampum belt. The officers watched him closely. Once, it is said, he was about to make the signal; but, at a sign from Gladwyn, the drums at the door began beating the charge, and the hurried tramp of men was heard in the adjoining passage. The officers kept their seats. Gladwyn wished to destroy the plot, without bringing on an open rupture. The din ceased, and Gladwyn replied, that the Indians should have his friendship as long as they deserved it; but that he would punish the first act of aggression. The gates were again flung open, and the baffled chiefs departed. The plot had failed.

The Indians began falling off, and in a little while the fort was clear. In their view, artifice was wisdom.

With them, the object of the war was to destroy their enemies; and, for that purpose, all means seemed alike honorable. The Indians would have regarded a needless risk as a great folly. Had Pontiac ordered his followers to charge upon the armed garrison, probably not one of them would have obeyed him. In accordance with their strange superstition, they might, indeed, have reverenced him, afterward, as a madman; but his fame among them as a warrior, would have been lost forever.

Pontiac, though chagrined at the failure of his stratagem, was not discouraged in the prosecution of his war. He immediately laid siege to Detroit, hemming in the garrison within the fortress, and cutting off stragglers and supplies. For many weeks, the soldiers were constantly under arms, mostly on guard, the officers sleeping only in their clothes, with their swords beside them. At one time, a large detachment coming to their relief was captured on the river, and slaughtered. A schooner ascending from Lake Erie, with supplies for the famishing garrison, was attacked so vigorously that, although the desperate crew had slain three times their own number, the savages were thronging the deck, when the mate sung out below to fire the magazine. Some of the Indians understood the order. Then they began plunging overboard on all sides, bobbing, and ducking, and swimming for the shore, yelling with affright. Countermanding the order, the schooner was brought safely to the wharf. The Indians continued to press the siege of Detroit, with unexampled perseverance, for more than five months.

In the meanwhile, Sandusky, and St. Josephs, and Ouatanon, and Miamis, and Venango, and Presque Isle, had all fallen to the Indians, and the defenders had been butchered. Fort Pitt, which had been strongly fortified on the ruins of Fort Du Quesne, was also in a state of siege. The storm of war was sweeping along the whole border. The settlements had been attacked with frightful fury, the inhabitants murdered at their firesides, or shot down in the fields. Congregations had been surprised and slain in the act of public worship. School-houses had been captured, and teachers and children left in slaughtered heaps. Scores of captives had been burned alive at the stake. Hundreds more had been adopted into savage families, to fill the places of the Indians that had fallen. Terror reigned everywhere. Each neighborhood was occupied in providing for its own defense, so that none could lend assistance to the others. The settlements were being swept away in detail.

Michilimackinac had fallen at a single blow. That fortress, in 1763, consisted of a large area, inclosed by a high palisade, in the form of a square. It stood on the southern shore, close upon the margin of the lake. The houses, barracks, and other buildings, within it, had been built around a smaller square, in the center of the fort. These erections were of a single story, with bark roofs, and projections for stoops, opening toward the palisade. The settlement at Michilimackinac was composed of sixty families, half residing within, and half without the fortress. The garrison consisted of thirty-five men, with their officers, under the command of Captain Etherington. Two tribes of Indians were in that vicinity, in considerable force. The Ojibway village, which stood on the island of Mackinaw, contained more than two hundred warriors. They had another village, also, at the head of Thunder Bay. The Ottawas, to the number of two hundred and fifty warriors, were located on an arm of Lake Michigan, about twenty miles to the south-west. The Ottawas had become partially Christianized, and had made some progress toward civilization. Many among them were living in log houses, cultivating corn and vegetables beyond their own wants, and supplying the fort. But the Ojibways, in every respect, were thorough savages.

Toward the close of May, a runner had reached the Ojibway village from Detroit. "Pontiac," he said, "had already struck the English." The news created great excitement on the island; and the Indians there determined to attack the fort without delaying for reinforcements. Alexander Henry, who had resided at Michilimackinac, as a trader, since the fall of 1761, and who was one of the few that escaped the massacre, remembers to have seen the fort filled with Indians, on the third day of June, roving about among the soldiers with every appearance of friendship. His own house, too, had been thronged with them, coming there to buy knives and hatchets, often asking to look at his silver bracelets and other ornaments, with the intention, as would appear from their conduct afterward, of ascertaining where he kept them, that they might pillage him the more readily.

The fourth of June, 1763, was a warm and sultry day. It was the birthday of King George. And on that account the discipline of the garrison had been relaxed, and considerable license was allowed to the soldiers. A large party of Ojibways had crossed over, and encamped in the woods near by, together with several bands of Sac Indians, from the Wisconsin River. In the forenoon, some of the Ojibways invited the officers to come out and see a grand game of ball played by their nation against the Sacs. In a little while the fortress was half deserted. A few soldiers, indeed, lounged in the doorways and windows of the barracks; but most of them were outside the fort, scattered along in the shadow of the palisade, watching the game. Scarcely one of them had his arms.

The Canadians were squatted in groups on the grass, smoking; and a great many squaws were hovering around, wrapped in their blankets. Captain Etherington and Lieutenant Leslie were standing near the open gateway, — the former, a thorough Englishman, offering to bet on the Ojibways, that they would win.

The plain before them was swarming with the players. The game was a great favorite with all the Indian tribes. Two tall posts had been erected wide apart, to mark the stations of the rival parties, and each was striving to drive the ball beyond its adversary. Hundreds of lithe, dark forms, half naked, their hair streaming out as they ran, were racing and bounding hither and thither, to smite the ball with their long bats. In fact, the ball was scarcely permitted to reach the ground at all. Whenever it flew, the yelling and screeching crowd followed at the top of their speed, and drove it again into the air. Suddenly, the ball was sent spinning up to a great hight, and it descended swiftly to the foot of the palisade, while the tumultuous throng came rushing on, as if in pursuit, to the very gateway. In they swept, jostling the officers aside, crowding upon one another, choking the passage, till the fort was alive with Indians. It was the work of an instant. Before the English could recover their composure, the startling warwhoop was raised within the fortress, and responded to from the plain and from the woods. The squaws threw open their blankets, and furnished the warriors with knives and tomahawks. Then ensued a terrible scene of blood. The unguarded English were slaughtered without resistance. Mr. Henry says that he saw several of his companions scalped while yet alive and struggling between the knees of their savage butchers. Shrieks, groans, and yells, filled the air. Then for a few moments nothing would be heard but the trampling of moccasined feet, till some new victim had been dragged from his concealment.

Captain Etherington and Lieutenant Leslie had been seized at the outset, and hurried off to the woods. Mr. Henry clambered over a fence, and hid away in a Canadian garret. From thence he beheld the closing scenes of the tragedy. "Through an aperture which afforded me a view of the arena of the fort, I beheld, in shapes the foulest and most terrible, the ferocious triumphs of the barbarian conquerors. The dead were scalped and mangled; the dying were writhing and shrieking under the unsatiated knife and tomahawk; and from the bodies of some, ripped open, their butchers were drinking the blood, scooped up in the hollow of joined hands, and quaffed amid shouts of rage and victory."

The posts at St. Mary's and Green Bay did not share the fate of Michilimackinac. St. Mary's had been partially destroyed by fire the previous winter, and had been abandoned. At Green Bay, Lieutenant Gorrell had conducted his command with great prudence. Having with him only seventeen men, he had enlisted the Dacotahs, from beyond the Mississippi, to overawe the Menominees and Winnebagoes. But it was deemed not advisable to maintain so feeble a post. With a large party of warriors, he crossed Lake Michigan to the Ottawa village, where Etherington and Leslie were held as prisoners. A council was called, and those gentlemen set at liberty. The Ojibways had been seized with a sudden panic after the taking of Michilimackinac, and consented that the English might return to Montreal, where they arrived on the thirteenth day of August.

The fate of Venango, on the southern border of the wilderness, was for a long time shrouded in mystery. It had been destroyed, with its garrison, and by fire; but under what circumstances was wholly unknown. The charred and blackened ruins alone remained, with the fragments of bursted stones, pieces of melted glass and iron, fire-eaten knives and gun-barrels, and calcined bones — to tell their dreadful story. The friends and relatives of the garrison kept hoping that some of them might have escaped through the wilderness, or that they would be restored from captivity. But they had been smitten, every one, and had fallen the victims of treachery. After the war was over, a Seneca Indian related to Sir William Johnson the fall of Venango. He said that, long before a breath of suspicion had been whispered along the border, a band of Senecas, far outnumbering the garrison, had presented themselves at the fort with many expressions of friendship, and had been hospitably received and entertained. While they were being feasted, a few of them had withdrawn, and surprised the sentinels, and closed the gates. Then, turning upon their unsuspecting hosts, they had put them to death with the knife and the tomahawk. The fortress was burned over the scalped and mutilated slain. Lieutenant Gordon, the commandant, had alone been reserved for a most awful fate. Tied hand and foot, strung up on a bent sapling, over a slow fire, he had been roasted alive for several successive nights, his flesh burned with blazing brands, and tortured with whips, till exhausted nature could endure no longer, and he had expired.

Ensign Price, with a small detachment, had been stationed at Fort Le Bœuf. They had a narrow escape. The fortress was set on fire at midnight. It was a mere block-house, built of logs, the upper story projecting far over the lower one. While the whole structure above was in flames, and the Indians gathered in a half-circle before the entrance, yelling and screeching in savage glee, expecting the stifled inmates would soon rush forth to certain death, the brave men within took advantage of the uproar, cut a passage between the logs in the rear, and crawled out into the woods. They found shelter at Fort Pitt. In the morning, the Indians, poking up the ashes and embers, wondered what had become of the white men's bones.

The following extract from a letter, bearing date June 30th, 1763, will serve to show the terrible condition of the frontier settlements: "This morning a party of the enemy attacked fifteen persons, who were mowing in Mr. Croghan's field, within a mile of the garrison, (Fort Bedford,) and news is brought in of two men being killed. Eight o'clock. Two men are brought in, alive, tomahawked, and scalped more than half the head over. Our parade-ground, just now, presents a scene of bloody and savage cruelty; three men, two of which are in the bloom of life, the other an old man, lying scalped (two of them still alive) thereon. The gashes the poor people bear are most terrifying. Ten o'clock. They have just expired. One of them, after being tomahawked and scalped, ran a little way, and got on a loft in Mr. Croghan's house, where he lay till found by a party of the garrison."

A strong detachment was sent out through borders to reconnoiter, and they found every habitation in ashes, and,in many instances, the singed bodies of the inmates lying around. In addition to the slain, the inhabitants were flying for their lives. A person from the midst of those scenes wrote that a thousand families had been driven from their homes; that the woods were filled with fugitives, without shelter and without food. As the party advanced further, pausing at each smouldering ruin to bury the poor victims of savage fury, and hastening the flight of the living, they came into the region where the general massacre was yet going on. From every hill-top they beheld columns of smoke rising above the woods, each way, as far as the eye could see. Often they had to drive away the hogs from tearing and devouring the dead. Frequently they found the corpses of men and women still tied to the trees, where they had been tortured to death by fire.

The multitude of the fugitives was so great that the villages could not accommodate them. They had to encamp in the fields, in huts made of boughs and bark, living on charity. At one place, there were gathered three hundred men, and as many women, and seven hundred children. They were the remnants, in part, of murdered families. Many of them were utterly incapable of helping themselves, crazed with terror. Children cried and sobbed, fatherless and motherless, and sank to sleep among the leaves. Some of the grown people stood aghast and bewildered with griefs that were too deep for tears. Others settled down in the apathy of despair. Others kept weeping and moaning with irrepressible anguish. With not a few, every faculty had become absorbed in a burning thirst for vengeance. A dying boy, just expiring from his wounds, hoarsely whispered, "Here, take my gun, and kill the first Indian you see, and all shall be well."

In 1763, the transmission of intelligence through the West was made by the means of messengers, traversing the wilderness. These, the Indians waylaid and killed. A few reached their destination. Tidings of disaster on disaster kept coming in. It had become known that nine forts had been captured in quick succession. Detroit and Fort Pitt, each beleaguered with savages, alone held out. The vast territory, so lately won from the French, had been suddenly snatched from the conquerors. Sir

Jeffrey Amherst, the commander-in-chief, was forced to the conviction that the Indian tribes had risen in a general insurrection. He began immediately his preparations to put them down. It was, indeed, time for action. The western settlements, extending from north to south more than six hundred miles, were being wasted with fire and steel.

Colonel Henry Bouquet, with five hundred Highlanders, chiefly of the forty-second regiment, hastened from Philadelphia across the Alleghanies. By birth, a Swiss of the canton of Berne, Bouquet had been in the military from his boyhood. He was possessed of a fine person, and his bearing was composed and dignified. Distinguished by great activity, courage, and fertility of resource, he added to these qualities a power of adapting himself to the warfare of the woods. He was a thorough partisan soldier. He possessed a practical knowledge of the duties of his officers and men, for he would sometimes perform those duties himself. And at times, when it had become necessary to penetrate dark defiles, he was known to have taken the rifle, and to have gone out with his scouting parties, preferring his own eyes to the reports of others. In such a leader, the bold and hardy hunters could repose entire confidence; and they flocked to his banner as the little army was bearing it westward.

On the morning of the fifth day of August, the troops met the Indians in the vicinity of Fort Pitt. The battle raged all that day with doubtful success. Bouquet kept his camp in utter darkness during the following night. Not the slightest glimmer of a lamp should light the savage rifleman to his aim. The Indians whooped, yelled, and fired for a while at random; but they soon gave it up till morning. With the earliest dawn the battle was renewed. The rapid firing of the troops was followed by instantaneous charges into the cover, driving savages out of their hiding-places like startled wolves. The Indians were tasting for the first time the terrors of the English bayonet. Soon the approach of the bristling steel would send them flying in every direction. But they would come back again. In this way the fight had continued till nigh noon of the second day. In the meantime the condition of the army was becoming frightful. The wounded were dying of thirst. No water could be had. The suffering of the soldiers was intolerable. Then Bouquet's genius displayed itself. He had observed that the enemy would fire, and immediately run to escape the bayonet. How should he bring them into a body, so that a charge could be made effectual? Making his arrangements with great rapidity, the rear was strengthened, and the weakened front soon began to fall back, as if overpowered and about to retreat. To the Indians the battle seemed to be won. Leaping in fury forward, they became compacted together, completely exposed, and ardent in the pursuit. Suddenly they received a heavy flank fire, and through the smoke, at full run, came the dreaded bayonets. There was no place of concealment. There was no quarter shown. The savages crowded upon each other, writhed, dodged, and snatched at the gun-barrels, and threw themselves on the ground, thinking to crawl under the line of steel, to get at the advancing troops. It was all in vain. The incessant thug, thug, thug of the merciless weapon as it drove through their naked forms, was dropping them thickly over the ground. At last, with yells of terror, they broke and fled. But one prisoner had been taken; and him the exasperated borderers, in spite of remonstrance and of authority, shot to death like a captured wolf. The little army had lost eight officers and one hundred and fifteen men slain. During the battle the pack-horses, frightened by the uproar, had made a general stampede. Bouquet, therefore, had to destroy all the surplus baggage. Bearing the wounded along on litters, the troops reached Fort Pitt on the tenth.

The moral effect of the victory was very great. The despairing colonists were aroused to action. In western Pennsylvania, a body of riflemen was organized under the command of James Smith, who had been several years a prisoner among the Indians. He understood the Indian mode of fighting to perfection. He had his men dressed like warriors, and their faces painted, and he trained them in the Indian discipline. From Western Virginia a thousand riflemen had taken the field. The tide of war soon flowed back into the wilderness, and the Indian villages began to be smitten in their turn. Late in the fall, a large detachment had ascended Lake Erie, and raised the siege of Detroit. Pontiac retired into the country upon the head-waters of the Maumee. In the spring, a large body of English troops was gathered at Sandusky; and Bouquet, having been reinforced at Fort Pitt, took up his line of march through the heart of the Indian country. The savages abandoned their villages, and fled at the approach of so large an army.

The order of the march was such as to make an ambush, or a surprise, impossible. Far in advance, a body of scouts was exploring every hill, valley, thicket, and ravine. On either flank, the woods were scoured for miles by skillful hunters. At night, the great body of the troops slept outside of the camp-fires, among the trees. While advancing, in this guarded manner, upon the Indian villages within the recesses of the forest, a deputation of warriors was received, and they requested a council, and offered the submission of their tribes. But Bouquet, fearing treachery, while consenting to the council, determined that the negotiations should be conducted under the muzzles of his guns. He ordered that the chiefs should meet him the next day at a point on the Muskingum River, a little below his camp. Booths were erected for the officers and chiefs. In the morning, the army moved in order of battle to the place of council, and took up its position in a natural meadow in front of the booths. The spectacle of fifteen hundred Englishmen in arms was to the Indians new and astounding.

The silence that reigned along the lengthened lines, the barrels and bayonets flashing in the sun, the tartans of the Highlanders, the bright red of the Royal Americans, the dark uniforms and trappings of the colonial militia, the hunting frocks of the backwoodsmen, with their long rifles—all combined, formed an imposing display of military power that created a deep impression on the savage warriors, and made the chiefs quite sincere in their desires for peace.

The effect of the presence of a powerful army was immediately apparent. The chiefs endeavored to excuse the war, saying, that they had been driven into it by the western Indians, and by their own hot-headed young men; that they were now anxious to be at peace with the English, and to have protection against the tribes beyond them to the westward. Bouquet's reply is a masterpiece of diplomatic skill in dealing with Indians. Assuming great sternness, he said: "Your excuses are frivolous and unavailing. Your conduct is without apology. You could not have acted through fear of the western Indians, for you know, that, had you been faithful to us, we would have protected you against them. As for your young men, you should have punished them, if they did wrong. You have been violent and perfidious. You robbed and murdered in cold blood the traders among you. With base treachery you took our out-posts and garrisons, and assailed our troops — the same that now stand before you. Not content with that, you burned our houses, and killed our women and children, and have got many captives hidden away in the woods. You have been prowling around this army during its march, and would have attacked it, had you dared. The other Indians have made peace with us. You are now in our power. We can cut you off the face of the earth. But the English are great and powerful, and will let you live, if you will do as I bid you. I give you twelve days to bring to me all your prisoners: Englishmen, Frenchmen, women, and children; whether adopted into your tribes, married, or living among you on any pretense whatsoever. You shall furnish them with food, clothing, and horses, to carry them back to their homes again. Comply with these conditions, and then I will tell you on what terms I will let you live."

Bouquet required the chiefs to remain in his camp, as hostages, till the prisoners should all be brought in; and, in the meantime marched into the immediate vicinity of the Indian towns, and fortified his camp, dispatching bodies of troops to hasten the compliance with his terms. Band after band of captives were brought in daily, until more than two hundred had been collected, which was all that could be ascertained to be in that part of the country. Until then, Bouquet had refused all friendly intercourse with the Indians. And they, judging him by their own ferocity, were constantly in terror lest he should put them all to the sword. At last, he gave them the hand of friendship. A Delaware chief had refused to come in. Bouquet ordered the tribe to depose the refractory chief, and appoint another in his stead. The Indians were completely cowed. Upon his return, Bouquet carried with him the captives, and also a large number of chiefs, as hostages for the continuance of the peace.

When the army had drawn near to the frontier, it was met by a great company in search of lost relatives and friends. Husbands found their wives, and parents their children, from whom they had been separated for years. Women, frantic between hope and fear, were running hither and thither, looking piercingly into the face of every child, to find their own, which, perhaps, had died—and then such shrieks of agony! Some of the little captives shrank from their own forgotten mothers, and hid in terror in the blankets of the squaws that had adopted them. Some that had been taken away young, had grown up and married Indian husbands or Indian wives, and now stood utterly bewildered with conflicting emotions. A young Virginian had found his wife; but his little boy, not two years old when captured, had been torn from her, and had been carried off no one knew whither. One day, a warrior came in, leading a child. No one seemed to own it. But soon the mother knew her offspring, and screaming with joy, folded her son to her bosom. An old woman had lost her granddaughter in the French war, nine years before. All her other relatives had died under the knife. Searching, with trembling eagerness, in each face, she at last recognized the altered features of her child. But the girl had forgotten her native tongue, and returned no answer, and made no sign. The old woman groaned, and cried, and complained bitterly, that the daughter she had so often sung to sleep on her knees, had forgotten her in her old age. Soldiers and officers were alike overcome. "Sing," whispered Bouquet, "sing the song you used to sing." As the low, trembling tones began to ascend, the wild girl gave one sudden start, then listening for a moment longer, her frame shaking like an ague, she burst into a passionate flood of tears. That was sufficient. She was the lost child. All else had been effaced from her memory but the music of the nursery-song. During her captivity she had heard it in her dreams.

The war was over. The English provinces, relieved from their great burdens, soon began to grow rapidly. The time was nearly come for a civilized people to extend themselves over the uplands and prairies, and along the lakes and rivers, and occupy permanently the West. In the meantime, France, by the treaty of 1763, had ceded to England all the territory east of the Mississippi River. The French inhabitants of the Illinois country received the news of their transfer with sorrow and anger. Many of them, unwilling to live under the shadow of the British flag, fled to New Orleans. Others removed to the opposite bank of the river at St. Geneviève. But a far greater number took the route by the way of Cahokia, and joined the new settlement on the western bank, that had been established by Pierre Laclede. That adventurer, in August, 1763, had set out with a large party of traders and hunters from New Orleans, and had ascended to the mouth of the Illinois River. The journey had been made in boats, and had occupied three months. Selecting a spot on the Mississippi, where a line of bluffs, beautifully wooded, rose with an easy ascent from the water, to a high, rolling prairie, Laclede had erected a storehouse, a few cabins, and a slight palisade. This was at the close of November. Those erections constituted the first foundations of the city of St. Louis.

But the French flag was still flying at Fort Chartres, and the smaller posts in that vicinity. Major Loftus, with four hundred regulars, had attempted to ascend the Mississippi, and take possession of the Illinois country. He had embarked at New Orleans in March, 1764, when the river was at its flood; but the repeated attacks of the Indians, together with the swiftness of the current, had compelled him to return. Captain Sterling, however, had better success in reaching those distant fortresses. Setting out from Fort Pitt, toward the close of the winter following, with one hundred Highlanders, he had floated down the Ohio with the drifting ice. To him the French flag descended from the ramparts of Fort Chartres, and the neighboring posts, and the English were completely in possession of the western country, after having endured the horrors of two sanguinary wars. Four years later, Pontiac was assassinated at Cahokia. The remains of the great chief were buried at St. Louis, where the race he so much hated are trampling with unceasing footsteps over his forgotten grave.

CHAPTER VIII.

CONQUEST OF THE WEST BY THE UNITED STATES.

English and French settlements contrasted — Want of elbow-room — The Yankee pioneers — Their character — Recklessness — Peculiar dress — Their Houses, etc. — "Hog and hominy" — "Old Ned" — Tomahawk rights — Col. Clark at the West — His character — Descends the Ohio — Sinks his boats — Surprises Kaskaskia — Inhabitants declare for the United States — British Lieutenant-governor, Rocheblane, captured — Vincennes taken — Militia organized — Clark among the Indians — "Courts of Illinois" — British governor, Hamilton, descends the Wabash with one thousand men — Ruse of Capt. Helm — Clark's winter march — Hamilton surrenders — Territory held by Col. Clark until the close of the war.

After the general peace with the Indians, it was to have been expected that settlements might be made at the West with safety. The late military achievements in the vicinity of the lakes and in the valley of the Ohio had established the supremacy of the English. The British flag was waving over the wilderness, from Niagara to the Mississippi. Nothing seems then to have been standing in the way of the speedy colonization of the country. Bold, adventurous men were pining for the larger liberty of the woods. Moreover, the fearful struggle through which the colonists had just been passing had called into existence a restless courage, that could not remain satisfied with the repose of a quiet time. A new want, also, strangely inconsistent with a sparse and scattered population, began to be felt; and it soon drove hundreds of men off in a westerly direction. It was the want of "elbow-room." The spirit of the borderers was impelling them to seek in the excitements of the forest a substitute for the excitements of war. A peaceful life seemed dull and insipid to them. They had actually acquired a relish for danger.

Large numbers were hastening forward to secure to themselves the choice of the best locations. For that purpose, the pioneers set out in parties, and traveled together far beyond the border; then, separating, they roamed over a vast extent of country, selecting each a place for himself. Thus settling down alone, and living in entire seclusion, they in a short time acquired habits utterly inconsistent with the development of civilization A close, compact neighborhood soon came to be unendurable. One man is said to have abandoned his clearing, and removed further west, because somebody else had come so near to him that he could hear the crack of his rifle. And another, observing a smoke rising over the other side of the valley where he had located, traveled fifteen miles to reach it; and, finding a settler there, quit the country in disgust, population having become too dense for him. But these, probably, are extreme cases. It is well known, however, that, when the English had undertaken the subjugation of the wilderness, they attempted it in a manner without a precedent in history. They did not sweep down suddenly upon it, with a force that would reduce its savage inhabitants at once into submission; but, by a sort of hectoring process, they wore away upon the woods, chafing and exasperating the Indians while gradually exterminating them. The English colonists, in the West, did not compromise with danger—they boldly took it by the beard.

The success of these early adventurers is almost a miracle in colonization. Nation has heretofore precipitated itself upon nation, conquering the occupants of the soil, and seizing upon their possessions. But in the case of the English settlement of the western country, we find that isolated emigrants, without the benefits of a military or of a civil organization, relying solely upon their own bravery, and the assistance of each other, took and held the possession of an extensive country, and laid the foundations of powerful states. They kept falling, it is true, under the knife and the tomahawk, and would have become entirely cut off, had it not been for the incessant streams of population supplying the waste of life, until the Indians, discouraged in a contest with an enemy whom no defeat could dishearten, sought safety in the most abject submission.

Such men, exposed to constant peril, and compelled to be on their guard at all times and places to avoid being surprised and slain, driven by necessity into fearful encounters with the wily savages in the defense of home and kindred, of necessity became fearless, reckless, implacable, and eager for victory and for vengeance. In time it was ascertained that the hostility of the Indian races was not so much excited against the English as a people, as against the settlers that were crowding in upon them. It was, therefore, an easy matter, after the breaking out of the war between Great Britain and her revolted colonies, to array the exasperated tribes of the West against the Anglo-Americans.

One general trait has always characterized the frontier settlers of the wilderness. They were daring, boisterous, enterprising men. They were robust, rugged, tough — caring nothing for luxuries or for comforts, and capable of enduring any amount of exposure without injury. The forerunners of civilization were not carpet knights, basking in the sunshine of a smile, and trembling at a frown, but men of iron nerves. Wild as untamed nature, they could scream with the panther, howl with the wolf, whoop with the Indian, and fight all creation. Forever going through hair-breadth escapes, some of them became indifferent to every peril, and would "chaw" two inches of live bear's tail for the toothache, quite careless whether bruin was pleased with the performance or not. One grizzly old fellow, slightly stoop-shouldered, with a great burned strip down his cheek, his left eye twisted round sideways, having been tomahawked, and had his scalp started, said he believed he might yet be killed sometime, as the lightning had tried him on once, and would have done the business for him, if he had n't dodged.

The pioneers, living in constant contact with the Indians, necessarily became more than half savages in appearance, habits, and manners; and frequently the whole savage character was assumed. Their ordinary dress was too unique to be forgotten. A coonskin cap, with the tail dangling at the back of the neck, and the snout drooping upon the forehead; long buckskin leggins, sewed with a wide, fringed welt, down the outside of the leg; a long, narrow strip of coarse cloth, passing around the hips and between the thighs, was brought up before and behind under the belt, and hung down flapping as they walked; a loose, deerskin frock, open in front, and lapping once and a half round the body, was belted at the middle, forming convenient wallets on each side for chunks of hoe-cake, tow, jerked venison, screw drivers, and other fixings; and Indian moccasins completed the hunter's apparel. Over the whole was slung a bullet-pouch and powder-horn. From behind the left hip dangled a scalping-knife; from the right protruded the handle of a hatchet; both weapons stuck in leathern cases. Every hunter carried an awl, a roll of buckskin, and strings of hide, called "whangs," for thread. In the winter loose deer-hair was stuffed into the moccasins to keep the feet warm.

The pioneers lived in rude log-houses, covered, generally, with pieces of timber, about three feet in length and six inches in width, called "shakes," and laid over the roof instead of shingles. They had neither nails, glass, saws, nor brick. The houses had huge slab doors, pinned together. The light came down the chimney, or through a hole in the logs, covered with greased cloth. A scraggy hemlock sapling, the knots left a foot long, served for a stairway to the upper story. Their furniture consisted of tamarack bedsteads framed into the walls, a few shelves supported on long wooden pins; sometimes a chair or two, but more often, a piece split off a tree, and so trimmed, that the branches served for legs. Their utensils were very simple; generally nothing but a skillet, which served for baking, boiling, roasting, washing dishes, making mush, scalding turkeys, cooking sassafras tea, and making soap. A Johnny-cake board, instead of a dripping-pan, hung on a peg in every house. The corn was cracked into a coarse meal, by pounding it in a wooden mortar. As soon as swine could be kept away from the bears, or, rather, the bears away from them, the pioneers indulged in a dish of pork and corn, boiled together, and known among them as "hog and hominy." Fried pork they called "old Ned."

Unlike the French, who clustered in villages, and had their common fields, our Yankee settlers went the whole length for individual property. Each settler claimed for himself four hundred acres of land, and the privilege of taking a thousand acres more, contiguous to his clearing. Each one run out his own lines for himself, chipping the bark off the trees, and cutting his name in the wood. These claims, so loosely asserted, were called "tomahawk rights," and were respected by all the emigrants. Each settler went to felling the timber and chopping house-logs, sleeping, meanwhile, under a bark cover raised on crotches, or under a tree. It is said of one of them that he could hardly stomach his house, after it was done. The door-way was open, the logs unchinked, and the chimney gaped wide above him; but the air was too "cluss,"—he had to sleep outside for a night or two to get used to it.

Such were the people, and such their modes of living, that began to spread themselves throughout the West, between the close of Pontiac's war and the commencement of the American Revolution. Then, when that struggle came on, new difficulties gathered thickly around the scattered settlements. The reduction of the wilderness was a huge task of itself, even with every encouragement, and without opposition of any sort. But the Anglo-Saxon seems to have had everything arranged against him. Not only the forest, and the wild beasts, and untold privations, stood in the way of his progress; but the French first tried to crowd him out; then the Indians sought to kill him; and, lastly, the British turned against their own flesh and blood, and bribed the savages to take his life. While the armies of England were ravaging and wasting the whole Atlantic coast, from Massachusetts to Georgia, the British governor at Detroit, and his agents at the forts on the Wabash and Maumee rivers, and at Kaskaskia, were busily engaged in inciting the Indians to deeds of rapine and murder on the western frontier. The terrible scenes of the old French war, and of Pontiac's war, were beginning to be reënacted. But the pioneers were now of a different temper altogether from those who had suffered previously in Pennsylvania and Virginia, and who had fled in terror from their own burning habitations. The Yankee pioneers did not wait to be smoked out, and have their throats cut, and their scalps torn off their heads. That was a game they could participate in as well as their enemies.

No sooner, therefore, was it known that British emissaries were at work among the savages, stirring them up to deadly strife against the American settlers, than it was determined upon to carry the war into the wilderness itself,—to the very doors of the enemy. Patrick Henry was one of the first to set the ball of the Revolution in motion. His eloquence as an orator was not greater than his foresight as a statesman. It is to his perception of the designs of Great Britain upon the western country, that the United States are indebted for the preservation of the immense region to the north of the river Ohio. In 1778, Patrick Henry was the governor of Virginia. He had planned a secret expedition against the British forts in the Illinois country. And on the second day of January, Governor Henry issued his instructions to Lieutenant-colonel George Rogers Clark, directing him to "Proceed with all convenient speed to raise seven companies of soldiers, to consist of fifty men each, officered in the usual manner, and armed most properly for the enterprise, and with that force to attack the British fort at Kaskaskia." His Excellency also directed Colonel Clark "to apply to the commanding officer at Fort Pitt for boats." He further cautioned him: "During the whole transaction, you are to take especial care to keep the true destination of your force secret;—its success depends on this."

The evidence of British agency among the Indians was full and complete. It had been ascertained that the British commissioners, at a great council, had told the chiefs that the people of the States were few in number, and might easily be subdued; and that, on account of their disobedience to the king, they justly merited all the punishment which white men and Indians could possibly inflict upon them. They had added, that the king was rich and powerful, both in subjects and in money; that his rum was as plenty as the water in the lakes; and that, if the Indians would assist in the war until its close, they should never want for money or goods. To complete the atrocity, they offered rewards for the scalps of men, women, and children. In consequence of these representations and persuasions, the tribes had eagerly espoused the quarrel of Great Britain, and were being supplied with their weapons, and ammunition, and with presents, at the various British forts from Detroit to Kaskaskia. Fort Chartres was now no longer occupied. It had been undermined in 1772, by the Mississippi, and since then it had been abandoned.

Now, the expedition through the hostile wilderness, for the reduction of those forts, and for the purpose of overawing the Indians, could not have been confided to better hands. George Rogers Clark was a Virginian by birth. He had become a pioneer from choice. His military genius made him the most prominent defender of the West, at the most critical period of American history. Colonel Clark was one of the finest appearing men of his time. He would have attracted attention among a thousand. Conscious dignity sat gracefully upon him. His commanding presence was made pleasing by uncommon sweetness of temper, and particularly agreeable by the manliness of his deportment, the intelligence of his conversation, and, above all, by the vivacity and boldness of his spirit. Colonel Clark was born a general. He certainly was the most competent officer that ever led an army against the Indians; and he seems to have had a tact for managing those impulsive, uncontrollable beings better than any other person. He possessed extraordinary military talents, and an energy of character that enabled him to plan with consummate wisdom, and to execute his designs with great decision and promptitude. He seems to have been able to penetrate the designs of the enemy with the utmost exactness, and never once failed in anticipating and defeating their hostile movements. His judgment was unerring. He never hesitated. He never was rash. And he was successful where failure would seem to have been inevitable.

The only means that were furnished to Colonel Clark for his expedition, besides the order for boats and ammunition, consisted of twelve hundred dollars in depreciated paper, and a promised bounty of three hundred acres of land to each private. He encountered great difficulty in recruiting his companies from the settlements, which already were too feeble for their own protection. And a secret enterprise was decidedly unpopular. Colonel Clark set about his preparations in January, but it was not till in June following, that his captains reached Fort Pitt with their levies, in all less than six, in complete companies. With these he descended the Ohio to the falls, and encamped a while on Corn Island, in hopes of receiving additions from the Kentucky stations; but it was deemed inexpedient to reduce their strength. With one hundred and fifty-three men, armed after the Indian fashion, Colonel Clark floated down the river below the mouth of the Tennessee. Having there obtained information relative to the actual condition of the British posts on the Upper Mississippi, he determined to march overland, and surprise Kaskaskia. Causing his boats to be sunk for concealment, he led his force through the wilderness, across extensive marshes, a distance of one hundred and twenty miles, each man carrying his own rations and baggage. The troops were often knee-deep in the water upon the marshes.

They arrived in the vicinity of Kaskaskia on the evening of the fourth of July, 1778. At midnight, Colonel Clark told his men "That the town and fort were to be taken at all hazards." The principal street was immediately secured, and a guard stationed at every avenue. All was still. Lieutenant-governor Rocheblanc, the British commandant, believing his post was entirely safe at so great a distance from the American settlements, had neglected setting a guard. The very gate of Fort Gage had been left open. Colonel Clark had captured a guide, and he compelled him to lead the way into the fort. The sleeping garrison were entirely surrounded. Rocheblane, while reposing with his wife, was awakened by a gentle tap on the shoulder, to find himself a prisoner, and to order the unconditional surrender of the fortress.

The town of Kaskaskia then contained two hundred and fifty houses, and about three thousand inhabitants, having become reduced somewhat since the English had gone into possession. It was now two o'clock in the morning. Runners were dispatched, to warn the people, in the French tongue, that every enemy found in the streets should be instantly shot. A strict patrol was established, and the inhabitants were commanded to be quiet within doors, on peril of their lives. The Americans kept up a terrible tumult in the streets, rattling their arms, and whooping and yelling like so many savages; during which, a sergeant's guard entered the houses, and completely disarmed the frightened population before daylight. All intercourse from house to house had been strictly prohibited; and Colonel Clark, in full possession of the fort, had every part of the town within range of its guns. During the next day, communications with the troops were forbidden. Several British militia officers were unceremoniously put in irons. The words of the commander were few and stern. Every movement of his men was made with the most rigid military discipline. The town was placed under martial law. The mongrel population, terribly scared, felt themselves prisoners in the hands of an inexorable enemy — the dreaded "*Bostonais*," whom they had been taught to fear and hate from childhood. At length a deputation, headed by the village priest, besought Colonel Clark not to tear them from each other, and from their wives and children, and that something might be allowed their families for their support. Colonel Clark replied: "Do you think Americans will make war on women and children, and take the bread out of their mouths? To prevent the butchery of our own wives and children, we have taken arms, and penetrated to this remote stronghold of British and Indian barbarity; and not for the purpose of plundering you. The people of Kaskaskia, their families and property, shall be safe. They shall not be molested by Americans. The British have told you lies concerning us. Tell your people they are at liberty to do as they please." Soon the bells were ringing, and the whole population came forth to profess themselves firmly attached to the United States.

Cahokia was captured with equal secrecy and celerity. Colonel Clark then proceeded to reorganize the civil government; and he placed in office prominent French residents. The people rejoiced at this change from British rule, and seemed gladly to espouse the American cause. From being enemies they had become friends. That was the result of Colonel Clark's firm and prudent management with them. The imperious and insolent Rocheblane was sent, under guard, to Virginia as a prisoner of war. After that, through the influence of the Kaskaskians, the inhabitants of Virginia also were induced to declare themselves for the United States. And the new commandant for that post, Captain Helm, was received with acclamations by the people.

With the first of September came new difficulties. The troops had been enlisted for three months only. Seventy of his men had returned home. To supply their places, Colonel Clark organized one company of the inhabitants under their own officers; and before the close of September, alarmed at his inroads into their country, the Indians were seeking to open negotiations with him. From long acquaintance with the Indian character, Colonel Clark maintained a stern reserve, until they should ask for peace; and he kept on fighting them fiercely until they did sue for it in earnest. And whenever he treated with them, he made them but few presents, because the giving of presents was regarded by them as indicative of fear. In all his negotiations, he made a deep impression on the Indians, by his fearlessness, reserve, and prompt decision; and in a little while they began to feel a wholesome dread of his authority, which had been wholly unknown before.

The name of Clark soon became a terror among the north-western tribes, because of his rapid movements, and the daring courage of his troops; and before the middle of December, Indian hostilities had nearly ceased. So friendly had the French become to the Americans, under his skillful treatment of them, that Captain Helm, with two soldiers only, and the volunteer militia, held possession of the Fort of Vincennes. The whole regular force at Kaskaskia and Cahokia was less than one hundred men. In the meantime, the jurisdiction of Virginia had been formally extended over the settlements of the Wabash and the Upper Mississippi, by the organization of the "County of Illinois." Colonel John Todd had been appointed civil commandant.

Soon the state of things in Indiana and Illinois had

become known at Detroit. The British governor, Hamilton, determined on recapturing the military posts that had fallen into Colonel Clark's hands. With eighty regulars, a large body of Canadian militia, and six hundred Indians, Hamilton ascended the Maumee, crossed over to the Wabash, and made a rapid descent upon Vincennes. He was going to take the fort by storm, and put the garrison to the sword. On came the red-coats and savages, certain of success. But Captain Helm was not a man to be frightened from his self-possession. With an air of confidence, as if the fort was filled with soldiers to back him, he sprang upon a bastion near a cannon, and swinging his lighted match, shouted in a voice of thunder to the advancing column to "Halt!" or he would "blow them to atoms!" The Indians scud for the woods, and the Canadians fell back a little, to get out of range. Hamilton was surprised, and thought possibly, the fort might be well manned, and that it might make a desperate resistance. So he stopped to parley. Captain Helm declared he would fight as long as a soldier remained to shoulder a rifle, unless he was allowed to march out with the full honors of war. At last, the honors of war were agreed to, and then the fort was thrown open, and Captain Helm and five men, all told, marched out, with due formality. The astonished Briton could hardly believe his eyes.

After his great achievement in taking Vincennes, Hamilton, as the winter had set in with much rain and snow, concluded to postpone the recapture of Kaskaskia until the return of spring, when he expected to be largely reinforced by Indians from Michilimackinac. Permitting the Canadian militia to return home, he dispatched the Indian warriors to ravage the borders of Pennsylvania and Virginia. Late in January, Colonel Clark received intelligence that Hamilton was at Vincennes, with only fifty soldiers, and that the savages had departed for the east. Now, therefore, his time for action was come. The British instigator of Indian barbarities might be captured. Fitting up a large keel-boat with two four-pounders and four swivels, under the command of Captain Rodgers, with forty men, Colonel Clark ordered it to ascend the Wabash to within a few miles of the mouth of the White River; and there Rodgers was to await further orders.

On the seventh day of February, Colonel Clark, with one hundred and thirty men, began a march for Vincennes. The distance was one hundred and fifty miles, through forest and prairie. The only road-mark was an Indian trail, beaten deep in the ground. All the streams were very much swollen. The rivers had inundated their bottoms from bluff to bluff, often several miles in width. In addition to their rifles, the soldiers carried knapsacks, filled with parched corn and jerked beef. When they had arrived at the Little Wabash, the bottom-lands were inundated to the width of three or four miles. The water was four feet deep. Through these lowlands the battalion were under the necessity of marching, feeling for the trail with their feet, and holding their guns and ammunition high above their heads. In five days more they reached the Wabash, nine miles below Vincennes. The boat had not arrived. Two days were spent in unavailing efforts to cross the river. At length, on the twentieth, a boat was captured. And when the troops had been carried over, they had afterward to wade up to their armpits before reaching the highlands.

At twilight, on the evening of the twenty-third, Colonel Clark ordered the soldiers on parade, near the summit of a hill, within sight of the fort; and kept them marching for a long time, in such manner, that, to Hamilton, a great army appeared to be approaching. He had seen, he thought, nigh a thousand men, well appointed, and in good order, with colors flying. Many of the inhabitants of Vincennes, friendly to the Americans, assisted to invest the fort. In the dead of night a deep ditch was dug, within rifle-shot of the fortress; and before morning a body of marksmen had been stationed therein to pick off the garrison. Every gunner that attempted to squint along the cannon of the fort was killed. Not a British soldier dared so much as show an eye at a loop-hole. On the twenty-fifth Hamilton surrendered.

During the siege, a war-party of British Indians was discovered on their return from the east, with two white prisoners. Clark gave them battle, and defeated them, recapturing the prisoners. A few days later, it was reported that a great quantity of military stores, together with Indian goods, were approaching from Detroit, guarded by an escort of forty men. Captain Helm was dispatched with two companies to intercept them. He captured the entire party, without the loss of a man, and he brought in the goods, which amounted to ten thousand pounds in value. The British soldiers were dismissed on parole; but Hamilton, Major Hay, and a few subordinate officers, were sent, strongly guarded, to Virginia, to answer for the crime of inciting Indian murders along the frontiers. Governor Hamilton and his associates were put in irons, and kept in close confinement, in retaliation for the massacres that had been planned and instigated by them.

After that, no further attempts were ever made by the British to recover the posts on the Wabash and Upper Mississippi. Colonel Clark, having achieved the conquest of the West, continued to hold military possession of it until the close of the Revolution, recruiting his troops, supplying his stores, keeping the Indians in check, unaided, alone, and without money, a thousand miles in the wilderness. And at the treaty for peace, Great Britain conceded that this territory belonged to the United States, mainly on the ground of its having been conquered by Colonel Clark.

CHAPTER IX.

THE NORTHWESTERN TERRITORY.

Political organization — Permanent territorial laws — First and second grade — First church and schools — Cincinnati and North Bend — First civil court in the territory — Lawyers of the Northwestern Territory — Their manner of traveling from one court to another — The British posts in the territory surrendered to the United States.

The review which has thus far been taken, of the early history of the great West, has brought us down to a period when society there first began to assume a political form. No longer dealing with the general affairs of the whole boundless region, our course hereafter will lead to the contemplation of those states and territories which have been carved out of the wilderness, and to a consideration of some of the advantages of position, of soils, of climate; the facilities for farming, mining, lumbering, manufacturing, and for commercial pursuits possessed by each of them.

The first political designation of the western country, under the authority of the Congress of the United States, was that of the "Northwestern Territory," comprising all the American possessions north-west of the River Ohio, over which, in 1787, a form of government was established, to continue until the inhabitants should increase to a sufficient number to entitle them to state governments. Previous to that time, Massachusetts, Connecticut, New York, and Virginia, had each laid claim to that region, by virtue of their royal charters, which had left their western boundaries undefined. And Virginia had claimed under another title, also, which was clearly indisputable — the title of conquest. For Colonel Clark, throughout all his campaigns on the Wabash and Mississippi, had been acting under a commission issued by that state. But, after the Revolution, these magnanimous states had consented to an amicable adjustment of their claims, and had relinquished each its individual interest to the federal government, for the common benefit of the whole Union. Connecticut and Virginia, however, made reservations in their acts of cession, but only for the purpose of liquidating their respective liabilities to Revolutionary soldiers. The reservation of the former state was laid in that part of Ohio lying north of the forty-first parallel of latitude, and west of the line of Pennsylvania; that of the latter included the land between the Sciota and Little Miami rivers. The former has been known as the "Western Reserve," the latter as the "Virginia Military District." For that same noble purpose, the Congress also appropriated a large tract along the eastern side of the Sciota River, known as the "United States Military District." With these exceptions, the whole region of the north-west had passed under the authority of the Federal government, and become the property of the Union. It may be well to state, that the acts of cession were made as follows, viz: That of New York, March first, 1789; that of Virginia, April twenty-third, 1784; that of Massachusetts, April nineteenth, 1785; that of Connecticut, September thirteenth, 1786—the Empire State taking the lead.

The ordinance of 1787 made provision for the subsequent division of the Northwestern Territory into not less than three, nor more than five states, the Congress having been restricted to these numbers by the stipulations of the compact with Virginia, as a condition of the act of cession. That ordinance contained several articles that were "to remain forever unalterable, unless by common consent." Among them are the following:

"No person shall ever be molested on account of his mode of worship or religious sentiments.

"No law shall be passed that shall in any manner whatever interfere with or affect private interests or engagements, bona-fide, and without fraud, previously formed.

"No tax shall be imposed on lands, the property of the United States, and in no case shall non-resident proprietors be taxed higher than resident.

"There shall be neither slavery nor involuntary servi tude in the said territory, otherwise than in the punishment of crimes, whereof the party shall have been duly convicted; provided, always, that any person escaping into the same, from whom labor or service is lawfully claimed in any of the original states, such fugitive may be lawfully reclaimed and conveyed to the person claiming his or her labor in service, as aforesaid."

The ordinance provided for the establishment of two grades of territorial government. The territory, in the earlier grade, would seem to have been regarded as a political infant, that would need wet-nurses, and dry-nurses, and swaddling-clothes. Its jurisdiction was confided to a governor, a secretary, and three judges. And the governor was authorized to "adopt and publish such laws of the original states, civil and criminal, as might be necessary, and best adapted to the circumstances of the district." In the absence of the governor, the secretary was to perform the duties of that officer. The first grade of territorial dependence was to continue until the number of free white males over twenty-one years should amount to five thousand. Under the second grade, a general assembly of the territory was provided for, to consist of the governor, the legislative council, and the legislative assembly. The governor was authorized to convene, prorogue, or dissolve, the general assembly, whenever he might deem it expedient to do so. The second grade was to continue until the territory should contain sixty thousand souls.

The next summer after the passage of the ordinance, the officers of the new territorial government arrived, and took up their residence at Campus Martius, now Marietta. They were General Arthur St. Clair, governor; Winthrop Sargent, secretary; and the three judges for the executive council. Campus Martius had the form of a square, and was one hundred and eighty feet on each side. On the top of the block-houses were small steeples for sentry-boxes, bullet-proof. It was surrounded by a strong palisade, ten feet high. And the buildings, which were all within the inclosure, had been constructed of whip-sawed timbers, four inches thick, dove-tailed at the corners, and covered with shingle roofs. The various rooms had fire-places and brick chimneys. The bastions and towers were glistening with whitewash.

Most of the settlers in the Northwestern Territory were men who had spent the prime of their lives, and had exhausted their fortunes, in the Revolutionary War. A body of emigrants of that character left New England in 1787, under the lead of General Rufus Putnam, and, descending the river, below Marietta, to a beautiful plain, formed the settlement of Belpre. The people carried with them into the woods the good old customs and steady habits of their pilgrim ancestors. With characteristic energy, they had no sooner provided shelter for their families, than they set about organizing a church and establishing a school, toward which all the inhabitants made contributions with right good will. These were the first institutions of learning and religion ever built up in the Northwestern Territory.

In 1789, Israel Ludlow and Robert Patterson, with twenty persons, erected the first houses at Cincinnati, then called Losanteville. The site of that great city was a beautiful woodland bottom, on the bank of the river, sixty feet above low-water mark, and extending back three hundred yards to the base of a second bank, which rose forty feet higher, and then sloped gently more than a half mile to the foot of the bluff. The first bottom was covered with a heavy growth of sycamore, sugar-maple, and black-walnut; the second with beeches, oak, and hickory. And in January of that year, another party passed down the river to North Bend. Their boats were novelties of river craft, consisting each of a frame-work of logs, covered with green oak plank, and caulked with rags. Stowed snugly in these rude "arks," men, women, and children, together with their goods, floated down the current with the drifting ice, secure from rifle-shots. The Indians kept popping away at them from the river-banks; but no one was harmed. When the company had landed, they picked out quite a little supply of lead from the solid planking.

For several years there was a continual strife between Cincinnati and North Bend for superiority in the infant territory. At first, North Bend had a decided advantage over its rival. Judge Symmes, the principal proprietor, had prevailed with General Harmar to have the troops of the territory stationed at that place; and emigrants came flocking thither, because they believed it was greatly more secure from Indian attacks than any other settlement in the wilderness. But, shortly afterward, the officer in command became very much smitten with the charms of a beautiful woman, the wife of one of the settlers, and paid to her the most assiduous attentions. The husband, fully aware of his danger, broke up his establishment, and removed his family to Cincinnati. Immediately North Bend became totally unfit for military occupation, and

Cincinnati was represented to be the only point from which the whole territory could be reached with the protecting arm of government. The troops in a little while were removed from North Bend, and the advantages of military occupation conferred upon the rival settlement. The population of Cincinnati began rapidly to increase; business seemed to center there; and from a rude log village, the lonely settlement on the bank of the river, has been growing and thriving, and has become the Queen City of the West. The beautiful Helen of Troy was the cause of the destruction of that ancient city. A modern Helen gave strength to the foundations of Cincinnati.

The first civil court ever held in the Northwestern Territory was convened on the second day of September, 1788, in the hall of the Campus Martius. It was the court of common pleas, Rufus Putnam and Benjamin Tupper, justices. The opening of that court in the remote wilderness was attended with an imposing ceremony. A procession having been formed in the street, the sheriff led the way with a drawn sword, followed by the officers of the garrison, members of the bar, the supreme court judges, the governor, and a clergyman, and the judges of the common pleas. On arriving at the door of the hall, the procession was countermarched into it, and their honors, judges Putnam and Tupper, took their seats on the bench. The prayer was offered by the Rev. Dr. Cutler. Then the sheriff cried aloud: "Oyez! Oyez! Oyez! A court is opened for the administration of even-handed justice to the poor and the rich, to the guilty and the innocent, without respect of persons; none to be punished without a trial by their peers, and in pursuance of the laws and evidence in the case." There were present a great crowd of settlers, and several hundred Indians.

After the territory had become more thickly settled, the general court was held at Cincinnati, Marietta, and Detroit. The journeys of court and bar, in those early times, to those remote places, would have taken all the conceit out of Blackstone. They would generally travel with five or six in company, with a pack-horse to carry provisions. Frequently they would be ten days together in the wilderness, camping out at night, and swimming every stream that was too deep to be forded. On one of those excursions, the learned gentlemen were kept awake all night by the caterwauling of a couple of panthers, that seemed to be hankering for a taste of judicial flesh. Sometimes, in the winter season, the party would stop by the trail-side, brush the snow off a log, and sit down to frozen chicken and biscuit, warming the frigid fare in the stomach with frequent "nips" of peach brandy. Once, in a summer tramp, the whole bar got lost in a swamp, and had to stand on their feet all night, doing penance for their sins by liquidating the bills of the musquitoes. That was a night of exquisite torment, and some of the gentlemen must have had vivid impressions of what they were coming to some time or other. At another time it rained daily and nightly, and the dripping limbs of the law shook and shivered in the wind. Even the court was moved. They all had to lie down and soak from dusk till morning, with wet knapsacks for pillows, and their smoking saddles drawn over their faces. The lawyers of the Northwestern Territory must have had some "high old times," if all be true that has come down to us concerning them. If they did run the risk of losing their scalps on the way to court, they could easily make it up by skinning a client or two.

The settlements of the Northwestern Territory were constantly annoyed by Indian hostilities, instigated by

British agents, residing at posts surreptitiously erected along the Maumee River. General Wayne advanced with a large army down that river, and gave the Indians and Canadians battle, within sight of a British fort. That was on the twentieth day of August, 1794. During the battle, the Indians were fiercely driven at the point of the bayonet more than two miles, through thick-fallen timber and brush; and the Canadians fled in terror to the fort. A spicy correspondence then followed between General Wayne and Major Campbell, the British commandant. The former reconnoitered the fort within range of its guns, and caused the troops to destroy all the property around it; and they burned the house and store of the British agent, Alexander McKay. The spirit of the Indians was completely broken. And in 1769, all the British posts in the territory were formally surrendered to the United States.

OHIO.

CHAPTER X.

OHIO.

Division of the Northwestern Territory — State government — Early politics of the state — Rapid growth of the state — Its climate and soil — Minerals — Salt springs — Water communications — Crops — Domestic commerce — Railroads — Institutions of learning — Churches — Taxable property, etc.

THE Buckeye State came into the Union in 1803. Since General Wayne's successful campaign, the population of the river counties had been rapidly increasing. A general feeling of security pervaded the entire Northwestern Territory. The eastern part had been separated, by act of Congress, from the western, by a line to be run due north from the mouth of the Great Miami, until it should intersect the parallel of latitude which passes through the southern extremity of Lake Michigan. The northern boundary of the proposed state remained undefined, by actual survey, for several years, and once came near involving Ohio and Michigan in a war for the possession of the great Cotton wood Swamp, back of Toledo.

The controversy between the executive and legislature of the Northwestern Territory was the immediate cause of an early attempt at the formation of a state government. Arthur St. Clair, the governor of the territory, was a staunch federalist. The majority of the prominent men were republicans. Party politics were running high, and the executive and legislative departments could not act in harmony upon any question whatever. It is due to the character of Governor St. Clair to say, that he enjoyed the respect of the people generally. In his manners, he was unassuming. In his dress, plain and simple, without ostentation or gaudy equipage. In his deportment, he was easy and frank. Holding himself accessible to all persons, he presented a strong contrast with the austere, haughty, and repulsive bearing of his secretary, Colonel Winthrop Sargent. But Governor St. Clair seems to have placed a high estimate upon his own judgment, and he rarely yielded to the opinions of others. He was stubborn, and the legislature was zealous.

The administration of the general government had passed into the hands of the republican party. Thomas Jefferson was President. The advocates of a state government had made application directly to Congress, to authorize the people of the territory to elect delegates, for the purpose of framing and adopting a constitution. Congress had granted the prayer of the petitioners, and had directed the convention to assemble at Chilicothe on the first Monday of November, 1802. The returns of the territorial census, taken during the summer of that year, had shown the aggregate white population of the eastern division to be forty-five thousand persons. While the convention was in session, Governor St. Clair, desirous of participating in its deliberations, had sent word that he would forward a communication in his official capacity. But so zealously republican was that body, so fearful of executive influence, that the proposition to listen to St. Clair, as governor, had been voted down. And then the convention coolly resolved, "That Arthur St. Clair, Senior, Esquire, be permitted to address the convention on those subjects which he deems of importance." The convention had stopped his mouth, as chief magistrate, but would listen to him as a man.

A constitution had been adopted on the twenty-ninth of November, and, with strange inconsistency, had been declared obligatory, without having been submitted to the people for their assent. A proposition to that effect had been rejected by a large majority. The delegates would seem to have stood in as great fear of the people as of the governor. Although the ordinance of 1787 required a population of sixty thousand souls to entitle the people to a state government, yet Congress had seen fit to waive that requirement; and, on the nineteenth day of February, 1803, an act was approved by the President, fully recognizing the admission of the State of Ohio into the Federal Union, as a free and independent state. Ohio, the eldest born of republicanism, has retained its republican proclivities to the present day.

The growth of the Buckeye State has been rapid, beyond all example, beyond all calculation or expectation. In the beginning of this century, it was a territory just emerging from the wilderness—just clear of savage marauders; in the middle of it, a state, populous, powerful, and controlling, in the midst of the greatest confederacy that has ever existed on earth. Ohio is eminently an agricultural state. The soil is fertile as a garden. The land, descending gently toward the south, is warm and quick; and the climate, on that account, is far more mild than would seem to be indicated by the latitude. The general length of the state, from east to west, is two hundred miles, and its breadth about one hundred and forty miles, with an area of thirty-nine thousand nine hundred and sixty-four square miles. More than nine-tenths of the state is susceptible of cultivation, and three-fourths of the soil is eminently productive. The river bottoms are wide and fertile. In the central portions, natural meadows are numerous; but the greater part of the country was originally covered with magnificent forests of oak, beech, sugar-maple, hickory, and whitewood.

The state of Ohio is rich in minerals. Its coal is bituminous, and the vast fields lie so near the surface that, in many places, it is easier to dig for fuel than to chop for it. The principal points where coal mines are worked, are at Talmadge, Summit county; Pomeroy, Meigs county; Nelsonville, Athens county, and some parts of Starke and Coshocton counties. The coal trade of Ohio might easily be increased to twenty million dollars annually. The iron business of the state will some time be of great magnitude and importance. Extending through the counties of Lawrence, Gallia, Jackson, Meigs, Vinton, Athens, and Hocking, is a vast belt of iron ore, some twelve miles in width, and more than one hundred miles in length. It has been estimated that the ore, so rich and abundant, is susceptible of feeding a furnace on every square mile, that would require each one hundred hands, and yield eight tons of iron per day, for ages. Coal underlies the same region, and the field there is of the best quality, and from twenty to thirty feet in thickness. England, with a coal region less extensive than the two counties, Meigs and Athens, produces, annually, fifty million dollars' worth of iron. From that, we may form some estimate as to what Ohio will be capable of doing, when her mineral resources shall have been fully developed.

Ohio has salt springs that might be made to compete with those of Onondaga. The salt wells are on Yellow creek, above Steubenville; on Will's creek; on the Muskingum river, from the Coshocton to its mouth; on the Hockhocking, and on Leading creek. The depth of the salt rock, below the surface, varies from six hundred feet to nine hundred feet. The brine, at the lower wells on the Muskingum, yields one hundred pounds of salt from one hundred gallons of water.

Ohio, moreover, has direct communication with the

copper regions of the north, the cotton fields of the south, and, in addition to the domestic growth of wool, might draw largely from the prairies of Illinois. There is no reason why Ohio shall not become one of the most successful manufacturing states in the world. Although the streams are mostly "dry-weather" streams, and swell full only with freshets; although there are no mountains to give velocity and force to running water; yet steam can be cheaply substituted for water-power. Along the whole southern border, vessels may be freighted with goods, and dispatched to one-half the states and territories of the Union, to the Gulf of Mexico, and the Atlantic ocean. And from the northern border, rich cargoes may be sent to the Gulf of St. Lawrence, and also up Lake Superior and Michigan, more than a thousand miles inland. Thus, with an abundance of material, Ohio has also a reliable and extensive market for all kinds of produce and manufactures.

The population of Ohio, in 1790, was three thousand; after sixty years, it had increased to two millions. While manufactures, and the mineral resources of the state, have been but little developed, its agriculture has become unusually prosperous. The corn crop of Ohio is one-tenth of the whole crop of the United States; its wheat crop, one-seventh; its crops of oats and buckwheat are exceeded only by those of New York and Pennsylvania, and its barley by New York alone. Ohio owns one-tenth of all the horses in the Union. It ranks next to New York in the number of its milch cows and other cattle. It has more sheep than any other state. One-fifth of all the wool in the United States is clipped in Ohio.

The domestic commerce of Ohio is astonishingly large, and has been estimated, in its annual value, as high as one hundred and sixty million dollars. Surprising as that

8

amount may seem, it is certain, that the domestic commerce is greatly on the increase. The exports of Sandusky, in 1850, amounted to three million one hundred thousand dollars; but in 1852 they had increased to upwards of twenty million dollars. The growth of the imports, at Sandusky, during those two years, was from seven million dollars to forty-five millions.

The capital of Ohio is very largely invested in internal improvements. One of the largest canals in America connects Lake Erie, at Cleveland, with the Ohio River, at Portsmouth; another from Cincinnati stretches across to Toledo;—affording the productions of the interior a convenient outlet to the north and the south. The railroads cross each other in all directions throughout the state. They center, chiefly, at Cleveland and Sandusky, on the lake coast; at Mansfield, Newark, Zanesville, Columbus, Xenia, Bellefontaine, Springfield, and Dayton, in the interior; and at Cincinnati, on the river. Among these roads, the most important are, the Bellefontaine and Indiana, one hundred and eighteen miles in length; the Cincinnati, Cleveland and Columbus, one hundred and thirty-five miles; the Cleveland and Pittsburg, one hundred miles; the Mad River and Lake Erie, one hundred and thirty-four miles; the Ohio and Pennsylvania, one hundred and eighty-seven miles; all of which are completed, and have several daily trains running on them. These roads, with their numerous branches, stretch far out into the adjoining states, and connect with other lines from Boston, in Massachusetts, to St. Louis, in Missouri, and bind the lakes in iron bands with the Atlantic coast and with the Mississippi River.

In Ohio, great attention has been paid to the establishment of institutions of learning. There are about twelve thousand common schools in the state, and the average daily attendance of scholars is four hundred thousand. There are twelve universities and colleges, and four medical schools. The number of libraries is forty-eight, with nearly two hundred thousand volumes. The number of churches is about four thousand, accommodating near one and a half millions of persons, and owning property to the value of six million dollars. Ohio has twenty-one representatives in the Congress of the United States. And the total value of the taxable property of the state is about four hundred and fifty million dollars. It seems almost incredible that so much wealth should have been created, on a tract of land two hundred miles long and one hundred and forty broad, in sixty years. With all this increase, Ohio, in fact, has but just begun the development of its resources. The present prosperous condition of that state may be regarded merely as an indication of its future greatness.

CHAPTER XI.

MICHIGAN.

French agriculture — Population — Geography — Geology — The lower peninsula — White-oak openings — Burr-oak openings — "Cat-holes" — Pine woods of the north — Windfalls — Soil and fruits of the lower peninsula — Pasturage — Settlements of Michigan — Commercial advantages — Detroit and other ports — Site for a great central city — The rivers — The lakes around Michigan — Improved lands — Annual products — Schools, churches, and other institutions — Attractions to the settler — Exemption laws.

MICHIGAN, on the first day of July, 1805, entered upon the first grade of territorial government, under the provisions of the ordinance of 1787. General William Hull was appointed governor; and Detroit was the seat of government. The southern boundary of Michigan Territory, according to the act of Congress, was to be a line running due east from the most southern part of Lake Michigan to Maumee Bay. At the time of its organization, the population of the territory, exclusive of the troops of the western army, did not exceed three thousand; for the early emigration to the West, at the beginning of this century, before the era of steam navigation on the lakes, had taken a more southern route, and had flowed into the country bordering upon the Ohio River. Michigan was then very difficult of access. The territory was little known, and but few persons attempted to reach its borders. The increase in the number of the inhabitants went on so slowly that, in 1810, it contained only eight thousand four hundred souls.

In 1796, when Michigan, for the first time, had come

into the hands of the Americans, the population, on both sides of the strait, from Lake St. Clair to the River Raisin, was almost exclusively Canadian French. They were an extremely ignorant people, and made most miserable cultivators of the soil. Their farms were only a few rods in width upon the river, and ran back nearly two miles, for quantity. The Canadian French seem to have had no idea of any improvement in agriculture having been made by any body, since Noah had planted his vineyard at the foot of Mount Ararat. They continued to plow, and sow, and reap, just as their fathers had done time out of mind. Whenever a field had become exhausted, it was abandoned. Instead of striving to enrich their lands, the people trusted to the efficacy of prayers, and threw the manure into the river. Under such treatment, the soil, of necessity, had become reduced, yielding light crops, and provisions were extravagantly high.

About the year 1830, the tide of emigration began to set toward that territory. The population had then become increased to twenty-eight thousand. Steamboat navigation had been opening a new commerce upon the lakes, encircling all the lower peninsula of Michigan. A fleet of an hundred sail, sloops and schooners, was engaged in traversing every part of these inland waters. On the fifteenth day of June, 1836, a state constitution had been adopted, and Michigan was admitted into the Union in the January following, with a population of nearly an hundred thousand. Emigrants began to flock in rapidly from the middle states, and from New England. The number of inhabitants, at the present time, is about three hundred and ninety-eight thousand; of which Connecticut has furnished seven thousand; Massachusetts, eight thousand; Vermont, twelve thousand; and New York, one hundred and thirty-four thousand.

The lower peninsula of Michigan is nearly three hundred miles in length, from north to south, and one hundred and twenty miles in width, having an area of about forty thousand square miles. It is skirted by a belt of heavily-timbered land, about twenty-five miles deep, surrounding the entire lake coast, and lying several feet below the level of the adjoining openings. The tract of timbered land, along the eastern side of the peninsula, is generally a dead level. The whole interior, however, is gently rolling, and, in some parts, hilly, though but slightly so, just sufficient for wholesome running water. The dividing ridge which gives rise to the river system of Michigan, is considerably east of a line drawn from Michilimackinac through the center of the state to the boundary of Ohio; and the whole western slope descends gradually from that ridge, with an even, unbroken surface, to Lake Michigan. The coast, however, is everywhere high above the level of the lakes; and along lakes Huron and Michigan the banks are steep, and varying from one hundred to three hundred feet in hight.

The lower peninsula is of the same geological formation as western New York. Its rocks consist of horizontal strata of limestones, sandstones, and slates; the limestones being found along the rivers near the lakes, and the sandstones in the interior. The soil is either alluvial or diluvial, and has a depth varying from one foot to one hundred and fifty feet. Quarries of sandstone have been opened at several places on the Grand River. It admits of being easily quarried, furnishing a good building material, and is frequently used for grindstones. The limestone of Michigan is, for the most part, quite compact, and well adapted to agricultural purposes, generally producing a valuable lime upon burning, though sometimes too silicious to be of the best quality.

Gypsum has been found in several localities. And in all those places where the limestone formation exists, there are indications of bituminous coal.

The lower peninsula presents three different general aspects to the traveler passing through it, from south to north. The first is the region of plains or openings. These are not bare of trees, like prairies, nor are they covered uniformly and evenly with timber. The growth and density of the wood that is scattered over them is extremely various, though all the openings are alike free from underbrush, and a wagon might be driven miles on miles without obstruction, or having scarcely to turn out for a fallen tree. The timber of the openings consists entirely of oak and hickory. The latter clusters almost always in groves, to the exclusion of other varieties, the trees being merely young, thrifty saplings, from three inches to ten inches through, at the root, and from twenty to thirty feet high. These groves are found mostly upon the elevated portions of gentle swells of ground, covering a few acres, and surrounded every way by oak. The hickories generally stand quite thickly, as though they had been purposely planted for the sake of nurseries of that timber, as the locust tree is raised in some parts of New York.

The name of the white-oak openings will indicate the variety of timber to be found wherever they exist. The trees will be seen standing far apart, in size from one to two feet through, the lower limbs, ten or twelve feet above the ground, huge and gnarled, spreading out wide, and supporting magnificent tops of branches and leaves, precisely like the cherished homestead trees of an older country. On the "timbered" openings, the oaks grow taller, and the bark is smoother; but they do not attain to the hight of those on timbered lands. Then, again, there are plains of red-oak, a tree which frequently stretches up higher than the white-oak, its bark almost black, its body covered with pins formed of the hearts of burnt limbs, rough, scraggy, and so fastened together with knots as to bid defiance to wedges and beetles. Here and there, however, will be found one, large and tall, that will split as free as a shingle. Such are selected for "shakes," and the settler delights in them for rails.

Also the bur-oak openings will inform the reader of the variety of oak growing upon them. These openings are the pride of Michigan. The bur-oak is slender and tapering like a poplar. The bark is lighter and spongier than the white-oak, the tree altogether more delicate, and the limbs more graceful. Scattered over the surface at regular intervals, nearly uniform in size, and about twenty-five feet in hight, they present the appearance of pear-trees planted in immense orchards. The bur-oak derives its name from the clusters of acorns which hang like burs upon the ends of the slender twigs, and crown the very top of the tree. A drove of hogs, turned out to feed, will start on a run for a bur-oak opening, and champ the acorns as they would corn. Bruin knows how sweet these acorns are, and he frequently leaves his mark on the limbs and on the bark. The wild pigeons, in countless numbers, will hover, and flutter, and flap among the bur-oaks.

The openings of Michigan do not, by any means, present an uniform appearance. Beside the different varieties of timber, and the gentle undulation of the surface, there are frequent springs of water, forming into streams, along which the woods, preserved from the ravages of fire, grow up thick and dark, stretching out like long arms and elbows throughout the country, adding to the interest and beauty of the landscapes. There are also frepuent "cat-holes," or little circular basins, some of them as regular as a bowl, from a few rods to two or three acres over, grown up to whortleberry bushes and alders. And sometimes, sunk down below the general level of the country, one will find wet meadows of rank grass, among which the cranberry stretches out its delicate vine. It is doubtful whether there is a more beautiful region in the United States than that of the openings of Michigan, which, commencing near Detroit, extend clear across the state.

On going toward the north, the timber becomes more and more plentiful. Beeches begin to mingle with the oaks. And, in a day or two, beeches and maples will predominate over other varieties of timber. Huge white-woods and basswoods will be seen towering above the forest. The white-ash, the shag-bark, the black-cherry, will have become abundant. The woods will seem to have been growing darker and denser every mile of the way. Soon the traveler will doubt whether Omnipotence himself could have planted the trees larger, taller, and thicker together than they are. A broad-horned ox would have to tip his head on one side, in order to pass through between them. The ground is slippery with decaying leaves. Further on, the timber gradually begins to lessen, and, after a while, openings again appear along the high, abrupt banks of the Grand River. These northern openings, some thirty miles in width, are not so beautiful as the southern, but they spread out fairer and more invitingly to the settler. For there, little prairies abound, just big enough for farms, and belted with timber.

Pressing still forward, the emigrant will enter the great pine woods of the north. For a while, however, before reaching them, he will have been wandering through groves of oak, and along the borders of natural meadows, and through clumps of beech and maple. Now and then a pine or two will have been seen standing out like sentinels. But soon, as with a single step, the timber has become all pine — yellow pine; moaning overhead, darkening all the ground, shutting out the sun, shutting out the wind. With outstretched arms, the trees might almost be reached on either hand, while passing along. The tall trunks support the dark-green canopy full fifty feet above the earth. Many of the trunks from the base of the leafy top, half way down to the ground, are thorny and jagged with the stubs of dead limbs. But the trees are, nevertheless, sound and thrifty.

The belt of pine timber, and nothing but pine, is about twenty-five miles in width, stretching from Saginaw Bay directly across the peninsula of Michigan. Wherever in all that region there have been windfalls, the pine has been replaced by the thickest masses of oak and beech saplings that ever was contemplated by man. A wolf could hardly crawl through one of them without taking every hair off his hide. In vain you poke the bushes aside, to look in; you can not see a foot beyond your nose; it is all bushes, thick as a hatchel, and limbs intertwining. On asking a surveyor of the government lands how they managed with the windfalls, he replied: "O that's nothing. We clomb on top and walked over, just as easy." After a while, to the northward, the pine appears to be confined to the little ridges, that rise up like back-bones between the streams. Wherever the rivers make a bend, on the hollowing side will be found a heavy growth of black ash. Now and then a clump of cedars will appear, each tree leaning away from the rest, and some of them twisting round at least "sixteen times in a foot." The level lands have again become covered with beech and maple, of a full, luxuriant growth, with here and there a gigantic

Norway pine, six feet through, without a limb, till it begins to stretch up half its length above the surrounding trees. These are the general aspects of Michigan, as seen on a tour through the center of the peninsula, from Coldwater, in Branch county, to the straits of Michilimackinac.

The soil of the lower peninsula is of great depth and fertility. That which covers the openings and the pine lands is a sandy loam, easily worked, and yielding large crops of wheat, corn, and potatoes. All the varieties of fruits to be found in western New York thrive there in great vigor and productiveness. The apple, the peach, the pear, seem native to the climate. Garden vegetables attain a surprising growth. The plains abound in strawberries. Throughout all the timbered lowlands there are thick clusters of wild currants and gooseberries. The whortleberries grow large and luscious. The wild cranberries furnish a convenient sauce, and an article of great market value. The soil of the timbered lands is slightly heavier than that of the openings, but it is still sandy rather than clayey. Vines of all kinds are astonishingly thrifty. A tomato plant will grow as high as a man's head, and will yield bushels of fruit. The pumpkin vine will run over logs, stumps, brush-heaps, and cover half a field with great yellow pumpkins. A single cantaloupe vine has been known to yield twenty large, delicious melons.

In all the openings, "the mast" is abundant. Hogs turned out to grass will become fat on the acorns alone. Pasturage is every where plentiful, on the plains until after the frosts of October, and then it is found in the timbered swales. Many of the wet meadows will yield red-top at the rate of two and three tons to the acre. And further north, among the heavy timber, there are marshes covered with a hardy reed, or flag, which the frost never kills to the ground, but a green, juicy stub, six inches in length, will remain all winter, just beneath the snow; and great droves of cattle, turned out in the sheltering woods, will thrive on these, alone, and come out in good condition in the spring.

The settlements of Michigan are mostly confined to the openings, and to the intervening belt of timber. Population has not extended more than thirty miles north of the Grand River. Emigration would seem to have swept straight across the southern half of the peninsula. In earlier times, two principal wagon roads existed; the old Territorial Road, through Ann Arbor, Jackson, and Marshall, and the South or State Road, through Ypsilanti, Tecumseh, and Jonesville; and the settlers, arriving at Detroit and at Toledo, would follow one or the other of these routes. Those who designed going to the Grand River country, had to make the voyage of the lakes. And now, the two great thoroughfares of the peninsula, the Michigan Central Railroad, and the Michigan Southern Railroad, are laid along those same lines of travel. Michigan would seem to have been made a mere roadway for the states beyond it. Population, therefore, has not reached far above these principal routes; for it has been easier to go to Iowa than to the central parts of Michigan. Some time or other, a railroad will be built on the line from Michilimackinac through Lansing, the capital of the state, and, intersecting the Central and Southern roads at Jackson and at Jonesville, will make easily accessible the pine region north of the Grand River.

There is probably no state in the Union which surpasses Michigan in its commercial advantages. It is admirably situated for drawing to itself the interior trade of America. The lower peninsula is inclosed on all sides but one, by four lakes: Erie, St. Clair, Huron, and Michigan. The extent of the coast line, thus furnished, is about seven hundred and fifty miles. Unlike most other commercial states, that are considered to be favorably situated if they have one border only lying along the sea, Michigan is nearly surrounded by water, scarcely an acre of its land is anywhere over seventy miles from a lake shore. Its ports, large and commodious, open toward all the points of the compass, except the south. Its productions, therefore, can easily be floated off westward, and northward, and eastward; and from these same directions, every species of merchandise that may be desirable can be imported into the state. Michigan has more natural harbors, that will involve little expense and labor to render them available in all seasons to all classes of shipping, than any other state bordering on the lakes. An enumeration of the ports and harbors will show how grandly Michigan is situated for carrying on an extensive commerce with the lakes.

First in order, along the great watery girdle around the state, is the city of Monroe, in the south-eastern part, at the base of the peninsula. Monroe is finely located on the River Raisin, two and one-half miles above Lake Erie. It is distant from Lansing, the capital of Michigan, eighty-seven miles, and from Detroit, forty miles. The country back of Monroe is level, having a sandy and fertile soil, and yielding largely of all the grains, fruits, and grasses. Building stone is found in that vicinity, of an excellent quality. And the sulphur springs are beginning to attract attention. The river, above the city, affords exhaustless supplies of water-power. The harbor, at all times, is accessible to vessels of the largest class. Monroe is an important point in the great thoroughfare of western travel and transportation. It is the eastern terminus of the Michigan Southern Railroad, and it has daily lines of steamboats, which connect it with Buffalo, and all the ports on Lake Erie. The Toledo, Norwalk, and Cleveland Railroad has brought Monroe into communication, overland, with the Atlantic cities; and its railroad connections with the country to the far West are interrupted only by the Mississippi River.

But Detroit is the great commercial center of the state, although located upon the extreme eastern border. The city extends along the bank of the river for more than three miles. The business part of it is about seven miles below Lake St. Clair, and eighteen miles above Lake Erie. It has the finest harbor in all the west. The French word, *D'Etroit*, signifies strait, which is a more appropriate appellation for the connecting stream between the upper and the lower lakes than the word river, which usually is applied to it. That strait, of an average depth of thirty-two feet, with an equable current of two and one-half miles an hour, is half a mile wide between the docks at Detroit and the docks opposite, at Sandwich. The channel is nowhere interrupted by rocks, and the stream is so deep and swift that it keeps itself clear of sand-bars and sawyers. The strait is closed but a little while during the winter, for its powerful current will wear away the thickest ice in a short time; and the floating ice, drifting from the lakes above, is borne along with an uniform movement, which does not permit of the formation of dams, like those of the St. Lawrence, at Montreal. These peculiarities of the strait make Detroit a secure and accessible harbor, at all seasons of the year. It is thronged with shipping. Detroit is the eastern terminus of the Michigan Central Railroad, as Sandwich, immediately opposite, is the western terminus of the Great Western Railway through Canada.

Mount Clemens is situated on the Clinton River, which empties into Lake St. Clair. Algonac, Newport, and St. Clair are situated upon the St. Clair River. All of these ports have good harbors. The St. Clair river is forty miles long, with a broad, deep current, of three miles an hour. The average depth of the channel is fifty feet. The river is half a mile wide. Five miles above Lake St. Clair, the river divides, and flows through six channels into the lake; the more northerly one alone is navigable. Port Huron, situated at the mouth of Black River, two miles south of Lake Huron, has a good harbor, and possesses superior advantages for ship-building. Saginaw is situated near the head of the bay of the same name. The city stands on the west bank of the Saginaw River, at an elevation of thirty feet above the water. The Saginaw River has a depth of twenty-five feet, and upon the bar, at its mouth, eight feet. The bay is sixty miles long, and thirty miles wide, and its shores are indented with innumerable coves, which form some of the most convenient harbors on Lake Huron. Further up the lake, Thunder Bay is a most excellent harbor. The depth of water is thirty feet. The bay is sheltered by several islands at its entrance. A considerable river of the same name comes in at the head, and a number of smaller streams; and at the extreme north is Michilimackinac. If one were to point out on the map of North America, a site for a great central city in the lake region, it would be in the immediate vicinity of the straits of Michilimackinac. A city so located would have the control of the mineral trade, the fisheries, the furs, and the lumber of the entire north. It might become the metropolis of a great commercial empire. It would be the Venice of the lakes. Following along down Lake Michigan, we come to Little Traverse Bay, and Grand Traverse Bay, each magnificent harbors. A railroad constructed from the latter bay to Saginaw would open all the upper half of the southern peninsula of Michigan. Next in order, are the mouths of the Manistee,

White, and Muskegon Rivers, which are said to have convenient harbors.

Grand Haven, at the mouth of the Grand River, is one of the best harbors on Lake Michigan. The water, on the bar, is never less than twelve feet deep; in the harbor it averages twenty-five feet. The Grand River is about one-fourth of a mile wide, and is navigable by steamboats, forty miles, to the rapids, at all seasons, and at high water to Ionia and Lyons. It is a noble river of clear and swift water, two hundred and seventy miles in length. The principal branches are the Rogue, Flat, Maple, Looking-glass, Red Cedar, and Thorn-apple rivers — all large streams, flowing through some of the choicest lands in the state, and furnishing an abundance of water-power. Kalamazoo River is a magnificent stream, two hundred miles in length, and navigable for vessels of forty tons, to Allegan, thirty-eight miles above its mouth. The depth of water on the bar is eight feet. St. Josephs River is two hundred and fifty miles long, and winds round through northern Indiana. At its mouth is a sand-bar with six feet of water. The river is a thousand feet in width. At its mouth, the village of St. Josephs occupies a commanding site, at an elevation of sixty feet above the water.

These are the harbors, and these the rivers of the lower peninsula of Michigan. The majority of them are, as yet, appropriated, almost exclusively, to the lumber trade. The northern branches of the Grand River; the Muskegon, White, and Manistee rivers; the Thunder Bay, and the Audable rivers; the Saginaw River, and its branches; the Cass, and Flint, and Shiawasse, and Tittibawasse, and the Black, and the Clinton rivers — all open into a region of the choicest timber. The pine lumber of

Michigan is equal to any in the world, and the demand for it has increased prodigiously within a few years.

The lakes around Michigan furnish that state with a theater for the grandest display of commercial enterprise. Lake Erie is two hundred and sixty-five miles in length, and averages thirty-five miles in width. Its mean depth is one hundred and thirty feet. It opens to Michigan the trade of the East. Lake St. Clair is about ninety miles in circumference, and twenty feet deep. The passage at the head of that lake into the St. Clair River is, for a little way, extremely difficult. At a trifling expense, the channel might be kept open to vessels of the largest class. The general government, heretofore, has neglected to make appropriations for the improvement of the channel through the St. Clair Flats, leaving millions of dollars annually to be stuck in the mud, because, forsooth, the mud is fresh-water mud, instead of salt. The policy of certain American statesmen, respecting the improvement of western rivers, has been childish in the extreme. Who ever heard, before, of the constitutional rights of a great commercial people being regulated by the ebbings and flowings of the tides? It is a wonder that it has not been suggested to those astute minds, to put the constitution itself into pickle. Now, the St. Clair Flats, (out of Congress,) lie between Algonac and the mouth of the Thames River. They are extremely shoal, covered all over with luxuriant crops of wild rice, through which the channel, crooked and narrow, rarely has a depth of water to exceed nine feet. From the principal passage, looking toward the Canadian coast, the whole expanse, for miles, is a waving morass of rice, intersected by small, winding bayous. Every northern state has an immediate interest in the removal of the obstructions of the St. Clair River. A commerce of the value of more than a hundred million dollars, and a licensed tonnage of steam and sail-craft, amounting in the aggregate to forty thousand tons, are put in jeopardy every year.

Lake Huron is two hundred and sixty miles in length, and one hundred and sixty in width, inclusive of the Georgian Bay, a vast expanse of itself, almost divided from the lake by a continuous chain of islands. Lake Huron is said to contain more than thirty thousand islands, principally near the northern shore. Its greatest depth is one thousand feet. A railroad runs across through Canada, from Toronto to Collingwood, at the head of Nottawasaga Bay on Georgian Bay; and another from Buffalo through Brantford, to be completed to Goderich, on the eastern shore of the lake. The principal harbors of Lake Huron are on the western side, which will give to Michigan the largest share of its commerce.

Lake Michigan is three hundred and sixty miles in length, with an average breadth of sixty miles. It has a mean depth of nine hundred feet. Its surface is four feet higher than that of Lake Huron, and six hundred feet above the level of the Atlantic Ocean. On the western side is Green Bay, one hundred miles long and thirty broad, through which, and the Fox and Wisconsin rivers, navigation can easily be opened between the lakes and the Mississippi. The same communication has been effected by the canal at Chicago, connecting with the Illinois River.

Being so situated in the heart of the lake country, Michigan may participate very largely in the commerce of the whole interior of the continent. And that state possesses within itself the means of supporting the most extensive commercial enterprises. Its soil, throughout, is of surpassing fertility. Only one-third of the land is improved; yet the produce annually is, as follows: Wheat, five million bushels; corn, six million bushels; oats, three million bushels; and potatoes, three million bushels. The yield of maple-sugar is two and one-half million pounds. The live stock within the state is valued at ten million dollars. The wool clipped annually, is about three million pounds; the butter made, seven and one-half million pounds; cheese, near two million pounds. The value of the animals slaughtered is about one and one-half million of dollars. The total amount of the yearly products of manufactures is nearly eleven million dollars. The whole northern half of the lower peninsula, covered with magnificent forests, though scarcely yet broken into, yields astonishing quantities of lumber. The saw-mills are already cutting over three hundred and ten million feet of sawed lumber annually.

The ports of Algonac, Mount Clemens, St. Clair, Port Huron, and Saginaw, on the eastern side, and the Grand River, the Muskegon, White, and Manistee rivers, on the western side, are the avenues through which the lumber of Michigan finds its way to market. While the ports at Grand Haven, Allegan, and St. Josephs, and at Detroit and Monroe, are crowded with grain and other agricultural productions.

The whole amount of property owned in the state is valued at sixty million dollars. Michigan is entitled to four representatives in Congress. The number of public schools is about three thousand five hundred. A State Normal School has been established at Ypsilanti, with an ample endowment of school lands. The principal collegiate institution is the University at Ann Arbor. The total number of libraries is three hundred and eighty-one, containing about seventy thousand volumes. About seventy periodicals are published in the State, of which thirty are of a literary, scientific, or religious character.

Michigan contains about four hundred churches, accommodating nearly an hundred and twenty-five thousand persons. Michigan may be far behind Ohio; but it should be remembered that Ohio has had more than thirty years the start.

Michigan presents many attractions to the settler; and among those, the beautiful little lakes, scattered profusely over its surface, through the openings and the timbered lands alike, must not be forgotten. These cover from one acre to five hundred acres, clear and deep waters, alive with fish. Some of the lakes have neither inlet nor outlet, being fed with springs just equal to the evaporation. But most of them send forth copious streams. There are places, among the openings, where, standing on a hill, one may see half a dozen of these lakelets, nestling together. Another advantage in settling in Michigan is, that it is about half-way between the East and the West. One does not have to go to the other side of creation to get there; and the inhabitants may well deem themselves located just about in the center of the world. A strong inducement, also, is found in the fact, that the government lands in Michigan have been in market, most of them, over ten years, and have fallen in prices to one dollar an acre. The land-offices are situated at Detroit, Ionia, and Michilimackinac.

The exemption laws of Michigan are extremely liberal toward her citizens. A correct view of household property would seem to have been taken by the legislature; that the property of the husband necessary to the sustenance of the family belongs to the family, and should not be alienated by mortgage, or lien, without the consent of the wife.

In addition to the usual exemption of a seat in a church, a cemetery, arms, and accouterments, and household utensils, and stores, the exemption includes the following property, viz.: All wearing apparel of every person or family; school books and library, to the value of one hundred and fifty dollars; household goods and furniture, to the same amount; ten sheep, two cows, five swine, and feed for them; and provisions and fuel for the family for six months; tools, implements, materials, stocks, apparatus, team, vehicle, horses, harness, or other things, to carry on a trade, occupation, or business, not exceeding in value two hundred and fifty dollars. And all chattel mortgages, bills of sale, or other liens on such property, are declared void, unless signed by the wife. In addition to the foregoing, forty acres of land, the dwelling-house thereon, and the appurtenances, are also exempt. So, where a man shall occupy a house or land not his own, the house is exempt.

INDIANA.

CHAPTER XII.

INDIANA.

Yankee emigrants — Emigration checked by the war of 1812 — Admission as a state — Rapid settlement of the state — Where the settlers came from — Soil of the state — The Ohio and Whitewater valleys — The White River Valley — The Wabash Valley — River navigation — Canals — Railroads — Agricultural products — Charitable institutions, churches, colleges, and schools.

Upon the organization of the eastern portion of the Northwestern Territory into a separate territorial government, the remaining portion of it, extending westward to the Mississippi, and northward to the lakes, became known as the Indiana Territory. In 1804, it entered upon the first grade of territorial government, as prescribed by the ordinances of 1787. William Henry Harrison was appointed governor. Vincennes was selected as the capital. The north-western tribes had continued to be peaceable, since the conquest of that region by Colonel Clark. The French settlements on the Wabash soon began to receive additions of Yankee emigrants. The rambling disposition of the people, their curiosity to see and explore new and beautiful regions, led them to plunge into the wilderness, and seek out those remote and lonely settlements. Road-traces, or lines of blazed trees, marked out the routes to be pursued by the emigrants. Previous to 1805, the Indian title to nearly all the southern half of Indiana had been extinguished, removing the chief obstacle to the peaceful settlement of the country.

Three years later, the population having increased to five thousand free white males, Congress, with a view to a future state government, assigned the limits of Indiana, and authorized the election of a territorial legislature. The prosperity of Indiana was considerably checked by the last war with Great Britain. Indian hostilities were at once resumed, and many of the advanced settlements had to be abandoned. It was not until the summer of 1815 that the population of Indiana began rapidly to increase. For the various campaigns of that war, and the mounted expeditions that had traversed the territory, were virtual explorations of that fertile and beautiful country by thousands of young, hardy, and enterprising pioneers, who, upon the return of peace, moved thither with their families, and formed settlements upon all the water-courses. Many of the inhabitants came into the territory from Ohio and Kentucky. So great was the rush of emigration that, early the next season, the population had become sufficiently large to entitle them to a state government. In April, 1816, Indiana was admitted into the Union as a free and independent state.

None of the western states have become settled with greater rapidity than Indiana. Four years after the adoption of the state constitution, the population numbered one hundred and forty-eight thousand souls; five years afterward, two hundred and fifty thousand; in 1830, three hundred and forty-two thousand; and in 1835, six hundred thousand. The present population is over one million. Of that number, New York has furnished twenty-four thousand; Pennsylvania, forty-four thousand; Maryland, ten thousand; Virginia, forty-five thousand; Kentucky, sixty-nine thousand; and Ohio, one hundred and twenty thousand. In 1850, the improved farm lands in the state amounted to five million acres; the unimproved, over seven million acres.

The remarkable fertility of the soil of Indiana arises mainly from its geological position. Situated nearly in the center of the great American valley, far distant from the primitive ranges of mountains, the surface-earth is accordingly formed from the destruction of a vast variety of rocks, both crystalline and sedimentary, which have been minutely divided, and intimately blended, by the action of air and water. That soil is known to be the most productive which has been formed from the destruction of the greatest variety of rocks, by which is produced the due mixture of gravel, sand, clay, and limestone, necessary for the nutrition of plants. Two-thirds of the state of Indiana is level land, slightly undulating, and the water-shed, or divide, within its borders, is scarcely perceptible. But the country has continuous slopes of vast extent, and the highest elevation of the surface is six hundred feet above the Ohio River at the falls. Along the rivers are ranges of low hills, which extend back in spurs a little way into the country. Those on the banks of the streams, where the water-courses have torn through them, present much imposing scenery. Back of the hills is the table-land of the interior country; and that lies gently rolling, as if formed into billows. Occasionally there are small conical elevations, from one hundred feet to two hundred feet in hight. Inclosed within the river hills are the rich bottom-lands, which, originally, were covered with mighty forests. The predominant timber of the state is oak and beech. Next in order are the sugar-maple, hickory, ash, poplar, elm, cherry, hackberry, whitewood, coffee-tree, and honey-locust. Chestnut is found only on the east fork of the White River.

Indiana has four distinct natural divisions. First, the Ohio and Whitewater valleys, comprising about five thousand square miles. It is a limestone region, heavily timbered, and the soil of great depth and fertility. The hills are abrupt, and broken through by numerous streams, that in dry weather show only the marks where torrents have disappeared almost as soon as the storms which had occasioned them. About two-thirds of this division consists of choice farming lands. The residue is too much broken to be cultivated profitably. The poorest land is in the flats at the heads of the streams, which would seem to have washed the substance of the soil upon the bottoms below.

Second, the White River Valley, which extends back, through the center of the state, from the Wabash to the boundary of Ohio, and contains about nine thousand square miles. The surface is uniformly level, originally covered with a heavy growth of forest — except in the western part, where there are some small prairies and low, rugged hills. This valley is wholly destitute of rock. The soil is the best in the state, with but very little that is not fit for cultivation. It is supplied with never-failing streams, and an abundance of water-power.

Third, the Wabash Valley, which constitutes the largest division, as it contains upward of twelve thousand square miles. It interlocks with the White River Valley, which it resembles, in the eastern part. The Wabash Valley is more broken, but not less fertile. The middle of this region is supplied with running water; but the upper and the lower portions are nearly destitute of it. From the river-hills along the Ohio, the land inclines to the Wabash; and it is a curiosity of the Indiana river system, that the streams rising near the former river flow off to a great distance, and form junctions with the latter.

Fourth, the northern part of the state, which is watered by the St. Joseph's and its tributaries, and the Kankakee, a branch of the Illinois. It resembles very much the Wabash country, only that it is rather more swampy, and, near the lake, quite sandy. The extreme northern counties have extensive ranges of sand-hills, covered only with shriveled pines and bur-oaks. This region, however, constitutes only a small portion of the state.

The principal rivers are the Ohio, the Wabash, and the White. The first named forms the southern boundary of the state, for a distance, following the windings of the river, of three hundred and eighty miles. The White-water joins the Miami six miles above its entrance into the Ohio. The Wabash, entering Indiana from the east, flows clear across it, and thence, turning south, forms the western boundary. It is six hundred miles in length, and for more than half that distance it is navigable. The confluence of the White River with the Wabash is one hundred miles above the mouth of the latter river. The Kankakee is lined with extensive marshes. Deep and Calumet rivers lie just south of Lake Michigan, separated from it, in some places, only by sand-banks.

The river navigation of Indiana is rendered difficult by frequent shallows. The boats are of light draft, flat-bottomed; and the paddle-wheel — for they have but one — is placed across the stern, and appears like a huge under-shot wheel, revolving behind. It has been said of the Indiana boats, that, in making headway down stream, they contrive to keep up with the current. They draw about as much water as a sap-trough. When they get stuck in the sand, all hands will jump out and push them off. It is related of an exasperated Hoosier, who had refused to pay his fare till there should be some prospect of his getting somewhere or other, that, being ordered ashore from the middle of the river, he stepped into the water, seized the craft by the bows, and gave it a shove half a mile down stream, stern foremost; and when it had worked back up again to where he was standing, he placed his foot against it, and held it, fluttering and puffing, without letting it make any headway. The engineer put on the steam, and the captain "cussed;" but it was no use. The Hoosier was too much for it. A compromise had to be effected. The Hoosier was hired for the rest of the voyage to help the engine.

Indiana is two hundred and seventy-six miles in extreme length, from north to south, and one hundred and sixty-miles in width, with an area of about thirty-four thousand square miles. It has a magnificent system of internal improvements. The Wabash and Erie Canal—from Toledo, on Lake Erie, to Evansville, on the Ohio River—is four hundred and sixty-seven miles in length, more than three-fourths of which are in Indiana. Indianapolis, the capital, is situated in the center of the state; and from that point the railroad lines radiate in every direction. One line stretches up north-east, through Bellefontaine to Cleveland, and connects with the Lake Shore road; another runs south to Louisville; another, west to Terra Haute, on the Wabash River; another, north through Lafayette to Michigan City, connecting with the Michigan Southern road; and another, east to Dayton, connecting with the Cincinnati, Cleveland, and Columbus road.

Indiana produced in 1850, of wheat, over six million bushels; corn, fifty-three million bushels; and oats, six million bushels. The corn crop had nearly doubled since 1840. The products of its manufactures is of the annual value of twenty million dollars. The total value of its live stock is about twenty-two million dollars. It produces annually about thirteen million pounds of butter; and the value of the animals slaughtered yearly is about seven million dollars.

Colored people are not permitted to come into, or settle in the state. All contracts made with them are declared void. And all persons employing them are liable to be fined from ten dollars to five hundred dollars. Notwithstanding its illiberality toward that unfortunate class of people, the state has adopted an humane policy in other respects. It has built an asylum for the deaf and dumb, and an institution for the blind, and a hospital for the insane, at Indianapolis. There are in the state about two thousand churches, accommodating seven hundred thousand persons. The common schools and colleges are endowed more liberally than those of any other new state. The constitution provides that "the common school fund shall consist of the congressional township fund, and the lands belonging thereto; of the surplus revenue, saline, and bank-stock funds; the fund derived from the sale of county seminaries, and money and property heretofore held for such seminaries; all fines, forfeitures, and escheats, and lands not otherwise specially granted, including the net proceeds of the sales of the swamp-lands granted to the state by the Act of Congress, September twenty eighth, one thousand eight hundred and fifty. The principal of the fund may be increased, but shall never be diminished; and its income shall be devoted solely to the support of common schools."

ILLINOIS.

CHAPTER XIII.

ILLINOIS.

Extinguishment of the Indian titles — Admission as a state — Great earthquake of 1811 — Effect on the Mississippi — Effect on the Indians — First steamboat on the Mississippi — Keel-boat navigation — Keel-boatmen — Nature of the population — Length and breadth of the state — Number of counties — Lands improved and unimproved — Number of farms — Value of farming implements — Annual products — The soil — The "American Bottom" — Prairie lands — Grand Prairie — Coal regions — Yankee fences in Illinois — Mode of forming settlements on the prairie — Plowing the prairie — The timber region — Minerals — Lead region — Chicago — Rivers, canals, and railroads — Varieties of climate — The winter of 1855-56 — Seasons of the greatest cold — Schools, colleges, and libraries — Exemption laws.

WHEN, in 1809, Congress, by the Act of February 3d, had restricted the limits of Indiana, and had authorized a territorial legislature, the region to the westward of the Wabash was erected into a territorial government of the first grade, and designated as the Illinois Territory. Ninian Edwards was appointed governor. Congress had already taken measures for the extinguishment of the Indian title. By the treaty of Fort Wayne, which was ratified at Vincennes, on the seventh day of August, 1803, by the Eel River Indians, the Wyandots, the Kaskaskias, and the Kickapoos, over three hundred and thirty-six thousand acres had been ceded to the United States. By a subsequent treaty, made only six days later, with the Kaskaskias alone, that tribe had ceded eight and one-half million acres. On the third day of November, 1804, the Sacs and Foxes, by treaty, had relinquished fourteen million acres, principally situated in Illinois. At Vincennes, December 30th, 1805, the Piankeshas had ceded their claim to about three million acres. So that, with the spring following, one-third part of Illinois was open for settlement.

The balance of the territory still remained in the possession of the Indians, and they continued lingering around the old familiar hunting-grounds which they had ceded away, although they had received the stipulated price, and had consented to retire. For several years. the settlements of Illinois increased in number but very slowly. The country was so remote, so much exposed to Indian depredations, and so destitute of the comforts of civilized life, that it did not attract many emigrants, while other lands, equally good and far more easily accessible, were to be had. But, notwithstanding the distance and the danger, the inhabitants began to come in slowly around the older villages of the French, and along the west bank of the Wabash, and upon the lower tributaries of the Illinois, and the east bank of the Mississippi, until about the close of 1817, when it was ascertained that the population had become equal to the population of Ohio at the time of its admission into the Union. The territorial legislature, at the next session, made application to Congress for authority to establish a state government. A constitution, adopted in August, 1818, had been approved in December following, and Illinois was admitted within about two years after the admission of Indiana.

The census of 1820 gave the entire population at the number of fifty-five thousand two hundred and ten souls. During the five years next succeeding, the increase was about seventeen thousand. Many persons had been deterred from going to Illinois by the erroneous supposition that the country was subject to volcanic action. This had originated from the great earthquake of 1811, by which the valley of the Mississippi had been greatly shaken, the shocks having continued for nearly three months. The country just below the mouth of the Ohio River would seem to have been near the center of the agitation. For miles, the land had been seamed with yawning chasms and deep holes, the remains of which are still visible. The bluff on which New Madrid had been built had sunk to the level of the river, and had become, soon afterward, totally submerged. The commotion in the Mississippi had been very great: the banks had caved in, islands had dissolved, and the channel had become changed.

At every shock, the surface of the river had risen and fallen like the waves of the sea. An eye-witness, who was coming down on a flat-boat, says: "After escaping many dangers, my boat suddenly swung round in the conflicting currents, and rapidly shot up the river. Looking ahead, I beheld the mighty Mississippi *cut in twain*, and pouring down a vast opening into the bowels of the earth. A moment more and the chasm filled; but the strong sides of the flat-boat were crumbled to pieces in the convulsive efforts of the flood to obtain its wonted level." The Indians had been utterly bewildered by the earthquake, and could account for the physical tumult only upon the supposition that things generally had been getting drunk. It is said of one of them, who had given himself up for lost, that, upon being questioned as to what the matter was, he had replied, while at the same time pointing fearfully to the heavens, "Great Spirit — whisky too much!"

It was not until after the commencement of steam navigation that Illinois received its great accessions of population. The first steamboat that ever plowed the Mississippi was built at Pittsburg in 1812, and made the voyage to New Orleans the next season. The Enterprise, in December, 1814, was the first to make the entire trip up the river, from New Orleans to Pittsburg. That is said to have been considered a great triumph, "for it was doubted whether this new power could displace the strong arms of the keel-boatmen in stemming the powerful tide." Several years more had elapsed before steam vessels were introduced upon the lakes. The first that was built upon Lake Erie was in 1818; and from that time until 1825, when the Erie Canal had become completed, the shipping upon the lakes was principally employed in carrying westward supplies and trinkets for the Indian trade, and returning with cargoes of furs and peltries. The influence of the canal was immediately felt throughout the entire West, in facilitating emigration; and Illinois began rapidly to fill up with an enterprising population.

Previous to the era of steam navigation upon the western waters, the transportation of emigrants, and merchandise, and produce, was effected by means of keel-boats, that would drift down well enough with the current, but had to be forced up stream with setting-poles. "The keel-boat was long and narrow, sharp at the bow and stern, and of light draft. From fifteen to twenty hands were required to propel it along. The crew, divided equally on each side, took their places upon the running boards, extending along the whole length of the craft; and each man, setting one end of a long pole in the bottom of the river, brought the other to the shoulder, and bending down upon it, his face nearly to the plank, exerted all his force against the boat, treading it from under him." While those on one side were thus passing down in line to the stern, those on the other, having faced about, were passing up toward the bow, drawing their poles floating on the water. One man always stood leisurely steering, astraddle of the oar; and generally, some one of the men might have been seen on the deck, sawing away upon a fiddle, with as much energy as if he were scalping an Indian. In this way, they would walk up the whole length of the Mississippi.

The keel-boatmen kept their rifles constantly within reach. They were the most athletic, restless, and reckless set of men the country ever produced. Constantly exposed, they despised danger, and were ready to drop their poles and have a fight, just for the fun of the thing. Going shirtless, wearing nothing but trowsers and hats, they were tanned and swarthy from the head to the waist. They seemed to live and thrive on grog, which they took in a manner peculiar to themselves — first a cup of whisky, and then a cup of river water, mixing it in the stomach. Whoever among them could boast that he had never been whipped, was bound to fight any one that might dare to dispute his superiority. The keel-boatmen were great sticklers for "fair play," and would permit of no interference with either of the combatants. Their arrival in port was a general jubilee, where hundreds often met together for the noisiest and most outlandish diversions. In their habits, the keel-boatmen were lawless in the extreme, and would set the civil authorities at defiance for days together. Had their numbers increased with the population of the West, they would have endangered the peace of the country; but they went out with the commencement of steam navigation, and have gradually disappeared.

Now and then a "specimen" of the by-gone race of river boatmen, who have mostly settled down to farming, will turn up on the western steamboats; and on such occasions their propensity to "rough fun" will break out afresh. Some years since, one of them took passage down for New Orleans, and for several days he seemed quite desponding for want of excitement. At last the boat put into Napoleon, in the state of Arkansas, for supplies. Just at the moment there was a general fight, extending all along in front of the town, which, at that time, consisted of a single grocery. The unhappy passenger, fidgeting about, jerking his feet up and down as if they were touching upon hot bricks, inquired of a spectator: "Stranger, is this 'ere a free fight?" The reply was prompt: "Wall, it ar'. If you want to go in, you need n't stand on ceremony." The passenger went in, and soon after came out again, appearing to be reasonably satisfied. Groping his way on board, his hair half torn out, his coat in tatters, one eye closed up, and several of his teeth knocked into his throat, he sat down on a hen-coop, and soliloquized: "So this is Na-po-le-on, is it? It's jeest the most refreshing place I 've seen in many a day."

After 1825, the number of inhabitants in Illinois increased with great rapidity. The fame of its prairies had reached the eastern states, and the Erie Canal and the steamboats on the lakes afforded a continuous chain of water communication to its distant borders. The ease and speed of the new modes of conveyance and transportation seemed to have shortened the journey by more than one-half. The states which bordered upon Illinois to the east and south sent forth constant streams of enterprising families, that were seeking, among its choice lands and rich mines, to secure a competence to themselves and to their children. Cities began to spring up, like Jonah's gourd, almost in a night. The edges of its prairies were beginning to be dotted with villages. And fields of luxuriant grain had taken the place of the tall, rank grass. The population, in 1830, numbered over one hundred and fifty-seven thousand; in 1840, four hundred and seventy six thousand; and in 1850, eight hundred and fifty-one thousand. During these last two periods, the decennial increase had been about three hundred and fifty thousand.

Of the whole number of people, in 1850, about three hundred and forty-four thousand had been born within the state. Nearly one hundred and eleven thousand were of foreign birth. Of the rest, twenty-six thousand had come from New England; sixty-seven thousand from New York; seven thousand from New Jersey; thirty-eight thousand from Pennsylvania; seven thousand each from Maryland and Missouri; from Virginia, twenty-four thousand; North Carolina, thirteen thousand; Georgia and Alabama, each one thousand; Tennessee, thirty-two thousand; Kentucky, fifty thousand; Ohio, sixty-four thousand; and Indiana, thirty-one thousand. Of the foreign population, eighteen thousand were from England; twenty-eight thousand from Ireland; thirty-eight thousand from Germany; and eleven thousand from British America. Illinois is entitled to nine members of the House of Representatives of the United States.

The extreme length of the state, on the meridian of Cairo city, is three hundred and seventy-eight miles, and its greatest breadth is two hundred and twelve miles; but the average length and breadth is considerably less than that. The state comprises an area of fifty-five thousand four hundred and five square miles. It is divided into ninety-nine counties. Illinois contains about five and one-half million acres of improved farm lands, and six and one-half million acres unimproved. The number of farms under cultivation is nearly one hundred thousand; and the value of the farming implements and machinery has been estimated as high as seven million dollars. The annual production of wheat and oats is, for each, ten million bushels; Indian corn, about sixty million bushels; and potatoes, three million bushels.

Generally, it may be said of Illinois, that it occupies the lower part of the great plain, inclining to the south-west, of which the shores of Lake Michigan are the highest part. Down this plain flow the Wabash, Kaskaskia, and Illinois rivers. The lowest section, in the extreme southern angle of the state, at the mouth of the Ohio River, is about three hundred and forty feet above tide-water in the Gulf of Mexico; and the mean hight of the arable lands above tide-water may be stated at six hundred feet.

It has been supposed that, at some former period, an obstruction existed in the channel of the Mississippi, at the Grand Tower, producing a stagnation in the current, at an elevation of about one hundred feet, above the present ordinary water-mark. At that place, the hills, which, for several hundred miles above, are separated by a valley of twenty-five miles in width, approach near each other, and line both banks with precipitous shores. The walls of rock that frown upon the river have, upon their abrupt fronts, a series of water lines, uniformly presenting their greatest depression toward the sources of the river. At Grand Tower, those rocks of dark-colored limestone, which pervade a very considerable portion of the country, project toward each other, and seem to indicate that, at a remote period, they must have been disunited by some convulsion of nature, which opened for the Mississippi its present channel, and gave vent to the waters stagnating upon the prairies above.

The surface of Illinois is almost uniformly level, the most so of any other of the American states, with the exception of Louisiana and Delaware. A small section in the southern part may be denominated hilly, and the more northern portion is broken and uneven. Along the Illinois River there are, likewise, considerable elevations; and the Mississippi bluffs in some places might pass for mountains; but the far greater portion of the state is distributed in vast plains, that are gently rolling like the waves of the sea after a storm. The surface is remarkably free from stone. A few of the northern counties are somewhat stony, yet, in every other part, the plow may pass over millions of acres without striking as much as a pebble big enough to fling at a humming-bird.

The portion of the soil most celebrated for its fertility and productiveness consists of the rich bottoms or alluvial borders of the rivers, which have been formed from the deposits of the waters during floods. On some of these the surface mold is more than thirty feet in depth; but, at present, nearly one-sixth of the bottom-lands in the state are unfit for cultivation, though productive of valuable timber. A tract, called the "American Bottom," extending along the Mississippi for ninety miles, and about five miles in average width, is of this formation. In the vicinity of the French towns, it has been under cultivation, and has produced great crops of corn every year, without manuring, for one hundred and fifty years.

The prairie lands of Illinois are less fertile than the river bottoms, yet they are not inferior for many agricultural purposes, and are greatly preferable, where timber can be had, on account of the salubrity of the climate. The soil of the oak openings is still thinner and lighter than the prairies. The level region, embracing the whole country lying between the waters which flow into the Mississippi and the waters which flow into the Wabash, is denominated the "Grand Prairie." The surface is undulating, and the wave-like ridges, with a long, gentle slope on one side, precipitous on the other, frequently rise into quite respectable hills. But the general aspect of the country is that of a dead level sea of grass. Grand Prairie does not consist of one vast tract alone—it is made up of a great number of continuous tracts, centering upon an immense plain. Long reaches of timber stretch, in narrow lines, far into that plain, while broad arms of prairie are extended out between. The central plain itself is utterly destitute of trees and shrubbery.

The southern points of the Grand Prairie are formed in Jackson county; and from thence, extending in a north-easterly direction, varying in width from five to twenty miles, through the counties of Perry, Washington, Jefferson, Marion, Fayette, Effingham, Coles, Champaign, and Iroquois, it becomes connected with those prairies which project eastward from the Illinois River. A very large arm stretches up through Marion county, between the Crooked Creek and the east fork of the Kaskaskia River. This latter part, alone, is frequently spoken of as the Grand Prairie, though, in fact, it is but a single branch of it. The Grand Prairie comprises territory sufficient for a state, respectable in size. The Vincennes road passes through it in Marion county. The soil is mostly fertile; but in the southern part there are vast flats that are quite inferior.

No insurmountable obstacle exists in the way of settlements upon the Grand Prairie. Timber for buildings and fences alone is wanting. Fuel is plentiful; for the immense coal field which stretches away through western Kentucky, northern Missouri, and the greater part of Iowa, crosses the Mississippi to the eastward, and underlies almost every acre of the Grand Prairie. The coal region of Illinois is the most extensive of any state or country on the globe. It comprises an area of about forty-four thousand square miles—nearly three times larger than that of Pennsylvania. With the completion of the Illinois Central Railroad, the lumber regions of Michigan and Wisconsin will have been brought into connection with the Grand Prairie, and will furnish supplies of building material; while the Osage orange — a tough, hardy shrub — can be grown rapidly into hedges. In the meantime, resort must be had to turf fences and ditches. Those who have settled upon the prairie contrive to eke out their fencing timber so as to make the most of it. The Yankee settlers have introduced into Illinois a new kind of fence, that takes all the conceit out of the zigzag Virginia worm fences. Coming from the land of wooden nutmegs and basswood hams, they seem to possess a rare genius for working up wood to the best advantage. With an inveterate propensity for whittling, they rive out of oak logs narrow strips, and drive them into the ground, about three inches apart, along the line of the fence; and upon the tops nail a cap, to hold all secure. After a year or two, a furrow is thrown up, on each side, against the stakes, to give additional support. Fences can be made in that manner so tight that a grasshopper could hardly jump through. The amount of timber necessary to inclose a field is, in this way, greatly lessened — by nearly one-half.

Those who have witnessed the changes produced upon a prairie surface within a period of twenty-five years, by excluding the fires from them, consider the extensive prairies of Illinois as offering no serious impediment to the future growth of the state. The effect of protecting the surface from the ravages of fire may be seen in St. Louis county, in the state of Missouri, which, down to 1823, was pretty much all prairie. But now that tract is covered with a thrifty growth of timber, and it would be difficult to find an acre of prairie in the county. The mode of forming settlements upon prairie lands has been thus described: "The first improvements are usually made on that part of the prairie which adjoins the timber; and thus we may see, at the commencement, a range of farms circumscribing the entire prairie. The burning of the prairies is then stopped, through the whole distance of the circuit in the neighborhood of these farms, to prevent injury to the fences and other improvements. This is done, by plowing two or three furrows all round the settlement. In a short time the timber springs up spontaneously on all the parts not burned, and the groves and forests commence a gradual encroachment on the adjacent prairies. By and by you will see another tier of farms springing up on the outside of the first, and further out on the prairie; and thus farm succeeds farm, as the timber grows up, until the entire prairie is occupied."

The sward of the prairies is exceedingly tough, composed of the fibrous grass-roots; and, in turning it over, five or six yoke of cattle are required to draw the plow. Two drivers, generally a man and a boy, guide the team. Moving over an unbroken surface, uninterrupted by stones or stumps, the plow moves steadily along; the plowman having but little to do, except at the end of the "lands," where the direction has to be changed, and the plow set in at a proper distance for the furrow. The modern wheel plow is mostly in use; the wheel at the nose of the beam regulating the depth, and the sharp colter, its heel set against the point of the share, dividing the sward like a knife. It would be almost impossible for the plowman alone to regulate the depth without the wheel; for sometimes the plow would be thrown out by the sward, and at other times plunged into the ground to the beam. To procure steadiness, the plow is set by the dip of the share, so as to run too deep, which brings a constant pressure upon the wheel, and binds the whole machine steadily to the earth. In earlier times, before the invention of plows that were adapted to prairie service, the end of the beam

PRAIRIE PLOWING.

had to be attached to the axletree of a cart, the box of which served to carry an ax, mattock, chains, wrenches, screws, nuts, bolts, clevises, and pieces of timber for repairs, in case of accidents. The yield of wheat the third season is deemed the best. After that the surface of the ground will have become mellow as an ash heap.

Illinois has plenty of timber within its limits; and, were it equally distributed through the state, there would be no part deficient. The several species of oaks are most abundant. The other varieties are the black-walnut, the white-walnut, ash, elm, maple, honey-locust, hackberry, linden, or whitewood, pecan, cottonwood, mulberry, buckeye, sycamore, wild cherry, box, sassafras, and persimmon. The undergrowths are the red-bud, pawpaw, sumac, plum, crab-apple, dog-wood, spice-bush, greenbriar, and hazel. On the bottom-lands, the cottonwood and sycamore grow to amazing size.

The prairies of Illinois are finely adapted for grazing. Immense flocks and herds might find ample room and abundant supplies of pasturage. The inhabitants are turning their attention in that direction. The state has superior advantages for the growth of wool, and might supply half the manufactories of the Union with that great staple. The clipping of wool, in 1840, was only about six hundred thousand pounds; in 1850 it had increased to nearly two and one half million pounds. There need be no limit to the growth of wool but the demand for it in the market.

The northern part of the state is inexhaustibly rich in minerals. Iron ore is widely distributed. Copper and silver have been found in considerable quantities. But the great mining operations are confined to the lead region, in the north-western point, in the vicinity of Galena. The lead region embraces an area of about sixty square miles. Commencing at the mouth of the Little Moquaquity River, in Wisconsin, it extends along both banks of the Mississippi about sixty miles, in Wisconsin, Illinois, and Iowa. The surface of the earth is there poverty-stricken and desolate enough; the short, wiry, dwarf-grass is unpalatable even to goats; but riches lie below. Galena is situated on both sides of the Fever River, six miles above the Mississippi, and is accessible to the largest class of steamboats, at all seasons. In 1852, not less than forty million pounds of lead were shipped from Galena alone, valued at two million dollars.

The north-eastern corner of the state, for fifty miles, is washed by the waters of Lake Michigan, which open communication with the whole lake country to the north and east. Its principal port is Chicago. Chicago in 1833, was described as follows: "This little mushroom town is situated on the verge of a level tract of country, for the greater part consisting of open prairie lands, at a point where a small river—whose sources interlock, in the wet season, with those of the Illinois River—enters Lake Michigan. It, however, forms no harbor; and vessels must anchor in the open lake, which spreads to the horizon, north and east, in a sheet of uniform extent." The contrast between Chicago of 1833, and the Chicago of the present day, is truly startling. "This mushroom town" is now the focus of a commerce equal to that enjoyed by many of the states of Europe. In 1830, Chicago was a mere trading-post, and ten years later it had only four thousand four hundred and seventy inhabitants; but in 1850 its population was thirty thousand.

The Mississippi forms the western boundary of the state; the Ohio and the Wabash rivers demark its southern and eastern limits, together forming a natural highway, by water, of unexampled extent. The Illinois River, through the center of the state, is navigable over four hundred miles from its mouth, and it is connected with Lake Michigan by the Illinois and Michigan Canal, at Chicago. That canal is one hundred miles in length. The railroad lines from Chicago reach the Mississippi River at Galena, Rock Island, Quincy, Alton, and Cairo. The Illinois Central Railroad runs through the heart of the "Grand Prairie." A line stretches along the lake to Milwaukie, and other lines to Janesville, Madison, and Fond du Lac.

Illinois offers very great advantages to the settler; but, at the same time, it must be borne in mind that, as the state extends through five and one-half degrees of latitude, it possesses considerable variety of climate, and that the level surface, unsheltered by forests, exposes it alike to sun and storm. The summers are hot and prolonged, and the winters everywhere severe. The prevailing winds are the south-west, which blow three-fourths of the year. The northerly and westerly winds prevail in winter. On the whole, the climate may be regarded as favorable to outdoor employments, the proportion of clear weather being two hundred and forty-five days, to one hundred and twenty of cloudy. The general salubrity of Illinois is well attested, and few suffer from endemic diseases, except those who have settled near swamps and wet bottom-lands.

The winter of 1855–56 has been one of uncommon severity throughout the West. On the prairies, the cold has been intense. Ice has been formed as far down as the Gulf of Mexico. The cold weather in Illinois continued, uninterrupted, for more than two months. Such periods of intense cold, however, recur at wide intervals. Some may be curious to know the seasons of the greatest cold which have occurred. In 1133, the river Po, in Italy, was frozen from Cremona to the sea; wine burst the casks containing it, and the trees split with a loud report.

In 1234, the Mediterranean was frozen over, and merchandise was transported across it on the ice. The winter of 1681 was so severe that whole forests of oak were ruined, the trees being split with the cold.

In 1698, the wolves came into Vienna, and attacked men, women, and children, owing to the intense cold and hunger.

And in 1704, the most extraordinary storm of which there is any record, occurred in Scotland. The snow fell in a single night to the depth of ten feet.

The schools of Illinois are in a flourishing condition. The funds appropriated to their support amount to a million of dollars. The Illinois College is located at Jacksonville; the Shurtleff College, at Upper Alton; the McKendree College, at Lebanon; and the Knox College, at Galesburg. There are twenty-seven libraries in the state, containing about twenty thousand volumes. The Law Library contains four thousand volumes.

In Illinois, the necessary wearing apparel of every person is exempt from execution, and household furniture to the value of fifteen dollars, beside bedding and utensils for cooking. Also, one cow; two sheep for each member of the family; and sixty dollars' worth of property, to be selected by the debtor; provisions for three months; and, in case of fines, only one bed and bedding, one cow, and ten dollars' worth of household kitchen-furniture.

WISCONSIN.

CHAPTER XIV.

WISCONSIN.

Organized as a territory — First settlements — Rapid emigration — Source of emigration — Admission as a state — Number of counties, dwellings, and families — Nature of the population — State laws, with regard to voters — Courts — Interesting provisions of the constitution — Length, breadth, and general surface of the state — Southern Wisconsin — Superior natural advantages — Prairies — Oak openings — Abundant pasturages — Inducements to settlers — Southern Wisconsin compared with other states — Increase of Agricultural wealth — Lead mines — Iron region — Limestone — White marble — Northern Wisconsin — Extensive pine regions — Water-power — The Wisconsin pine — Annual amount sawed — Climate of Wisconsin — Health — Opinion of physicians — Commerce — Harbors — Milwaukie brick — Railroads — Educational institutions and laws — Exemption laws.

THE region of country west of Lake Michigan — formerly attached to the territorial jurisdiction of Michigan, and known as the "Huron District — was erected into a separate territorial government, under the name of the Wisconsin Territory, upon the admission of the State of Michigan into the Union in 1837. Henry Dodge was appointed governor, and John S. Horner, secretary. The territory, at that time, comprised within its limits all the country from Lake Michigan to Lake Superior, extending westward to the Missouri River, including all the sources of the Upper Mississippi. Its southern limits were the northern boundaries of Illinois and Missouri, and its extent, from north to south, was five hundred and eighty miles, and from east to west, six hundred and fifty miles.

Its settled portions consisted of a small tract near the shores of Lake Michigan, and the organized counties lay along the Fox River of Green Bay, as far as Fort Winnebago, and thence down the Wisconsin River, on the south-eastern side, for thirty miles below the portage. Immigrants, coming in by the way of Milwaukie and Racine, were advancing upon the tributaries of Rock River, as far west as the Four Lakes and Fort Madison. A few settlements had grown up on the banks of the Mississippi, north of Galena; and some where extending across the river upon the Des Moines, Skunk River, Lower Iowa, and Wapsipinicon. Those settlements upon the western side of the Mississippi were known as the District of Iowa. After the organization of a separate territorial government, and especially after the extinction of the Indian title, in 1837, the settlements began to extend in a remarkable manner, not only upon the western shores of Lake Michigan, but in an equal degree upon the Mississippi. About the same time, immense numbers of foreign immigrants from Europe, but chiefly from Germany, arriving at New York and New Orleans, took their way to Wisconsin, around the lakes, and up the Mississippi. And thousands of the early settlers of Ohio, Indiana, Kentucky, and Tennessee, or their descendants, were seeking new homes in the same direction.

During the years 1841, 1842, and 1843, emigration from the New England and middle states began sending its floods into Wisconsin Territory, to repose along the Wisconsin River. Inhabitants came crowding into the beautifully undulating lands near the shore of Lake Michigan, south of Green Bay, to the Illinois line, and around Lake Winnebago, and between the Fox and Wisconsin rivers. Settlements soon spread throughout this delightful country, diversified by lakes and rivers, in which the crystal tributaries of the Rock River take their rise. Thriving towns and villages were springing up in all parts of this region, which, but a few years previously, had been called the Far West, beyond the advance of white settlements and civilized life, in the sole occupancy of the most degraded and improvident of the savage tribes — the Winnebagoes, the Sacs, and the Foxes. During 1843, the aggregate number of persons that arrived in the Wisconsin Territory has been estimated at more than sixty thousand, embracing all ages, and both sexes. Of those, fifty thousand came by the route of the lakes.

In 1845, Wisconsin Territory contained more inhabitants than any other new territory had possessed upon admission into the Union; yet the people, satisfied with the territorial form of government, did not desire, the settlements having been made so recently, to incur the additional expenses of an independent state government. And although the population amounted to more than one hundred and forty thousand souls, they had not made application to Congress for authority to organize themselves into a state. Leave, however, having been granted by Congress, in 1846, for the holding of a convention, the delegates assembled at Madison, in October of that year, and adopted a constitution. But the people, at the next election, having rejected it, another convention was held in the winter of 1847, and the new constitution was approved in April following. On the twenty-ninth day of May, 1848, Wisconsin was admitted into the Union on an equal footing with the other states.

Wisconsin is divided into thirty-one counties, the most populous of which are, Dane, Dodge, Milwaukie, Racine, Rock, Walworth, Washington, Waukesha, Winnebago, Kenosha, Jefferson, Grant, and Fond du Lac counties; and the least populous are, Saint Croix, Richland, Marathon, La Pointe, Chippewa, and Adams. In 1850, the whole number of dwellings in the state was fifty-six thousand three hundred and sixteen; of families, fifty-seven thousand six hundred and eight; and of inhabitants, three hundred and four thousand five hundred and sixty-five. Wisconsin contains twenty-one thousand more males than females; and a larger number of foreigners in proportion to the whole population than any other state — one-third being foreigners. Of the whole population, upward of sixty thousand were born in the state; the balance came, mainly as follows, viz.: From New England, twenty-seven thousand; from New York, sixty-nine thousand; New Jersey and Pennsylvania, eleven thousand; Kentucky and Michigan, each two thousand; Ohio, twelve thousand; and Illinois, six thousand. Of the foreign population, nineteen thousand came from England; twenty-two thousand from Ireland; three thousand five hundred from Scotland; twelve hundred from Russia; nine thousand from Norway; four thousand from Prussia; and nine thousand from British America. Wisconsin is entitled to three members of the House of Representatives of the United States.

The Legislature meets annually at Madison, on the first Monday of January. All males, twenty-one years old, residents of the state for one year next before the election, who are white citizens of the United States, or white foreigners who have declared their intention to become such citizens, or persons of Indian blood once declared by the laws of the United States to be citizens — subsequent laws to the contrary notwithstanding — or civilized persons of Indian descent, not members of a tribe, are entitled to vote at all elections. The elections are held on the Tuesday after the first Monday in November, in each year.

Wisconsin has an elective judiciary. The state is divided into six judicial districts, in each of which the people elect a supreme court judge, for six years. The circuit courts have original jurisdiction of all actions — civil, criminal, and equitable. The supreme court, with the exception of issuing writs of mandamus, quo warranto, and the like, has appellate jurisdiction only, and is the court of last resort. There can be no trial by jury in that court. The county courts are composed of a county judge for each county, elected for four years; and they have concurrent jurisdiction with the circuit court, where the damages claimed do not exceed five hundred dollars. Justices of the peace are elected in the several towns, and hold office for two years.

The state constitution contains some interesting miscellaneous provisions, among which are the following: No lottery or divorce can be granted by the legislature; laws shall be passed providing a way for suing the state; the credit of the state shall never be lent, nor shall any debt be contracted nor money paid for internal improvements, unless the state holds trust property dedicated to such uses; except in cases of war, invasion, or insurrection, no debt exceeding one hundred thousand dollars shall be contracted; an university, without sectarian instruction, shall be established; the legislature shall prevent towns and cities from contracting debts; no general or special law to create a bank or banks shall be passed, till a majority of the votes at a general election shall have been in favor of a bank, and until such majority have afterward approved the act passed; any person implicated in a duel loses the right of suffrage, and becomes ineligible to any office; no public defaulter shall hold any office; in criminal prosecutions for libel, the jury are judges of both law and fact; leases of agricultural lands for more than fifteen years are void; resident aliens have all the property rights of citizens; imprisonment for debt is abolished; no religious opinions shall disqualify a witness. Amendments to the constitution, agreed to by the legislature, shall be published for three months before the election, and again referred to the legislature then chosen; and if again approved, shall then be submitted to the people. And a convention may be called in like manner.

The State of Wisconsin in its greatest length, north and south, is two hundred and eighty-five miles, and its greatest breadth is two hundred and fifty-five miles. It comprises an area of about fifty-four thousand square miles. The surface of Wisconsin presents the appearance of a vast plain, extending from Lake Michigan to the Mississippi River. The water-shed, or divide, is near the lake; but it bears away to the north-west. The surface of the state possesses great uniformity of elevation, and it is neither mountainous, hilly, nor flat, but gently undulating throughout, presenting to the settler one of the most beautiful regions of country in America. Wisconsin is one of the highest, best-watered, and best-drained states in the Union. The country west of the Sugar River, and south of the Wisconsin, is somewhat broken, principally by the dividing ridge upon which the road from Madison to Prairie du Chien passes. West of the Wisconsin River is a range of hills, which might be dignified with the name of mountains, seeing they are situated in the heart of a level country.

The south-eastern portion of the state is one continuous table-land, marked and furrowed by ravines along the streams, which are depressed but little below the surrounding surface. The principal features of that region are the prairies, destitute of trees and shrubbery, covered by a luxuriant growth of grass, interspersed, in the spring, with flowers of every hue; the oak openings, which, like those of Michigan, have a sufficiency of timber for fencing and building purposes scattered over the surface; the wood-land borders of the little lakes and streams, running out into the prairies and openings in all directions; and the natural meadows, which supply any amount of pasturage, and a sufficient quantity of hay for the winter. The soil of the prairies and openings consists of a vegetable mold, dark-brown in color, and from one to two feet in depth, very mellow, and entirely destitute of stone or gravel. For fertility it is not, and can not be surpassed. The sub-soil is a clayey loam, preventing all danger of leaching, and furnishing, by deep plowing, a ready means for enriching the surface.

The prairies of Wisconsin are not so extensive as those of other states, and being skirted and belted with timber, within easy access from every part, they are adapted to immediate and profitable occupation. Nature has done all the clearing and preparing the lands; man has only to put in the plow, and reap abundant harvests. The openings comprise the finest portions of the state. The autumnal fires have kept down the under-growth, and destroyed all the varieties of timber, except the oak, which seems to be capable of withstanding the sweep of that element. That autumnal destruction of wood, and leaves, and grasses, has been adding to the richness of the land for ages; while, at the same time, there has been left a sufficient supply of timber for the immediate wants of the immigrant. These considerations explain, in a great measure, the wonderful capacity Wisconsin has displayed for rapid settlement. There is another fact, important to be noticed in this connection: "The low, level prairie, or natural meadow, of moderate extent, is so generally distributed over the face of the country, that the settler, on a fine section of arable lands, finds on his own farm, or in his immediate neighborhood, abundant pasturage for his stock in summer; and hay for the winter for the cutting — the bounty of Nature supplying his need in this behalf till the cultivated grasses can be introduced and become sufficient for his use."

Presenting such strong inducements to the actual settler, Wisconsin has been rapidly drawing within its borders an enterprising, industrious, and thrifty population. The increase has been almost unexampled. In 1840, the Territory of Wisconsin did not possess thirty-one thousand inbabitants; but in the ten years next succeeding, the number had increased to more than three hundred thousand. It may safely be presumed that the southern half of the state is capable of accommodating and supporting a denser population than any other part of America of the same extent. As rapidly as the country would appear to have been settling up, a small portion only of the choicest lands has been reduced to actual occupation. Thousands of acres, equal to the best in the world, are awaiting the hand of the husbandman to make them blossom like a garden. In 1850, the unimproved farm lands in Wisconsin numbered over one million nine hundred thousand acres; the improved lands, one million and forty-five thousand acres; the total number of cultivated farms, twenty thousand one hundred and seventy-seven. The farming implements and machinery were at the same time valued at more than a million and a half of dollars.

The following tables, extracted from Colton's Gazetteer, will show how rapidly Wisconsin has been increasing in agricultural wealth. The years compared are 1840 and 1850. We have no reliable data later than the last-mentioned year.

LIVE STOCK.	1840.	1850.	INCREASE.
Horses, . . .	5,735 hd.	30,179 hd.	24,600 head.
Asses & mules,		156 "	
Milch cows, . .		64,339 "	
Working oxen, .	30,269 "	42,801 "	153,164 "
Other cattle, . .		76,293 "	
Swine, ...	51,383 "	159,276 "	107,893 "
Sheep, ...	34,624 "	124,892 "	90,268 "

The growth of wool, in 1840, was . . . 6,777 pounds.
" " in 1850, was . . . 253,963 "

The grain crops of 1840, as compared with those of 1850, are as follows:

CROPS.	1840.	1850.
Wheat, ...	212,116 bushels.	4,286,131 bushels
Rye, ...	1,905 "	81,253 "
Indian corn, . .	379,359 "	1,988,979 "
Oats, ...	406,514 "	3,414,672 "
Potatoes, . . .	419,608 "	1,500,000 "

In 1850, the value of live stock amounted to nearly five million dollars.

But it is not to agriculture alone that the inhabitants of Wisconsin may look for increase of wealth. The mining and lumbering facilities of that state are on the grandest scale. The copper mines are reserved for the chapter on "The Superior Country." Wisconsin is best known as a mineral region by its lead mines, which comprise four-fifths of the entire lead district of the West. The lead-bearing rock is a porous limestone, and it prevails throughout the counties of Grant, Iowa, and Lafayette. Three-fourths of all the lead shipped at Galena is produced in

Wisconsin. There are, also, large quantities shipped at other places along the Mississippi, and on the Wisconsin River, the precise amounts of which no data has been furnished upon which an intelligent estimate can be made. The general appearance of the lead region of Wisconsin is precisely similar to that of Illinois,—a broken, desolate surface, covered with a wiry, unpalatable grass; but the rich mineral lies below.

The iron mines of Wisconsin have scarcely yet been opened; but they are well worthy of the attention of the immigrant. The ore exists in great abundance near the head-waters of the Rock River, on the upper tributaries of the Mississippi, and to the west of the sources of the Menominee. In respect to the iron, it is impossible to do more than point out, generally, the localities where it is known to exist. The region where the ore abounds is mostly a howling wilderness. The smelting of the ore requires a great outlay of capital in the first instance; and, in view of the present condition of the country, it will probably be several years before the iron of Wisconsin will become known in the market. But with the lead it is quite different. Very little capital is requisite. The exceeding abundance of the mineral, the comparative ease with which it may be mined, and the high price it commands, the moment it is brought to the surface, open to the industrious and prudent operative a highway to wealth.

"The limestone underlying the coal fields of Illinois forms the immediate basis of the alluvion of southern Wisconsin. This geological district, in addition to that portion of the state which lies southerly of the valley of the Wisconsin River, comprises the whole of the slope toward Lake Michigan." *In many places the lime rock* disappears, and the out-cropping sandstone furnishes a fine material for building. The region of primitive rock lies north of a line drawn from the Falls of St. Anthony across to Green Bay; and in that portion of the state between the primitive formation and the limestone to the south and east, the transition sandstone prevails, comprising the section drained by the rivers flowing south-westerly, and below the falls in those rivers. In all this middle region are found quarries of white marble, which promise to be abundant and valuable, rivaling those of Vermont.

Leaving the prairies and proceeding northward up the Wisconsin and Fox rivers, the timber constantly increases. The surface of the ground becomes more uneven. Large marshes are found, with a rank growth of cranberries and wild-rice. And still further north and north-west is one of the finest tracts of pine land in America, through which the streams, tumbling down frequent falls, afford an incalculable amount of water-power, just where it is most needed for the manufacture of lumber. The Wisconsin forest of evergreens is perfectly immense, covering fully one-third of the state. The pineries of the Upper Wisconsin and its tributaries are at present most extensive; and those are distinguished still more for the fine quality than for the inexhaustible quantities of the timber. The other localities of pine may be reached by going up the Wolf River, the great northern affluent of Fox River, the streams which pour into Green Bay, and the LaCrosse, the Black, Chippewa, and the St. Croix rivers, branches of the Mississippi. These are all streams having swift currents, broken by frequent rapids. With the annual floods and the occasional freshets, the yield of the mills on the Wolf River are floated down to Lake Winnebago and Green Bay, and on the north-western streams, to the Mississippi

Throughout all the west and south-west, the Wisconsin pine has taken the place of all other in the market. It is carried to Kansas and Nebraska; it is used throughout Missouri and Arkansas; it monopolizes the market at Natchez and New Orleans; it is taken up the Tennessee, the Cumberland, and the Green rivers; it is carried east by way of the lakes, and south into Indiana and Illinois. "Scarcely ten years have elapsed since the Alleghany pine of New York and Pennsylvania had undisputed possession of the market, not only of the Ohio valley, but of the Mississippi and its tributaries above New Orleans, at which point it competed with the lumber of Maine and New Brunswick. The course of the lumber trade may now be considered permanently changed. The pineries of Wisconsin control, and will hold possession of the market of the valley of the Mississippi and its great western affluents."

The amount of pine lumber estimated to be sawed in Wisconsin, annually, is as follows:

Black River, ...	15,000,000	feet.
Chippewa, ...	28,500,000	"
Green Bay, ...	21,000,000	"
Manitowoc, ...	24,500,000	"
St. Croix, ...	20,000,000	"
Wisconsin, ...	58,500,000	"
Wolf River, ...	25,500,000	"
Total number of feet, . . .	193,000,000	

And owing to the great demand for lumber upon the prairies, to the south and south-west, the lumbering business of Wisconsin is increasing more rapidly than any other in the state, not excepting the mining for lead.

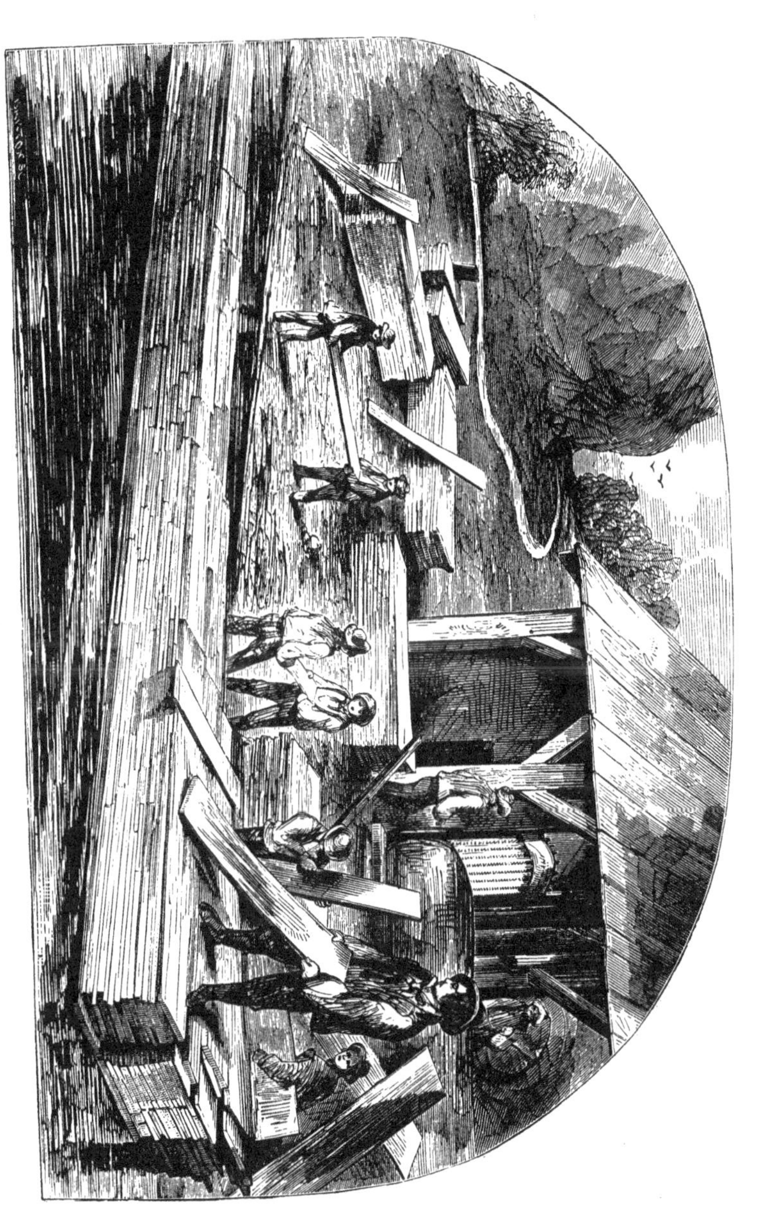

Aside from the pine lumber, a great number of saw-mills, driven by both steam and water-power, are in operation in all parts of the state, where timber is found, manufacturing large quantities of oak scantling and plank, and basswood siding and lath.

Wisconsin, in addition to its immense resources, has one very decided advantage over some of the other western states. It possesses a most salubrious climate. Its atmosphere is one of great purity. Every part of the state is supplied with copious, living springs. "The coolness and short duration of the summer," says Mr. Lapham, "and the dryness of the air during winter, conspire to render Wisconsin one of the most healthy portions of the United States. The wet-meadows, marshes, and swamps, are constantly supplied with pure water from springs; and as they are not exposed during summer to a burning heat, they do not send forth those noxious and deleterious qualities so much dreaded in more southern and less favored latitudes. Many of our most flourishing towns and settlements are in the immediate vicinity of large swamps, and partially overflown meadows; yet no injurious effects upon the general health are produced by them. It has usually been found, in making new settlements in the western wilderness, that, as the forests are cleared away, and the surface thereby exposed to the direct influence of the sun and winds, a deleterious effect is produced on the general health — the decaying vegetable matter being thus suddenly made to send forth its malarious qualities. But in Wisconsin no such result is apprehended, or can be produced; for a large proportion of the country consists of oak openings and prairie, and may therefore be considered as already cleaned. The removal of the few remaining bur-oaks can not have the same effect upon the soil as the cutting down of the dense forests of other states. And besides this, the fires that have annually raged over the surface have prevented that rapid accumulation of vegetable matter, which is always found in deep, shady woods." It is also stated to be the opinion of physicians, that Wisconsin is, and will continue to be, one of the healthiest regions in the world.

Wisconsin is finely located for carrying on an extensive commerce, with Lake Michigan on the east and the Mississippi on the west, besides the Wisconsin River, which flows in a south-westerly direction through the heart of the state. Its principal ports are Milwaukie, Racine, Sheboygan, and Green Bay, on the lake, and Prairie du Chien and Cassville, on the Mississippi.

Milwaukie is situated at the mouth of a river of the same name, ninety miles above Chicago. The shore of Lake Michigan consists of a bank of clay from twenty to one hundred feet high, and nearly perpendicular. The harbor lies at the head of a semi-circular bay, six miles across and three miles deep. The bottom affords the best anchoring ground to be found on Lake Michigan. In 1850, the city contained a population of more than twenty thousand persons. During the year 1855, six vessels were built at Milwaukie, having an aggregate tonnage of twelve hundred tons; and at the close of the season there were on the stocks one propeller and five vessels, estimated to have an aggregate tonnage of one thousand six hundred and thirty tons. The finest quality of brick in the world is manufactured at Milwaukie. In and about the city are six extensive yards, employing over two hundred men, and turning out upward of twenty-six million bricks annually, valued at nearly two hundred thousand dollars. Of that number, six and one-half millions are exported to Chicago and other lake ports Its external and domestic trade, and manufactures, are very rapidly on the increase.

Racine is situated at the mouth of Root River. It is a flourishing place, with a good harbor, and has already become an important commercial point in the state. The Green Bay, Milwaukie & Chicago Railroad passes through it. Sheboygan, at the mouth of Sheboygan River, is rapidly growing into a place of considerable importance. It is visited by regular lines of steamboats and vessels, and is surrounded by a fertile and well cultivated country. Green Bay is situated at the head of Green Bay, at the mouth of the Fox River. It occupies an important location, and has an excellent harbor. The village stands on a commanding eminence. It must become, in the natural course of events, a large commercial depot. Its population is about three thousand.

Prairie du Chien is situated on the Mississippi River, three miles above the mouth of the Wisconsin. The prairie from which it takes its name is ten miles long and three miles wide, and productive as a garden. The population is about three thousand. Its trade is very large, and rapidly increasing. There are rich mines of copper and lead in its immediate neighborhood. Cassville is situated in Grant county, in the midst of the lead region. It is one of the principal places for shipping that valuable metal, and for bringing in supplies for those engaged in mining. It is growing rapidly in size and in business.

Wisconsin is laying down lines of railroad in all directions across the state. The Lake Shore road, from Chicago, north, will soon be completed to Green Bay. The Milwaukie & Mississippi road, already opened to Madison, ninety-seven miles, will be completed during the season of 1856, to Prairie du Chien, one hundred and ninety-five miles. The LaCrosse & Milwaukie road, extending from the latter place to the Upper Mississippi, is open to Beaver Dam, sixty-one miles from Milwaukie, and is progressing toward a speedy completion. The Horicon road branches off from the LaCrosse at Horicon, and will strike the Wisconsin River at Stevens' Point, on the route toward St. Paul, in Minesota. A company has been organized to build a road from Stevens' Point to Lake Superior. Another road will intersect the LaCrosse at Ripon, and running through Oshkosh, on Lake Winnebago, will terminate at Green Bay. These roads are all upon important lines of transportation, and some of the last-named will open through the great pineries of Wisconsin.

Wisconsin is not behind-hand in promoting education. The school fund amounts to more than half a million dollars. Seventy thousand children attend her common schools. The value of the school-houses in the state is about two hundred thousand dollars. The school-houses would seem to vary some in the value set upon them, according to the report of the superintendent of public instruction, one being valued at five thousand dollars, and another at five cents. There are also about ninety private or select schools, averaging seventy-five pupils each. The State University is located at Madison, the capital of the state, and is well endowed. The Beloit College is an older institution. Both are in a flourishing condition. The State Library contains over four thousand volumes. In the state there are thirty-five libraries, containing, in all, about eight thousand volumes.

Wisconsin has a liberal homestead exemption law, securing to the occupant forty acres, together with the necessary buildings. The statute would seem to have been copied from the statute of Michigan, being almost precisely similar to it. The mechanic's lien law is more liberal than in most states. It is not confined in its operation to cities, but extends throughout the entire state, as all such laws should do. Every contract not to be performed within one year, and every promise to answer for the debt, default, or miscarriage of a third person, and every agreement made upon consideration of marriage — except mutual promises to marry — must be in writing. Every contract for the sale of goods for the price of fifty dollars or more, must be in writing, and subscribed by the parties thereto, unless the buyer receive part of the goods, or pay part of the purchase money.

It is clear that Wisconsin is destined to become one of the most populous, enterprising and wealthy states in the Union. Her people are steady, industrious, and loyal. Having commercial intercourse with the east and with the south, her influence will be felt and respected in the most extreme portions of our common country.

IOWA.

CHAPTER XV.

IOWA.

The Black Hawk purchase — First settlements — Second Indian pur chase — Reports of the surveyors — Erected into a Territory — Garden of the West — Constitution formed — Provisions of the constitution — Refuses the terms of admission as a state — A new constitution — Admission as a state — Length and breadth of the state — Population — Number of dwellings and families — Number of counties — Amount of unimproved lands — Excess of male population — Source of emigration — Most populous counties — Land speculations — Advantageous geographical position — General appearance of the state — Agricultural condition and resources — Coal-fields — Limestone — Cedar Valley — Soil — Minerals — Commerce — Shipping ports — Capital of Iowa — Iowa City — Railroads — Advantage to settlers — Public institutions.

Iowa had attracted the attention of emigrants about the same time with Wisconsin. The region of country to the west of the Mississippi was easily accessible; for the settlers from the south could ascend that river; those from the east could float down the Ohio. Settlements, however, in that direction, had met with a sudden and terrible check, upon the breaking out of the Black Hawk war, in 1829, which for three years had laid waste all the north-western portions of Illinois. But at the close of that period, Black Hawk, utterly routed, driven from Wisconsin Territory, had retired to the distant border of Missouri, and there, upon the head-waters of the Iowa River, he had made overtures for a cessation of hostilities. In September, 1832, a treaty of peace had been concluded between the discomfited savages and the United States, by which it was provided that the Indians should relinquish nearly all the lands from the Mississippi westward, for fifty miles, between the Des Moines River on the south and the Yellow River on the north. That cession comprised not less than one-third part of the present State of Iowa, and became known, subsequently, as the "Black Hawk Purchase." By the treaty, it was stipulated that the Indians should retire from the ceded lands as early as the month of June of the next year.

The first settlement in the Black Hawk Purchase was made in the fall of 1832, at Fort Madison, on the Mississippi, just above the mouth of the Des Moines River, by Zachariah Hawkins and Benjamin Jennings. Three years afterward, the town was regularly laid out, and the lots exposed for sale. From that time, Fort Madison continued to grow rapidly; and in 1838, the beautiful grounds contained a thriving village of nearly six hundred inhabitants.

The next year after Fort Madison, another settlement was begun at Burlington, seventy-nine miles below Rock Island, by Morton M. M'Carver and Sampson S. White, while the land was still in the occupancy of the Indians. At the same time, two stores were opened there by Dr. W. R. Ross and Jeremiah Smith, each "well supplied with western merchandise." In less than four years, Burlington had become the seat of government for the Territory of Wisconsin, of which Iowa was then a district; and three years later, it contained a population of fourteen hundred persons.

Also, in 1833, the city of Dubuque, situated on the Mississippi, four hundred and twenty-five miles above St. Louis, received its first Anglo-American inhabitants; and so rapid was its growth, that, in seven years afterward, it had become a rich commercial town, of about fifteen hundred persons. Dubuque received its name in honor of Julien Dubuque, the early proprietor of the "Mines of Spain," upon the Upper Mississippi. A Canadian by birth, Dubuque had visited the lead region in 1786. Exploring its mineral resources, he had succeeded in obtaining from the Indians a grant of a tract of land, comprising about one hundred and forty thousand acres, upon the west bank of the river. Dubuque had acquired great wealth from his mining operations. He died in 1810. His monument may be seen, about one mile below the city, on a high bluff.

In 1835, the town of Salem was settled by Aaron Street, a member of the Society of Friends. It was upon the extreme frontier of the Black Hawk Purchase, and constituted the first Quaker settlement in Iowa. Five years afterward, the colony in the vicinity of Salem numbered one thousand persons, many of them aged patriarchs, surrounded by their descendants to the third and fourth generations. Many other settlements of less note had also been springing up along the Mississippi.

At the time of the organization of the Territory of Wisconsin, in 1836, the region of country west of the Mississippi was included within it, under the name of the District of Iowa, comprising but two counties — the county of Dubuque and the county of Des Moines — which together contained ten thousand five hundred and thirty-one inhabitants. In a little while, the District of Iowa had become noted throughout the West for its extraordinary beauty and fertility, and the great advantages which it afforded to agricultural enterprise. The first Black Hawk Purchase was speedily overrun by emigrants, who were advancing upon the Indian country beyond. A new treaty, in 1837, had to be negotiated with the Sacs and Foxes, by which they consented to the further extension of the western boundary, so as to include the principal sources of the Iowa River, opening a magnificent region to the progress of settlements. Emigration continued to augment the population. Land-offices were established at Dubuque and Burlington. The surveyors reported "the lands" to consist of "a beautiful, fertile, healthy, undulating region, interspersed with groves and prairies, abounding in springs of pure water, with numerous streams flowing through a soil abounding with limestone of divers varieties, and other kind of rock, and some coal."

Before the close of 1838, the counties of Dubuque and Des Moines had been broken up into sixteen counties, having in the aggregate a population of more than twenty thousand souls, widely distributed throughout those portions of the district to which the Indian title had been extinguished. In the meantime, on the fourth of July of that year, Iowa, having been erected into a territory, had become separated from Wisconsin. The first governor of the territory of Iowa was Robert Lucas, formerly governor of Ohio. James Clark was appointed secretary. Augustus C. Dodge was elected by the people to represent them in Congress. The territory, as first organized, comprised "all that region of country north of Missouri, which lies west of the Mississippi River, and of a line drawn due north from the source of the Mississippi to the northern limit of the United States."

The first general assembly of the Territory of Iowa, with a strong conviction of the certainty of the growth of the future state, proceeded to make provision for the seat of government, and ordained that it should spring up in the wilderness. "On the first day of May, 1839, the beautiful spot which is now occupied by the city of Iowa, was within the Indian hunting-grounds, from which the tribes had not then retired, and within twenty miles of the new Indian boundary, and fifty-two miles west of the Mississippi River. On the fourth, it was selected by the commissioners as the site of the future state capital. On the first day of July, the survey of the city was commenced, upon a scale of magnificence rarely equaled. The streets and avenues were wide, and spacious lots and squares were designated for the public use; and the city of Iowa commenced. Twelve months afterward, it contained a population of seven hundred persons.

The inhabitants of the territory continued to increase in number with astonishing rapidity. The Mississippi was crowded with steamers ascending to the north, and vast fleets were plowing the lakes westward, loaded with emigrants bound for the distant Garden of the West. The growth of the settlements in Iowa is unprecedented in the history of colonization. That territory was outstripping its former yoke-fellow upon the eastern bank of the river. According to the census of 1840, the population of Iowa Territory was forty-three thousand and seventeen persons; that of Wisconsin, thirty thousand nine hundred and forty-five persons. Foreign immigrants kept on coming into the territory, but not nearly so rapidly as into Wisconsin. The far greater portion of the settlers came from the other western states, and from the middle states. Internal navigation throughout the north, by means of the lakes and canals, had become so much perfected, that population, for many years, continued to flow toward the far west in one continuous stream.

The number of the inhabitants had become augmented to such a degree that, with the permission of Congress, a convention assembled in 1844; and on the seventh day of October it adopted a constitution for the proposed State of Iowa. Iowa was the fourth state organized within the limits of the province of Louisiana. The constitution was strongly democratic. It not only provided for an elective judiciary, but all officers, civil and military, were to be elected by the people. The legislature was prohibited from creating any debt in the name of the state, exceeding one hundred thousand dollars. But the people of Iowa, numbering about ninety thousand persons, were doomed to disappointment in the contemplated change of government. The constitution which they had adopted never went into operation; and they remained two years longer in a condition of territorial dependence. The difficulty between the state and the federal government grew out of the territorial limits which Iowa had assumed to herself; — Congress, having approved of the proposed constitution, by the act of the third day of March, 1845, provided for the admission of Iowa simultaneously with Florida; but with the condition attached, that the people of the former territory, at the next general election, should assent to the territorial limits imposed by Congress. The object of the condition was to reduce Iowa, so as to make it conform with the general area of the other western states. But the people refused to ratify the proposed limits, and they rejected the terms of admission by a majority of two thousand. Iowa, however, at last yielded, and, in 1846, through its legislature, signified its acquiescence in the terms which had been prescribed. A second convention was accordingly authorized, and the new constitution having also been approved, the State of Iowa was admitted into the Union on the third day of December.

The greatest length of the state, from east to west, is three hundred miles; and its breadth, one hundred and ninety-six miles, with an area of about fifty-one thousand square miles. In 1850, the population numbered one hundred and ninety-two thousand two hundred and fourteen persons. The number of dwellings in the state was about thirty-three thousand; and of families, thirty-three thousand five hundred. Iowa, at that time, contained forty-nine counties; but since the census of 1850 was taken, Pottawatamie county has been broken up into forty-nine additional counties, so that the number is now ninety-nine. The number of farms under cultivation, at that time, in the whole state, was fourteen thousand eight hundred and five, containing in all about nine hundred thousand acres. There were ten thousand more males than females in the state. *Of the entire population, a little over five thou*sand persons came from New England; New York, eight thousand one hundred and thirty-four; New Jersey and Pennsylvania, together, sixteen thousand; Delaware and South Carolina, each about five thousand; Maryland, two thousand; Virginia, eight thousand; Tennessee and Kentucky, thirteen thousand; Ohio, thirty-one thousand; Indiana, twenty thousand; Illinois and Missouri, eleven thousand. The foreign population consisted of nearly four thousand English, five thousand Irish, and over seven thousand Germans, and two thousand Canadians.

The most populous counties are as follows, viz: Lee, Van Buren, Des Moines, Dubuque, Jefferson, Henry, Wapello, Davis, Jackson, Muscatine, Scott, Marion, Mahaska, Linn, Louisa, Keokuk, Polk, Washington, Johnson, Clayton, Cedar, and Appanoose. The western and north-western parts of the state, though increasing in population, are, as yet, but thinly inhabited. Speculation in the lands of Iowa has run very high, and, in many of the newer regions, a very large proportion of the choicest lands has been taken up by non-residents. The land-offices, for weeks at a time, have been thronged with anxious buyers, crowding and pressing upon one another, at the doors and windows, to enter their selections.

It is not at all surprising that everybody should desire to own lands in Iowa. Its position, soil, climate, and resources, indicate that it will, one day, take rank among the first states in the Union. "Situated nearly midway between the two great oceans; bounded on both sides by the great rivers of the continent, and watered by innumerable smaller streams; possessing a fertile soil, inexhaustible mineral resources, a healthful climate, a free constitution, and a hardy, industrious population, the State of Iowa has commenced its career with prospects of far more than ordinary brilliancy. In extent of boundary, it is one of the largest in the Union; and it may safely be prophesied that, with these great advantages, it is destined, at no distant day, to rank among the first in point of wealth and political importance, as it already exceeds its compeers in rapidity of growth."

The general appearance of Iowa is that of a high, rolling prairie, watered by magnificent streams of the clearest water, flowing over pebbly and rocky beds. Interspersed, throughout the whole region, are beautiful groves of oak; and the river bottoms, and the margins of the smaller streams, are mostly covered with a dense and thrifty growth of timber. Iowa contains a smaller quantity of "poor land" than any other state in the Union. Upon traveling through the state, the eye is everywhere greeted with a succession of the finest landscapes in the world. The inland scenery is surpassingly beautiful. Iowa contains a great number of little lakes, set like crystals in the surface — clear and limpid — with gravelly bottoms and shores. Mostly the lake-margins are timbered; but sometimes the green-sward will be found sloping to the very edge of the water.

Iowa owes its present prosperous condition to its agricultural resources. It is indeed true, that the timbered lands in the state are less extensive than the prairies; but the timber is so uniformly and equally distributed, so easily accessible, that no reasonable objection can be taken to the openness of the country. "For all agricultural purposes, Iowa is perhaps as fine a region as ever the sun cherished by its beams."

In 1850, the value of the farming implements and machines was estimated at one million one hundred and seventy-two thousand eight hundred and sixty-nine dollars. The following table will show the condition of the agriculture of the state for that year.

Wheat,	1,530,581	bushels.
Rye,	19,916	"
Indian corn,	8,656,799	"
Oats,	1,524,345	"
Barley,	25,093	"
Buckwheat,	52,516	"
Irish potatoes,	276,120	"
Sweet potatoes,	6,243	"
Butter,	2,171,188	pounds.
Cheese,	209,840	"
Wool,	373,898	"
Flax,	62,553	"
Beeswax and honey,	321,711	"

The value of the animals slaughtered during the year was estimated at $821,164. The live stock was reported as follows: Horses, 38,546; milch cows, 45,704; working oxen, 21,892; other cattle, 69,025; sheep, 149,960; and swine, 323,247—estimated at the value of $3,689,275.

The most important mineral of Iowa is coal. The coal-field is of prodigious extent, of remarkable thickness, and lies quite near the surface. Coming into the state across the southern border, it stretches broadly off to the north, for more than one hundred and forty miles; and in length, from east to west, it is over two hundred miles. The coal-field of Iowa, therefore, underlies an area of about twenty-five thousand square miles. The beds of coal have been estimated, by geologists, to be of the average thickness of one hundred feet.

The principal limestone regions of the state are in the valleys of the Cedar and Iowa rivers. In the former valley, the limestone, commencing along the Mississippi, for thirty miles in width, between the head of Rock Rapids and the town of Wyoming, sweeps, with a north-westerly curve, up Cedar River, varying from twelve to fifteen miles in width; till, in latitude forty-three, it disappears under the drift of northern Iowa. The rock appears mostly in low ledges near the water-courses. On the Shell Rock, an eastern branch of the Cedar River, near the head of the latter, is a bold bluff of limestone, standing high above the bottom, and at right-angles with the stream. The country around is exceedingly picturesque, diversified with gentle swells of ground, groves of oak, and meandering streams. Cedar Valley is plentifully supplied with timber; but it contains no such dense forests as originally grew upon the river-banks of Indiana and Ohio. The soil is stiff, dark, calcareous, exceedingly strong and deep, richer and more retentive than that over the coal-fields. On the whole, Cedar Valley may be regarded as the finest portion of the state.

The Iowa River, also, flows through a limestone region; but the out-croppings of the rock are not, in general, so marked and distinct as along the Cedar River; nor is the valley so uniformly supplied with timber. In the elbows of the river are timbered bottoms; and, spreading off each way, are openings, with gentle swells of ground, from seventy to one hundred feet in hight; furnishing capital building sites, and delightful farms, within reach of both water and wood. The soil is similar, though slightly lighter, than that of Cedar Valley. There is but little choice between the two streams for desirable locations.

The rich, black soil of the prairies, and the lightly-timbered openings, which are found chiefly over the coal-field, throughout the southern portion of the state, is rather sandy and porous, but warm and quick, forcing vegetation rapidly, particularly early in the season. Crops there, however, are liable to suffer from the droughts of summer; and the higher grounds are generally gravelly. Notwithstanding that, the soil is considered to be equally advantageous, as it is adapted to all kinds of agricultural pursuits. The prairie-sod, matted and deep-rooted, usually requires from six to eight yoke of oxen effectually to break it up. The second year, it will have become rotted, and the surface of the fields will be mellow, and free from stone.

Iowa is justly numbered among the great mineral-producing states of the Union. In addition to its coal, the lead mines in the north-east, of which Dubuque is the center, have been worked for three-quarters of a century, and have been productive in proportion to the number of persons engaged in mining. The mines are contiguous to those of Illinois and Wisconsin, being separated from them only by the breadth of the Mississippi. Dr. Owen — who made a geological survey of this region — upon a review of its resources and capabilities, says, that ten thousand miners and laborers could find profitable employment within its confines. The mines furnish as much of that desirable metal as the whole continent of Europe; and there would seem to be no end to the quantities of the ore. Zinc, also, occurs in the fissures of the lead-bearing rock; and it sometimes appears in cellular masses. Iron ore has been found abundantly distributed throughout the state; but as yet no large amount has been converted into metal.

The three states, Ohio, Wisconsin, and Iowa, might produce sufficient iron to supply all America for ages. At the present time, instead of working and patronizing our own native mines, the people are largely engaged in importing iron from abroad, enriching Sweden and England at the expense of the Great West. It would seem to be a pity that it should be deemed the policy of the United States to bring railroad iron, for instance, across three thousand miles of ocean, exposed to the lightnings of heaven and the tumbling billows of the deep, and lay it down over the ore beds of the infant states of the west, crippling their energies, and restraining the development of their resources.

Iowa is finely situated with respect to inland commerce and navigation. On the map, the state presents the appearance of being upheld between the two principal rivers of the continent. The Mississippi forms the eastern boundary, throughout its windings, for nearly four hundred and fifty miles. On the west, the Missouri, from above latitude forty to the mouth of the Big Sioux River, washes the confines of the state for more than three hundred miles; so that both sides of Iowa are furnished with equal facilities for external commerce, and many fine sites for flourishing cities. The Des Moines River is the great central artery of the state. It enters Iowa from the north, and, flowing south-east for four hundred miles, empties into the Mississippi at the foot of the lower rapids. It is one of the most beautiful of all the noble rivers of the west, having a rock bottom, and high banks, which are not subject to overflow. It passes through the great coal-field, and through a country of surpassing fertility. The state has undertaken to render it navigable for steamboats of a medium size, to Fort Des Moines, two hundred miles above its mouth. Beside those three great rivers, there are many smaller ones — the Iowa River, the Skunk River, Wapsipinicon, Makoqueta, and the Turkey River, and numerous other streams, affluents of the Missouri. Most of these streams are navigable from twenty to sixty miles, and, with their branches, fur nish an abundance of water-power. Many of them pass over limestone or sandstone beds, and they are generally skirted with timber.

The principal shipping ports are Keokuk, at the mouth of the Des Moines; Fort Madison, just above, on the Mississippi, two hundred and forty-eight miles from St. Louis; Muscatine City, thirty-two miles below Davenport; Davenport, one hundred miles below Galena, and three hundred and thirty-eight above St. Louis. It is situated opposite Rock Island, and is connected by railroad with Chicago, and another line is projected westward to Council Bluffs. Also Lyons, Bellevue, and Dubuque. The annual value of the commerce of Keokuk is estimated as high as seven million dollars. It is the principal port of the entire Des Moines Valley, in which more than half the population and agricultural wealth of the state is concentrated. The city stands upon a high limestone bluff, which affords inexhaustible supplies of building stone. It is situated at the foot of the lower rapids of the Mississippi, which are eleven miles in length; and in that distance the water falls twenty-four feet. At low stages of the river upward-bound boats have to unload at Keokuk, and their cargoes are taken over the rapids on lighters.

The present capital of Iowa is Fort Des Moines; which is finely situated on the west bank of the Des Moines River, a little to the south of the center of the state, and one hundred and nine miles west of Iowa City. A large branch of the river comes in just below Fort Des Moines, and opens a communication with some of the western counties, while the Des Moines extends up beyond the northern boundary of the state. The railroad in contemplation from Davenport to Council Bluffs, passes through Fort Des Moines, and several other lines center in there. It is a place of great business facilities, surrounded by a delightful and exceedingly fertile country, with a good supply of water-power in its vicinity for manufacturing purposes. A land-office is situated there, besides other public buildings; and the crowd of emigrants in the streets gives it a business-like appearance.

Iowa City is destined to be one of the most attractive cities in America. It is situated on the east bank of the Iowa River, fifty-two miles from the Mississippi, sixty-three miles from Burlington, fifty-one miles from Davenport, and seventy miles from Dubuque. The river is navigable to Iowa City at all stages of the water, and regular lines of steamboats ascend and descend it daily. Railroads are centering toward it from all the ports on the Mississippi, to unite and stretch out from thence to Council Bluffs and the Pacific Ocean. A grand chain of railroads, north and south, will pass through it, connecting St. Louis with the great upland prairies of Minesota; and the last few miles of railroad are now being completed between Iowa City and Portland, in the State of Maine; and before the season of 1856 will have drawn to a close, a continuous track will exist between those places, one thousand four hundred and thirty-six miles distant from each other—the largest line of railroad on the globe.

The surface of the ground, at Iowa City, rises from the margin of the river in three successive plateaux: the first is about one hundred yards in width, and has been devoted to a public promenade; the second plain is about twelve feet higher than the first; and the third, eighteen feet above the second. On these two beautiful natural elevations the city is built. The principal avenues, nearly two hundred feet wide, run along the brows of the plateaux, and are intersected by Iowa Avenue — a magnificent street, ascending, one after another, these eminences, and reaching to the open prairie.

There are many reasons which should influence the emigrant to settle in Iowa; and not the least important is the acknowledged salubrity of the climate. The state is not exempt from those diseases incident to rich, luxuriant, and uncultivated soils; but from the openness of the landscape, warmed with sunshine, fanned with breezes, it is less liable to the scourge of malaria than most new countries. The temperature of the atmosphere is far more uniform than upon the Atlantic coast. It is exempt, too, from those chilling, piercing easterly winds, so withering to the consumptive. The air breathes over the elevated plains as regularly and as refreshing as from the ocean between the tropics, tempering the extremes incident to the high northern latitude.

Iowa has made noble provision for her public schools. All lands granted by Congress to the state, all escheated lands, and such per centage as may be granted on the sale of the public lands, constitute a perpetual fund for the support of schools. It is made the duty of the legislature to provide, in each district, a school, for at least three months in each year. All moneys received as a commutation instead of military duty, and moneys derived from fines imposed by the courts, are devoted to the same purpose, or for the establishment of school libraries. The school fund amounts to nearly three hundred thousand dollars. A State University, amply endowed, has been located at Iowa City. The State Library contains about three thousand volumes.

There are one hundred and forty-eight churches in the state, accommodating about thirty-eight thousand persons. Of the religious denominations, the Methodist is the most numerous; next the Presbyterian; then the Roman Catholic, the Baptist, and the Congregationalists.

Iowa, in every respect, is an important member of the Union. In its extent of surface, climate, productions, commercial position, institutions, and the enterprising spirit of the inhabitants, it promises soon to compete with the older states in everything which will tend to promote the prosperity of a great people.

MINESOTA TERRITORY.

CHAPTER XVI.

MINESOTA TERRITORY.

Explorations of the Upper Mississippi — Location of the Territory — "The New England of the West"— Territorial boundary — Laws — Counties — Population — Nature of the population — Crops —General surface of the territory — Geology — Above Crow Wing River — Chalk formation — James River — Buffalo pasture-ground — Big Sioux River — Red pipe-stone quarry— St. Peters River — Bottom lands — Blue Earth River — St. Peters Valley — The paradise of farmers — Lake Pepin — Terror of the lumbermen of the north — Timber — Wild rice — Soil and its products — The Red River of the North — Springs and lakes — Minesota the artesian fountain of the continent — Underground hydraulic power — Boiling springs — Magnificent forest — Destiny of Minesota — Indian summers — Manner of perfecting a squatter's title — St. Paul — Table of distances from Galena to St. Paul — Rates of fare.

The Mississippi River extends, in a direct line, through nineteen degrees of latitude. Nine states and one territory are watered by its magnificent stream. The great valley, which slopes from the east and from the west to the banks of that river, is barely cultivated sufficiently to afford an indication of its vast capabilities. The lower waters of the Mississippi had been explored nearly three hundred years before any white man ever stood upon the sources of its exhaustless tide. Countless steamboats were stemming the torrent, for a distance of two thousand miles, while yet the region whence it emanated was as unknown as the interior of Ethiopia. Lieutenant Zebulon Montgomery Pike, with a military expedition, in 1805, ascended the Mississippi one hundred and twenty miles above the Falls of St. Anthony; but he had set out late in the season, and the snows and ice compelled him to delay, for the purpose of erecting a block-house and securing his stores. Tramping about in the winter on snow-shoes did not afford him much opportunity for examining the country. With the spring, his expedition had returned.

In 1820, another expedition, which had been projected by Governor Cass, of Michigan, left Detroit in a fleet of birch-bark canoes, and, passing up through Lake Superior, crossed over the country between the St. Louis River and the Sandy Lake, in the valley of the Mississippi, and from thence explored the river as high as the Cass Lake. Twelve years afterward a third expedition, commencing its explorations at Cass Lake, followed up the channel of the river, through all its windings and lakes, to its source in Itasca Lake. The last two expeditions were fortunately accompanied by an intelligent chronicler of their adventures, in the person of Henry R. Schoolcraft, to whose narratives the public is indebted for much of the knowledge which it possessed of those distant regions.

Upon the head-waters of the Mississippi and of the Red River of the North lies the territory of Minesota, extending from Iowa to the British possessions, and from Lake Superior to the Missouri River. The most accurate information concerning the soil and climate of the various portions of the territory is derived from the geological surveys made under the authority of the federal government; and in the immediate vicinities of the settlements above the mouth of the St. Peter's, the country has been pretty thoroughly explored; but the extent of exact knowledge acquired in that manner is about as a stone's throw to the wide reach of the territory itself.

Concerning Minesota — "the New England of the

West"—but little, indeed, was heard or known until in 1849. Emigration had continued flowing, year after year, into regions further south, and not so far west. Fertile lands, comprising millions of acres, far easier of access, lay spread out invitingly to the settler, nearer home. The whole intervening country still contains but a sparse and scattered population. Wisconsin, which lies between the sources of population in the older states and the vast territory of the north, is yet a new country, more than half of it a wilderness, and but little explored. Iowa, too, is receiving an immense influx of immigration, the entire western and northern portions of the state being comparatively wild and tenantless. And for two years past, the political excitement in Kansas has been drawing public attention to that quarter, and political motives are urging on settlers from all parts of the Union to seek there for homes. Minesota, therefore, has been, and is, to some degree, neglected and forgotten.

The southern limit of the territory is the boundary of Iowa. On the east, the line follows up the Mississippi to Prescott, at the mouth of the St. Croix; thence up the latter river to Lake Superior. On the north, the line, commencing at the mouth of the Arrow River, opposite Isle Royale, runs north-westerly through Rainy Lake to the southern extremity of the Lake of the Woods; thence westerly to the White Earth River, which empties into the Missouri at its extreme northerly bend. The boundary on the west is, for a little way, along the White Earth River; thence, following down the Missouri, throughout its windings, for a thousand miles, it terminates at the mouth of the Big Sioux River. Minesota extends through more than six degrees of latitude and twelve degrees of longitude. Its extreme length, from east to west, has been computed at six hundred miles, and its breadth at four hundred and sixty miles, with an area of upward of one hundred and fifty thousand square miles.

Previous to the organization of the State of Wisconsin, all that part of Minesota lying on the east side of the Mississippi River had been included in the Territory of Wisconsin. All that portion west of the river had been comprised in the Territory of Iowa. By the Act of Congress, March 3d, 1849, Minesota was erected into a territory. Alexander Ramsey was appointed governor, and Charles H. Smith, secretary. The legislative power is vested in the governor and legislative assembly. The assembly consists of a council, and house of representatives. Councilors, to the number of nine, are elected every two years; representatives, annually. The number may be increased, from time to time, by the legislative assembly; but not to exceed fifteen councilors and thirty-nine representatives. No law shall be passed interfering with the primary disposal of the soil; no tax shall be imposed upon the property of the United States; nor shall the lands or other property of non-residents be taxed higher than the property of residents. All laws, passed by the legislative assembly and governor, shall be submitted to the Congress of the United States, and if disapproved, shall be null and of no effect. No one session of the legislature shall exceed the term of sixty days. All persons of a mixture of white and Indian blood, who have adopted the habits and customs of civilized men, are admitted to citizenship.

Minesota is divided into twenty counties; viz., Benton, Blue Earth, Cass, Chisago, Dakotah, Fillmore, Goodhue, Hennepin, Itasca, Kapasia, Le Seur, Nicollet, Pierce, Pembina, Ramsey, Rice, Scott, Sibley, Wabashaw, and Washington. St. Paul is the capital. The increase of population is seen by comparing the years of 1849 and 1850. In the former, the number was four thousand seven hundred and eighty; the latter, six thousand and seventy-seven. According to the census, there were nearly two thousand more males than females. Of the inhabitants, about seven hundred came from New England; New York, five hundred; Pennsylvania and New Jersey together, three hundred; Virginia, sixty; Illinois, two hundred; Ohio, three hundred; Wisconsin, three hundred and fifty; Missouri, ninety; South Carolina, Georgia, Alabama, and Louisiana, each about half a dozen. The foreigners consist of about ninety Englishmen, three hundred Irishmen, forty Scotchmen, one hundred and fifty Germans, thirty Frenchmen, thirty-five Swiss; Canadians, two thousand.

The number of farms, in 1850, was one hundred and fifty-seven, containing in all some thirty thousand acres, of which one fourth was under cultivation. The crops were reported as follows; viz,

Wheat,	1,401	bushels.
Rye,	125	"
Corn,	16,725	"
Oats,	38,582	"
Barley,	1,216	"
Buckwheat,	515	"
Peas and beans,	10,000	"
Irish potatoes,	21,145	"
Sweet potatoes,	200	"
Wool,	85	pounds.
Butter,	1,100	"
Maple-sugar,	3,000	"

The value of the animals slaughtered was estimated at three thousand dollars.

The general features of Minesota are those of a high,

rolling prairie, or elevated table-land. The surface of the territory is destitute of mountains; yet the land is the highest of any between the Gulf of Mexico and Hudson's Bay. The Mississippi, and the Red River of the north, each rising near the head-waters of the other, in the center of the great plain, flow off in opposite directions—the one to the tropics, the other half-way to the frozen ocean. The St. Lawrence, also, takes its rise in this favored territory. The average hight of the land above the Gulf of Mexico is about twelve hundred feet.

This vast northern region is one of great geological interest. The prevailing opinion of those who have studied the features of the rocks of Minesota would seem to be that, at some period, the whole region has been lifted up—projected outward from the center of the earth. On ascending the Mississippi, the layers of rock are seen to have a southern dip. At the entrance to Lake Pepin, the lower sandstone constitutes nearly three hundred and forty feet of the bluff; and the lower magnesian limestone, one hundred and fifty feet. Near the great bend of that lake, the latter rock forms a perpendicular wall of two hundred feet, the total elevation above the water being over four hundred feet. This is known as the celebrated "Maiden's Rock." Thirteen miles below the mouth of the St. Croix River, the sandstone has entirely disappeared, the lower limestone reaching to the hight of two hundred feet above the level of the Mississippi; and at St. Paul, the upper white sandstone rests above the terrace of lower magnesian limestone.

The sandstone at St. Paul is of the best quality, whiter and fairer than the Linn sand, used in the manufacture of flint-glass. The depth of the rock varies from forty to one hundred feet. Along the St. Peter's, as far up as Little Rapids, the sandstone is covered by a thin formation of shell limestone, which contains about sixty per cent. of carbonate of lime. And throughout the region of little lakes, south of the St. Peter's, known as the "Undine Region," the same formation continues, consisting of a friable sandstone basis, covered with a deposit of limestone. The undulating prairies of that tract of country support a calcareous soil, of excellent quality, producing heavy crops of grain. Other contiguous tracts rest upon a white shell marl and infusorial earth, possessing great fertilizing properties. Above Little Rapids, extending to White Rock, a distance of eighty miles, the bed of the St. Peter's is formed by ledges of soft, brown sandstone, supporting a layer of fawn-colored carboniferous limestone. Wherever that formation prevails, the soil is of excellent quality, rich, and capable of sustaining a long succession of crops.

Ascending the Mississippi, above the Crow Wing River, the country presents an entirely different aspect from that below. The forests become denser, and contain a greater variety of timber. The soil is alternately sandy, gravelly, clayey, and loamy; and lighter, except on the shores of the lakes and larger streams. The high lands are covered with white and yellow pines, spruce, and birch; the lowlands, by larches and willows. From the lake and river margins, the wood-lands extend back a mile and more, producing sugar-maple, oak, elm, ash, and basswood. Red cedar is found only on the islands of the Red Cedar Lakes. "The aspect of the country is greatly varied by hills, dales, copses, small prairies, and a great number of lakes. The climate is found to be well adapted to the culture of wheat, barley, oats, and corn. The potato is of a superior quality to that of the middle states of the Union."

On the western side of the territory, along the Missouri, the chalk formation sets in, just above the Big Sioux River, and extends indefinitely north-west. This region may possess great interest to the geologist; but it should be shunned by the agriculturist. The banks of the Missouri consist of argillaceous limestone, at the bottom, rising three feet above the bed of the river; next a calcareous marl, from thirty to forty feet thick; then a ferruginous clay bank, of a yellowish color, some twenty feet thick; and lastly a deposit of plastic clay, two hundred feet thick. Now a soil formed from such materials will produce only the most meager vegetation.

But that region of sterility is confined to the immediate vicinity of the Missouri. The valley of the Rivière à Jacques, or James River, is preëminently beautiful and fertile. That river, rising north of parallel forty-seven, winds along in a southerly direction, through more than four degrees of latitude, across the whole of western Minesota, for seven hundred miles, to the south-western extremity of the territory. Its shores are lined with beautiful groves of maple, elm, ash, and oak. Frequently the stream expands into picturesque lakes. Its waters are wide, deep, and clear, descending from an elevation of seven hundred feet. The immense basin of the river varies from fifty miles to one hundred miles in width, and constitutes one continuous prairie, interrupted only by the timbered branches of the main stream, unsurpassed by any other in the United States. The river is navigable throughout three-fourths of its entire length. The valley of the James River is the great pasture-ground of the buffaloes east of the Missouri.

The Big Sioux River is likewise a most interesting stream, flowing through a fertile country, except near its mouth, where the surface is broken into rugged hills. Its banks are continuously lined with timber. The river rises within a mile of the head-waters of the St. Peter's. About midway in its course, the Big Sioux breaks through a remarkable quartz formation, and seems to have ruptured the massive wall of rock. Within a distance of four hundred yards, the river leaps and plunges down three successive falls — one of twenty feet, one of eighteen feet, and one of ten feet — with rapids intervening, supplying an incalculable amount of water-power. Above and below, the valley rises gently, on either hand, to a hight of three hundred feet above the bed of the stream. Between the Big Sioux and the Des Moines is situated the celebrated red pipe-stone quarry, which the Indians believe was opened to them by the Great Spirit. The tribes all consider it to be consecrated grounds, and never chip off a bit of the rock, without many superstitious observances. The stone readily receives a dull polish. It is not affected by acids, and is said to be indestructible by fire. In color it is blood-red.

Before dismissing the western side of Minesota, it may be well to mention, that the Missouri River is navigable, for steamboats, as high up as the Yellow Stone — more than three thousand miles above St. Louis; but the channel is winding, intricate, and ever-shifting, thronged with snags and sawyers, and interrupted by sand-bars. The greatest freshets occur in July. Steamboats, stemming its impetuous current, require four months to complete the ascent.

The valley of the St. Peter's is one of the most attractive portions of the territory. The land rises from the water in three terraces, rather than bluffs. First, the alluvial border, about a mile in width, of natural meadow, some parts of it annually overflowed, and of inexhaustible fertility. Ten miles above Little Rapids, this bottom-land is elevated one hundred and thirty feet above the water, three-fourths of a mile wide on each side of the stream, and many miles in length, affording some of the best farming lands in the world. In that delightful region, the lower terrace is dotted with groves of sugar-maple, elm, ash, and oak. The second terrace is from fifty to one hundred feet higher than the first, and consists of openings, so interspersed with timber that it resembles a cultivated country. Fifty feet higher is the third elevation, spreading out, as far as the eye can reach, an illimitable rolling prairie.

Commencing at Traverse des Sioux, one hundred and sixteen miles above the mouth of the St. Peter's, the valley consists of an undulating, fertile prairie, with a background of forest, in which the basswood, and whitewood, the sugar-maple, elm, butternut, and hickory, abound. The underbrush is a mixture of prickly-ash, gooseberry bushes, and grape-vines. In many places, the terraces subside into a gentle slope, dotted with groves, with here and there among the shrubbery a huge bowlder, giving the landscape, at a little distance, the appearance of a settled country, with dwellings, and gardens, and orchards.

The Blue Earth River is the principal tributary of the St. Peter's, and it comes flowing in from the south. At its mouth it is very rapid; but above, the current is rather moderate. On the whole, it is a deep and important stream. The river takes its name from a bank of blue clay, six miles from the St. Peter's, which the Indians have been using as a paint for ages. The river banks are, in some places, almost perpendicular, and generally full sixty feet in hight. The Blue Earth has a very great number of branches spreading out through the country, like a fan. The valleys and the uplands are well supplied with timber. One of its branches is separated

MINNE-HA-HA FALLS.

from the Des Moines only by a narrow tongue of land, not more than a mile and a half broad.

The St. Peter's Valley is destined some day to support an immense population. It is in the same latitude of northern New York. The soil is inviting; the land cleared for the plow, yet timber sufficient for all purposes; and water-power always near at hand. The most important point in the whole course of the stream, which flows through a distance of nearly five hundred miles, is Traverse des Sioux. It has a good landing, a fine site for a city, in the midst of a lovely country; and from a back ridge of an elevation of two hundred feet, comes tumbling down a rapid creek, fed by constant springs.

Among the beautiful scenery of the St. Peter's Valley, the tourist should not fail to look for the Minnehaha Falls, about three miles distant from Fort Snelling. The outlets of a number of the upland lakes flow into each other, and form a single channel with a gentle descent to the edge of a precipice, down which the "Laughing Waters," as the Indians named them, leap into a secluded rocky chasm, throwing up spray, and roaring among the trees. But some egotistical "cuss," who deserves flinging over the cataract for his impudence, has stuck the name of his own "ugly mug" upon the picturesque locality, and called it "Brown's Falls." Let the public all unite in the spicy protest of the indignant tourist, who, upon the banks of the Minnehaha, in view of the "Laughing Waters," and of "Brown's" desecration of them, thus proclaimed aloud: "In the name of common-sense, and all that is poetic and pleasing in human nature, let us solemnly protest against those desecrations which rob our beautiful lakes, rivers, and cascades, of their charming and significant Indian names; and no longer allow every Brown, Smith, Snooks, and Fizzle, who happens to be the first to see some beautiful creation of Nature, with dull eyes which have no appreciation for any thing more sentimental than a lump of lead, a buffalo-hide, or a catfish, to perpetuate his cognomen at the expense of good taste and common honesty."

The tract of land sweeping away to the south of the St. Peter's, to the head-waters of the Cannon and the Wazi-oju rivers, is likewise fertile, undulating, dotted thickly with little lakes, of deep, clear, and sparkling water, belted with trees, and surrounded every way by wood-crowned hills and lovely prairies. So romantic is this region, so thickly strewn with lakes and ponds, that repose like gems on the bosom of the earth; so beautifully timbered with groves, free from underbrush; with such a gently-rising and falling surface of prairie and openings, that it may be denominated the paradise of farmers.

Approaching the Mississippi, from the country south of the St. Peter's, the traveler will come plump upon the yawning chasm of Lake Pepin, four hundred feet below him, where huge rafts, like river serpents, are floating along, and steamboats, diminutive in the depths, are coughing, and wheezing, and fluttering upon the water. But Lake Pepin is not all the way walled in by precipices. On the western shore, near the upper end of this remarkable expansion of the Mississippi, there is a beautiful prairie, commencing along the water's edge for four or five miles, and rising in a gentle slope, far back, where it is crowned with mounds and bluffs. Just above this prairie is La Grange Mountain, three hundred and twenty-two feet high.

Lake Pepin is ordinarily placid and smooth as a mirror. It has scarcely a perceptible current. Yet it is deceitful above all things — subject to gales and storms, when the wind will whistle and howl through the rocky chasm, and toss the water about like "all possessed." The French voyageurs regarded it as a natural contrivance for "raising the devil," generally. They would say of it: "*Le lac est petit, mais il est malin.*" It is the terror of all the lumbermen of the north. Their rafts often get knocked "endwise," and distributed pretty generally along down the Mississippi. One day, a steamboat was towing a huge raft of timber and sawed lumber over the lake, as proud as an old duck followed by her brood; but soon a gale pitched the raft to pieces, and tumbled the logs about, so fiercely that the boat had to cast loose, and scud for safety.

Proceeding up the Mississippi, the country, from St. Paul to Sauk Rapids, one hundred miles above the Falls of St. Anthony, is well adapted to agricultural purposes. The soil, sandy to the depth of six inches, rests on a bed of clay. The river banks vary from ten to twenty feet in hight; well timbered—particularly the western shore—with groves of sugar-maple, oak, ash, elm, and hickory. Many small streams wind through the prairies, skirted with woods; and, passing along the river road, one scarcely loses sight of the lakes,—for, in Minesota, lakes are everywhere—on the hills; in the valleys; among the woods; on the plains; and upon the banks of rivers. In some parts of the country, it is difficult to tell whether the land is surrounded by water, or the water by land.

"Crow Wing River is an important tributary of the Mississippi. It has its source in Lake Kaginogumaug, near Leech Lake, with which it is connected, in Indian navigation, by ten small lakes or ponds, separated by five small portages, of various lengths. It expands successively into eleven lakes, before it forms a junction with Shell River, which is nearly as large as the main stream. It has two large tributaries—Leaf and Long Prairie

FALLS OF ST. ANTHONY.

rivers, which flow from the west, and are rivers of considerable magnitude. Its banks are elevated, crowned with forests, yielding every variety of pine. Its alluvial bottoms are studded with elm, soft-maple, ash, and oak."

Further toward the north, in the vicinity of Red Lake, and Cass Lake, and Turtle River, the country abounds in wild rice. Immense fields of it — thousands of acres — grow up annually, without sowing or reaping, with large yield, sufficient to supply a dense population. The Indians push round in among it in the latter part of August, and thrash their canoes full of the grain, scaring innumerable water-fowl, that quack, and twitter, and flap about, gorged almost to suffocation. The wild rice makes a nourishing diet, — a bushel of it is said to contain as much nutritive matter as a bushel of wheat. There are likewise vast meadows of sweet grass, which the cattle eagerly crop. For the mere purpose of sustaining life, this is an incomparable region, — there is wood enough, cranberries, raspberries, rice, pasturage, game, and the finest varieties of fish; the soil is quick and warm, producing corn, potatoes, oats, peas, and all the substantial garden vegetables; and the woods abound in sugar-maple.

In no part of the country do the streams meander so beautifully as in this. They wind around in all shapes and directions, sweeping away for miles, to return within a few rods of their own banks. They interlace the entire region, and almost flow under, and over, and into, each other. The country rises to a high prairie, between those streams and the tributaries of the Red River of the north, possessing groves of timber, springs of water, and a sandy, loamy soil, bottomed on clay. From the Otter Tail Lake, the Red River makes a great southward bend, through a region unsurpassed for rural beauty. It resembles the most attractive portions of Iowa. The boundless prairie has a strong, calcareous soil, adapted to all the cereal grains. Voyaging down that noble river in midsummer, between its banks embowered in wild-roses, the air is loaded with perfume. When the river has again turned to the northward, it pours along through a plain of vast extent,— the eye seeks in vain for hills; but scattered about, as if planted by hand, are groves of oak. The timber continues growing sparser and thinner, till, before reaching Pembina, every vestige of shrubbery has disappeared from the plain. The river, however, has some few trees on its banks. Its ash attains a prodigious growth. One striking peculiarity of the Red River of the North is, that it has no bluffs, no hills, no rising background; but throughout its entire course it meanders in the midst of a high table-land. The river-bed is channeled into the surface of the plain. In the immediate neighborhood of Pembina, the timber increases, and becomes plentiful for all purposes.

No country of which we have any knowledge is so bountifully supplied with spring water as Minesota. The springs are constant and powerful: they are rather gushing fountains, supplying lakes innumerable, and filling the upper channels of the three largest rivers in North America. The rocks, dipping in either direction, here bring to the surface those water seams, which in other parts are only to be reached by deep boring. Minesota is the artesian fountain of the continent. A few miles above St. Anthony's Falls, at Cold Spring Prairie, the tourist may see a little of the working of that underground hydraulic power that pumps the territory full of lakes, and requires the Red River, and the Mississippi, and the St. Lawrence, for spout-ways to the ocean. Cold Spring Prairie takes its name from a spring in the bottom of the Mississippi. A traveler has described it as follows: "It was boiling up in the Mississippi like a pot, about a foot from the edge of the bank, and apparently in deep water, throwing up constantly gravel and pebble-stones. By scooping my hand two or three times along the surface, I obtained a handful of the latter. The noise made by this boiling spring could be heard some ten or twelve rods. The water, though mingled with that of the Mississippi, was nearly as cold as ice-water."

Minesota, notwithstanding its prairie features, has one magnificent forest. Commencing at a point on the west side of the river, about eight miles above St. Anthony, a remarkable belt of heavy timber extends in a southerly direction, at a right-angle across the St. Peter's, to the branches of the Blue Earth River, a distance of one hundred and twenty miles. This forest varies, in width, from fifteen to forty miles, resembling very much the "Cross Timbers" in the western part of Arkansas. The soil is unusually deep, covered with the mold of a thousand years. Wherever the sunlight penetrates the shade, the little lakes, with which the forest is studded, glisten and gleam like molten silver.

Minesota is destined to become a great agricultural and grazing region. Its upland and lowland pastures would support a dairy that would enrich an empire. All the principal grains and roots thrive there in great vigor, as high toward the north as Pembina, just below the dividing line between the United States and British America. Latitude does not always indicate the climate. The character of the soil has great influence upon the temperature of the air. A quick, warm soil makes a warm atmosphere. The autumns of Minesota are greatly lengthened out by the Indian summer — that smoky, dreamy, balmy season, which protects the surface from frost, like a mantle flung over the earth. The cold nips vegetation about as early along the Ohio as along the St. Peter's. The winters of Minesota are cold; but then they are still and calm, and the icy air does not penetrate as it does in a windy climate. The snow falls, and there it lies till spring; and does not, as in Virginia the present winter, drift over the tree-tops in the valleys, leaving the hills bare, to freeze any imaginable depth.

The manner of perfecting a squatter's title in the territory, upon the unsurveyed lands, is as follows: "First, some labor must be bestowed on the claim—such as plowing two or three furrows, or staking it out, so that the claim may be designated, or the intentions of the claimant made known. This causes it to be respected for one year. In the second year, improvements to the value of fifty dollars or more must be made. During the third year, it must be occupied, either by the claimant himself, or by some one for him." In Minesota, two sections of land in every township are devoted to the support of common schools.

The beautiful village of Mendota occupies a fine situation on the St. Peter's, five miles below St. Paul, and upon the west bank of the Mississippi. There is one serious drawback upon this attractive town: it is within the military reservation, and no white people are allowed to reside there without permission of the United States.

St. Paul, the seat of government, at the head of navigation from the Lower Mississippi, is built on a level plateau, terminating, on the river, in a precipitous bluff, about eighty feet high. But that bluff recedes from the margin of the river at both the upper and at the lower end of the town, forming two landings, creating a healthy rivalry in business. Part of the lower town is situated on a bench of land, about twenty feet below the level of the plateau. St. Paul has one disagreeable feature: the

MENDOTA.

streets are narrow; and the land on the edge of the bluff, instead of being reserved for a promenade, like that of Iowa City, is cut up into small lots, having their rear toward the Mississippi; and certain little, but very useful, buildings present an unpleasant aspect, when viewed from the river.

The religious statistics of the territory are as yet so imperfectly made up that but little can be said, with certainty, respecting the denominational character of the inhabitants. The Episcopalians have a church at St. Paul. The Roman Catholics have seven, in different parts — chiefly mission stations. The Methodists and Baptists are supposed to be numerous. On the whole, Minesota is one of the most promising regions of country in the world, and will richly repay the tourist in surveying the beauty of its scenery, and the settler in the productiveness of its soil.

A railroad now connects Chicago with Galena, and the remainder of the distance to St. Paul is by steamboat. The Upper Mississippi generally opens in April, and the boats continue running till about the first of December. The following table will show the distances from Galena, viz:

		Whole Distance.
	Miles.	Miles.
"To the mouth of Fever River, . .	6	6
Dubuque, ...	20	26
Cassville, ...	31	57
Wisconsin River, ...	26	83
Prairie du Chien, ...	5	88
Upper Iowa River, ...	38	126
Bad Ox, ...	12	138
Root River, ...	23	161
Black River, ...	12	173

	Miles.	Miles.
Chippewa River, ...	68	241
Head of Lake Pepin, ...	25	266
St. Croix, ...	35	301
St. Paul, ...	26	327

"From Galena to St. Peter's, the fare varies from five to six dollars, for cabin passage; two dollars and fifty cents for deck passage; freight, per hundred, twenty-five cents; horses and cattle, per head, four dollars. But families, with considerable freight, are taken at a much lower rate."

CHAPTER XVII.

THE SUPERIOR COUNTRY.

Lake Superior — American coast — Anchorage — Harbors — Danger of navigating the lake — Curious phenomena of the lake — Transparency of its waters — The *mirage* of Lake Superior — Islands — Isle Royale — Lakes in Isle Royale — Perennial ice — Effect of the extreme cold on the growth of the trees — Rock Harbor — Streams emptying into Lake Superior — Appearance of the shore — Iron-works of Carp River — Porcupine Mountains — Table of distances — The La Grande Sables — Pictured Rocks — Ontonagon River — Montreal River — Sturgeon River — The Iron region — The different beds, etc. — Geologists' opinion of the iron region — Location of good agricultural lands — Advantages of a railroad through the iron regions — The copper region of the Superior country — Lake Superior reverenced by the Indians — The first Englishman who visited the copper region — Extract from his journal — First mining company — Mining companies of Keweenaw — Trap rock — Silver among the copper — Cliff mine — Copper Falls mine, rich in silver — Largest mass of copper — Table of the products of foreign mines — Eagle Harbor — Game and speckled trout — Fisheries of Lake Superior — Climate, etc.

THE North American lakes, consisting of lakes Superior, Michigan, Huron, Erie, and Ontario, present a watery surface of ninety thousand square miles, of which more than one-third, or thirty-two thousand square miles, is comprised in Lake Superior alone. That vast inland sea lies between the forty-sixth and forty-ninth parallels of latitude, and the eighty-fourth and ninety-second degrees of longitude west of Greenwich. Its greatest length is four hundred miles. Its greatest breadth from Grand Island to Neepigon Bay is one hundred and sixty miles. The surface of the lake is six hundred feet above the level of the Atlantic Ocean; but its bottom is three hundred feet below; for it has a mean depth of nine hundred feet. The French, who were the first explorers of Lake Superior, fancifully described it as a watery bow, of which the southern shore was the string, and Keweenaw Point, the arrow. The lake discharges through the St. Mary's Strait into lake Huron, which occupies a lower level, by forty-four feet and eight inches. The strait is about seventy miles long; but it is divided into two sections by the Falls of St. Mary, fifteen miles below Lake Superior. The lower section is navigable for small steamboats, and vessels drawing six feet of water. This section contains four large islands and several smaller ones; but the principal channel — the westerly one — is nearly a mile in width. The Falls of St. Mary, or more properly, rapids, are three-fourths of a mile in length, having a fall, in that distance, of twenty-two feet and ten inches. The two sections are now united by a steamboat and ship canal.

Following along the indentations of the southern shore, around the westerly extremity of the lake, to Arrow River, opposite to Isle Royale, will give the extreme length of the American coast, which can not be much less than one thousand miles; a part of which is in Michigan, part in Wisconsin, and part in Minesota. Lake Superior is walled in by rocks, which, in some places, are piled in mountain masses upon the very shore. The waves dash against precipices and beetling crags, that threaten the unfortunate mariner, in a storm upon a lee shore, with almost inevitable destruction. There is tolerable anchorage at the head of St. Mary's Strait. Keweenaw Point has two sheltering bays; viz, Copper Harbor and Eagle Harbor. Protection may be found from the surf, under the lee of the Apostle Islands, at La Pointe. St. Louis

River, at the head of the lake, is a good harbor; but the best harbors are afforded by the indentations of the shores of Isle Royale.

"Owing to the lofty crags which surround Lake Superior, the winds, sweeping over the lake, impinge upon its surface so abruptly as to raise a peculiarly deep and combing sea, which is extremely dangerous to boats and small craft. It is not safe, on this account, to venture far out into the lake in bateaux; and hence voyagers generally hug the shore, in order to be able to take land, in case of sudden storms. During the months of June, July, and August, the navigation of the lake is ordinarily safe; but after the middle of September, great caution is required in navigating its waters; and boatmen of experience never venture far from land, or attempt long traverses across bays. Their boats are always drawn far up on the land at every camping-place for the night, lest they should be staved to pieces by the surf, which is liable, at any moment, to rise, and beat with great fury upon the beaches."

One of the most curious phenomena of the lake is the sudden and inexplicable heaving and swelling of its waters, when the air is still. Mr. Schoolcraft, who passed over Lake Superior, in 1820, thus describes it: "Although it was calm, and had been so all day, save a light breeze for a couple of hours after leaving the Ontonagon, the waters near the shore were in a perfect rage, heaving and lashing upon the rocks in a manner which rendered it difficult to land. At the same time, scarce a breath of air was stirring, and the atmosphere was beautifully serene." Now this agitation was observed at the close of the day's voyage, which had carried the party fifty miles from the Ontonagon; and the slight breeze had been blowing only a little while in the morning.

Another noticeable feature of Lake Superior is the extraordinary purity and transparency of the water, through which every pebble may be distinctly seen at the depth of twenty-five feet. When out in a canoe upon its surface, the frail vessel does not seem to be afloat upon a watery element, but suspended in mid-air, with ethereal depths around and below. Those who have visited both Lake George—the world-famous Horicon, whose waters were at one time carried to Rome to fill the papal fonts—and Lake Superior, affirm that the latter far surpasses the former in clearness and transparency. Indeed, they assure us that, often, while looking down from the hight at which the boat seems suspended, the head will grow dizzy, and a feeling of faintness be superinduced. The water of Lake Superior, like that of lakes Michigan, Huron, and Erie, is "hard," and unfit for laundry purposes, without a previous breaking by soda or other means. This can be accounted for only on the supposition that it rolls over calcareous beds in some part of its course, but what part has not yet been ascertained; for the water of all the streams and springs that flow into the lake, so far as they have been examined, is found to be "soft," and so entirely free from earthy or other foreign matter, "that the daguerreotypist finds it better for his purposes than the best distilled water of the chemist."

Not less peculiar is the atmosphere around and over the lake, which plays strange and fantastic tricks in the face of high heaven, seeming to possess a life and spirit strictly in unison with the wonderful expanse of waters that lies spread out below. The *mirage* of Lake Superior fills the spectator with astonishment. For weeks during the summer, the traveler along the shores of this inland sea may be gratified by a view of the most curious phantasmagoria—images of mountains and islands being vividly represented, in all their outlines, with their tufts of ever-green trees, precipices, and rocky pinnacles, all inverted in the air, and hanging high over their terrestrial originals, and then again repeated upright in another picture directly above the inverted one. Rock Harbor, in Isle Royale, is the most noted locality for observing these phantasmagoria. But the *mirage* is not confined to any particular part of the lake. Frequently, the voyager, long before he has hove in sight of land, will see the coast he is approaching pictured upon the skies along the horizon; and after the real shore has appeared, three views of it will be presented — two, right side up, according to the order of creation; and the middle one bottom upward. Vessels will appear to be sailing in the air, points of land bent up at right-angles, and the sun at setting twisted into astonishing shapes.

The skies and the waters seem to harmonize completely together. While the sky daguerreotypes all below, the water catches the tints of all that is above, and the ethereal dome is caverned in the deep. Mr. Jackson, United States geologist, says of the lake: "The color of the water, affected by the hues of the sky, and holding no sediment to dim its transparency, presents deeper tints than are seen on the lower lakes — deep tints of blue, green, and red prevailing, according to the color of the sky and clouds. I have seen at sunset the surface of the lake off Isle Royale of a deep-claret color — a tint much richer than ever is reflected from the waters of other lakes, or in any other country I have visited."

Lake Superior, unlike Lake Huron, has but few islands. The largest of these are Grand Island, situated near the southern shore, one hundred and thirty-two miles west of St. Mary's, and represented to have a deep and landlocked harbor; Middle Island, toward the westerly extremity of the lake, near the group of Apostle Islands; and Isle Royale, near the northern shore, and within the jurisdiction of the United States. Isle Royale is about forty miles long, and averages six miles in width. It is a most interesting island, "singularly formed, and sending out long spits of rocks into the lake at its north-eastern extremity; while at its south-western end, it shelves off far into the lake, presenting slightly-inclined beds of red sandstone; the tabular sheets of which, for miles from the coast, are barely covered with water, and offer dangerous shoals and reefs, on which vessels, and even boats would be quickly stranded, if they endeavored to pass near that shore." But igneous rocks constitute the rocky basis of more than four-fifths of the island, and in those portions of it where these exist, the shores are precipitous. "Bold cliffs of columnar trap and castellated rocks, with mural escarpments, sternly present themselves to the surf, and defy the storms. The waters of the lake are deep close to their very shores, and the largest ship might in many places lie close to the rocks, as at an artificial pier."

Isle Royale contains a great number of beautiful lakes, the largest of which is Siskawit Lake, on the southern side, near Siskawit Bay. It is also surrounded by innumerable small islands, which cluster close to its shores, as if for protection from the waves. Mr. Jackson, before referred to, gives the following interesting description of the general appearance of Isle Royale: "Added to the fantastic irregularities of the coast and its castle-like islands—the abrupt elevation of the hills inland rising like almost perpendicular walls from the shores of the numerous beautiful lakes which are scattered through the interior of the island, and corresponding with the lines of mountain upheaval—we observe occasionally rude crags detached from the main body of the mountains, and, in one place, two lofty twin towers, standing on a hillside, and rising perpendicularly, like huge chimneys, to the elevation of seventy feet, while they are surrounded by the deep-green foliage of the primeval forest."

In the secluded valleys between the hills of Isle Royale there are either little lakes, or swamps filled with a dense growth of white cedars. Upon the higher lands, the timber is a mixture of maple, birch, spruce, fir, and pine trees, which are of thrifty growth, and will afford both timber and fuel. The soil of more than nine-tenths of the island is formed by the decomposition of the trap rocks; and such a soil is well-known to be warm and fertile. In the lowlands, the springs from the hills will keep the soil cold and wet; but if properly drained, there is no doubt those lands might be cultivated, and would produce good crops. Indeed, this is said to have been proved in the vicinity of Rock Harbor, where the lowland soil, which was originally covered with swamp-muck, is now drained and made productive.

In the deep shadow of the crags, and in some of the thick swamps of cedar, it is said that perennial ice has been found upon the island; and on the immediate rocky border of the lake shore, the influence of the wintry winds from the lake is strikingly exemplified in the stunted growth of the fir and spruce trees, that get root in the crevices of the rocks. Mr. Jackson says: "In numerous instances, we were able to witness the joint effects of cold air and a limited supply of soil, in retarding the growth of trees, and giving the wood an extremely fine texture. Small trees have sprung up, having all the appearance of age which the dwarfed trees raised by the ingenious Chinese gardener are known to present. Those little trees, from four inches to a foot high, are covered with mosses like old trees, and the tiny stem presents in its bark and wood, the different layers, representing many seasons. In cutting through these little trees, they were found, in some instances, to possess forty different annual rings; and the wood was nearly as hard as boxwood, and as fine!"

Rock Harbor, on the southern side of the north-easterly end of Isle Royale, is the largest and most beautiful haven on Lake Superior. The bay extends about four miles up into the island. The water is deep enough for any vessels, and the harbor is perfectly sheltered from every wind. Around its entrance are numerous islands, that stand like so many rocky castles to break the heavy surges of the lake. "In some respects it resembles the Bay of Naples, with Procida, Capri, and Ischia, at its entrance; but no modern volcano completes the background of the picture, though there must at one time have been greater eruptions there than ever took place in Italy."

Lake Superior is fed by about eighty streams, which are represented to be not navigable, except for canoes, owing to the falls and rapids with which they abound. The principal ones that flow through American territory are the St. Louis, Montreal, Presque Isle, Arrow, Little Montreal, Ontonagon, Eagle, Sturgeon, Huron, Dead, Carp, Chocolate, La Prairie, Two-hearted, and Tequamenon rivers. The largest of these are the Ontonagon and Sturgeon rivers, which, by the removal of some obstructions at their mouths, and the construction of piers to prevent the formation of bars, might be converted into excellent and spacious harbors, in the immediate vicinity of some of the most valuable mines, where the want of safe anchorage is now severely felt; as at Eagle Harbor, for instance, where the propellers have to cast anchor over a hundred yards out, and the copper intended for shipment has to be first placed on board of a scow, on which passengers also take a position, and then floated out to the propellers. The copper is raised on board by means of a crane, which is stationary upon the side of the vessel.

The Twin River, or Two-hearted River, as it is called by the traders, consists in the union of two separate streams, near the point of its outlet. It empties into the lake seventy-two miles westward of St. Mary's. A short distance beyond Grand Island, at the mouth of a small stream known as Laughing-fish River, a curious flux and reflux of the water is maintained, similar to the tides of the ocean. At the mouth of Chocolate River, there is a large bay setting up deep into the shore, which requires a day's canoe-travel to circumnavigate it. Just beyond that, the traveler will first strike the old crystaline rocks, or primitive formation. From hence, for two days' travel to Huron Bay, the shore presents a continuous series of rough, conical peaks, which are noted for immense bodies of iron ore, chiefly in the condition of iron glance, from which the extensive iron-works of Carp River, seated at the foot of these mountains, are yielding such fine blooms. Continuing on westward across Keweenaw Bay, the canoe voyager will enter Portage Lake, embosomed near the base of Keweenaw Point, and, with a short portage, will reach the lake west of the Point without the toil and distance of circumnavigating it. And, in doing so, he will observe that the geology of the country has become entirely changed. He will have passed into the midst of a region of trap-dike—the great copper-bearing rock of Lake Superior. Passing onward along the lake, the dim-blue outlines of the Porcupine Mountains will rise to view on the edge of the horizon, directly ahead. These mountains, on a clear day, may be seen from a distance of sixty miles. Soon the voyager will be traversing the entrances of Little Salmon, Graverod, Misery, and Firesteel rivers, to the mouth of Ontonagon River, where a large body of water enters the lake; but the mouth of the river is very much obstructed by a sand-bar. There, likewise, may be observed another of those curious refluxes, where the water, impeded and dammed up by gales, reacts with unusual force.

The following table of distances is made up from the statements of voyagers, and is supposed to be exaggerated by about one-third, as that class of men always pride themselves on going long distances. Nevertheless, the table may be of value.

	Miles.	Whole No of Miles.
From Michilimackinac to Detour, .	40	
Sault Ste. Marie, ...	45	85
Point aux Pius, ...	6	91
Point Iroquois, entrance to Lake Superior, ...	9	100
Tequamenon River, ...	15	115
Shelldrake River, ...	9	124
White Fish Point, ...	9	133
Two-hearted River, ...	24	157
Grande Marrais, ...	21	178
La Point la Grand Sables, . . .	9	187
Pictured Rocks, ...	12	199
Miner's River, ...	6	205
Grande Island, ...	12	217
River aux Trains, ...	9	226
Isle aux Trains, ...	3	229
Laughing-fish River, ...	6	235
Chocolate River, ...	15	250
Dead River, and Presque Isle Bay,	6	256

	Miles.	Whole No. of Miles.
Granite Point, ...	6	. 262
Garlic River,.	9	. 271
St. John's River, ...	15	. 286
Salmon River, ...	12	. 298
Pine River, ...	6	. 304
Huron River, ...	9	. 313
East Cape of Keweenaw Bay, .	6	. 319
Mouth of Portage River, . . .	21	. 340
Head of Portage River, . . .	24	. 364
Lake Superior, at the end of the Portage, ...	1	. 365
Little Salmon River, ...	9	. 374
Graverod River, ...	6	. 380
Misery River, ...	12	. 392
Firesteel River,.	18	. 410
Ontonagon River, ...	5	. 416

In crossing the St. Mary's Strait, from Point aux Pius to Point Iroquois, the first view of Lake Superior is to be had, affording one of the most pleasing prospects in the world. The St. Mary's River passes out of the lake between two prominent capes; viz, Gros Cape and Point Iroquois. The former rises up in high, barren peaks, of hornblende rock; the latter consists of elevated masses of red sandstone, covered with a dense forest.

The La Grand Sables is an interesting feature of the lake coast. The shore consists of "several heavy strata of the drift era, reaching a hight of two or three hundred feet, with a precipitous front on the lake. The sands, driven up by the waters, are blown over these hights, forming a heavy deposit. It is this sandy deposit, falling down the face of the precipice, that appears to convert the whole formation into dunes, whereon the sandy coating rests like a vail. The number of rapacious birds, which are observed about these hights, adds to the interest of the prospect."

The pictured rocks of Lake Superior will always attract the attention of the tourist. That coast of rocks is twelve miles in length, consisting of a gray sandstone, and presenting perpendicular walls, which have been worn by the waves into pillared masses, and cavernous arches. These caverns yawn into the face of the cliff, and the winds howl, and the waves roar around their mouths. A small river leaps from the top of the precipice clear into the lake. At one place the "Doric Rock," a vast entablature, rests on two immense water-worn pillars. At another place, the precipice has been completely undermined, so that it rests solely on a single massive column, standing in the water. The dark-red clay, overlaying the rocks above, has been washed by the rains down the face of the precipice, and, being blended with the sand and dust blown about by the winds, presents a pictorial appearance. Schoolcraft says: "We almost held our breath in passing that coast."

The Ontonagon River, for four miles up from its mouth, is broad and deep, having a gentle current, flowing through a winding channel, between banks that are heavily wooded, the dark-green foliage overhanging the water. A long, narrow island divides the river into two channels, through which the current flows slowly and tranquilly to the lake. The stream above is broken by frequent rapids. The soil of the Ontonagon, near its mouth, is coarse and sandy; but it is said to be productive of garden vegetables. Further up the river the soil becomes clayey and loamy — very suitable for cultivation. Several mining companies have locations on this river; but at its mouth the land is reserved for the use of the government. The banks are from seven to ten feet high, supporting a fine growth of elm, whitewood, sugar-maple, birch, spruce, white-pine, and cedar; also, gooseberries and raspberries.

The Montreal River forms the boundary between Michigan and Wisconsin. It presents many attractions for the admirers of picturesque scenery, and exhibits the most beautiful waterfalls any where to be found along the entire coast of Lake Superior. A little way above its mouth, and within sight of the lake, the red sandstone rocks have a northerly dip of seventy degrees; and over this ledge, the river is precipitated eighty feet, into a deep circular basin, the sides of which have been excavated by the rushing waters into a spacious amphitheater. About three miles further up the river, in a direct line from the lake, is a second waterfall, said to be fully as beautiful as the first.

Sturgeon River rises in the country to the south of the head of Keweenaw Bay; and, running northerly, empties into Portage Lake. This lake is connected with Superior by Portage River, which may be ascended by vessels drawing eight feet of water, and to the head of the lake, twenty miles inland. Those streams, together with the Montreal River, are famous for their sturgeon fisheries. All the rivers that flow into Lake Superior, at a little distance inland, become very rapid, broken by frequent waterfalls, furnishing water-power in great abundance. The hights of land between Portage Lake and Montreal River vary from six hundred feet to thirteen hundred feet in hight.

The Superior country is celebrated alike for its iron, its copper, and its silver. It can never become much of an agricultural country; but its mineral resources are very great, beyond the power of calculation. The country has been explored just sufficiently to enable us to form a mere rough guess as to its capability of producing the most valuable metals in constant use by man. The iron occupies a region distinct by itself. The copper and silver are found blended together.

The iron region of Lake Superior, no less than the copper region, is one of the wonders of the world. It commences along the coast of the lake, with the metamorphic rocks, extending from the Chocolate River to the Dead River, a distance of ten miles, following the shore, and sweeps away southerly and westerly across the branches of the Menominee River—the Machi-gamig and the Brule—and the Sturgeon River, and the Esconaba River, that empties into Little Bay de Noquet, near the head of Green Bay. Now, it must be borne in mind, that the Chocolate River comes into Lake Superior from the south-east, and the Dead River from the west. On the meridian intersecting the mouth of the Dead River, the iron-bearing rocks extend directly south more than eleven miles; and on that of the Jackson Forge, nine miles west of the mouth of the river, the iron region is some fourteen miles in width. Its western limit has not been determined; but it must be far within the borders of Wisconsin, having been traced in that direction nearly one hundred miles. The northern limit is nearly on a line drawn due west from the mouth of the Dead River. The southerly limit also, from the Chocolate River, runs pretty much straight west, till beyond the Esconaba, where it turns off south along the Machi-gamig, and crosses the Menominee. There the width of the iron region is known to be more than fifty miles. This valuable mineral tract has been but partially explored, and no sufficient data have been furnished to estimate exactly its area.

There is the most abundant authority, however, for saying, that the iron of the Superior country is both rich and inexhaustible. The following statements, condensed from the reports made by the persons engaged in the United States geological survey of the mineral lands, will convey some idea of the extent and quality of the ore.

The first bed of magnetic ore is situated near the Menominee River, and in the direction of Fort River, a branch of the Esconaba, at the corner of townships forty-one and forty-two, north, and between ranges twenty-nine and thirty, west. It was found in a low ridge, some three chains in width, which appeared to be one mass of iron ore, stratified and jointed. The ore has generally a granular structure; color, iron-black, passing into steel-gray; luster, when fresh broken, metallic, but soon oxydizes, upon exposure to the atmosphere.

The second bed of ore is situated on the east boundary of township forty-six north, range thirty west, sections one and six, along the south-western shore of a small lake, in the Machi-gamig River. The extent of this bed of ore is unknown; but it borders that side of the lake, from twenty to fifty feet in hight. The ore is likewise stratified and jointed, so that it may be quarried with ease. In color and luster, it resembles the first—fresh fractures appearing like fine-grained cast-iron. Now, this bed of ore extends along through a range of hills on the north-easterly side also of that lake, to an unknown extent, and in a mass so great as to stagger belief. Let the surveyor speak for himself: "The river here forms a lake-like expansion, and is bounded on the north-east by a range of hills, which rise abruptly to the hight of two hundred feet above the water. We explored this ridge, and found that it was composed, for the most part, of nearly pure specular oxyd of iron. It shoots up in a perpendicular cliff, one hundred and thirteen feet in hight, so pure, that it is difficult to determine its mineral associations. We passed along the base of this cliff for more than a quarter of a mile, seeking for a gap, through which we might pass, and gain the summit. At length, and by clambering from one point to another, we succeeded. Passing along the brow of the cliff, forty feet, the mass was comparatively pure; then succeeded a bed of quartz, composed of grounded grains, with small specks of iron disseminated, and large, rounded masses of the same material inclosed, constituting a conglomerate. This bed was fifteen feet in thickness, and was succeeded again by specular iron, exposed in places to the width of one hundred feet; but the soil and trees prevented our determining its entire width. This one cliff contains iron sufficient to supply the world for ages; yet we saw neither its length nor its width, but only an outline of the mass."

It may be proper here to suggest, that the best possible use that can be made of the capital afloat in the importing trade, would be to make one more investment in English railroad iron, to lay a track from Green Bay up the Esconaba River, which reaches within a mile of this mountain of iron, and make it accessible. Whoever will do this will do more to promote the wealth of the country than ever has yet been done by opening mines; for iron is the most valuable mineral on the continent, despite the copper further north, and the gold of California. Set this native mountain of ore once to running, and it will flow throughout the earth, superseding the iron of all other countries.

The third bed of ore is situated on the east boundary of township forty-seven north, range twenty-nine west, near section thirteen, in another cliff, facing south-west, and varying from twenty to fifty feet in hight. The ore is stratified and jointed, and in quality similar to the other beds. The extent of this bed is likewise unknown. Thirteen chains distant, south-south-west, from the main mass, on the shore of a pond, the ore rises above the surface in the form of a knob, thirty feet in hight.

The fourth bed of ore is near the south boundary of township forty-eight north, range twenty-eight west, on section four, consisting of a knob of iron fifty feet in hight.

The fifth bed of ore is in the next township west of the fourth bed, on section thirty-two, consisting of a ridge of iron ore eight feet in hight. It was traced seventy-five chains. This bed is very extensive, and highly magnetic. In quality it is similar to the others.

In this manner the surveyors proceed to enumerate ore-bed after ore-bed, throughout the various townships of that great mineral tract. The foregoing is probably sufficient to satisfy the reader of the existence of exhaustless beds of that ore in the Superior country. With the mention of one more ore-bed, this enumeration shall cease. It is referred to because it is much nearer the Chocolate River than the others, being directly south of the Jackson furnace six miles, in township forty-seven, range twenty-six, sections twenty-nine, thirty, thirty-one, and thirty-two. There are two hills of the ore, made up almost entirely of granulated, magnetic, or specular iron, with small quantities of spathous and micaceous iron. The more northerly hill extends east and west full a quarter of a mile, and is over one thousand feet in width — a single mass of ore. The ore breaks readily into sub-rhomboidal fragments, in such manner as will greatly facilitate the operations of mining.

In conclusion, the geologists say: "This iron region is the most valuable and extensive in the world for the manufacture of the finer varieties of wrought-iron and steel.

When we consider the immense extent of the district, the mountain masses of the ore, its purity and adaptation to the manufacture of the most valuable kinds of iron, and the immense forests which cover the surface, suitable for charcoal, this district may be pronounced unrivaled. The ore consists mainly of the specular, or peroxyd of iron, an admixture of the fine-grained magnetic. In some instances, the whole ridge, or knob, appears to consist of one mass of pure ore—so pure that no selection is required; but an unlimited quantity might be quarried, or picked up in loose blocks around the slopes. In others, the ore is mixed with seams of quartz or jasper, which renders it less valuable, and requires some care for the selection. The iron in such cases presents a banded or contorted structure, or alternating seams of steel-gray and brilliant red. The appearance of a mountain cliff, thus made up, is extraordinary. The iron mountain of Missouri becomes insignificant compared with these immense deposits."

The surveyors report some good agricultural lands in this district. The following table will show the location of them, viz.:

Townships 42 north, in ranges 32, 33, 34, and 35 west.
Townships 43 north, in ranges 32, 33, 34, and 35 west.
Townships 47 north, in ranges 27 and 28 west.
Townships 48 north, in ranges 27 and 28 west.
Townships 49 north, in ranges 32, 33, 34, and 35 west.
Townships 50 north, in ranges 29, 30, 31, 32, 33, 34, and 35 west.

These tracts of fertile land will become of great value, when the rivers shall have been opened, and a mining population introduced, creating a sure and convenient home-market for the productions of the farm.

This bountiful iron region, in most part, sustains a

heavy growth of maple, birch, pine, and oak timber; and the streams, numerous and rapid, supply any amount of water-power. If a railroad was constructed from Little Bay de Noquet, on Green Bay, to Keweenaw Bay, on Lake Superior, a distance of one hundred and ten miles, through the heart of the iron region, those extensive ore-beds would be left no longer unoccupied and useless. It would seem to be like offering an indignity to Providence to neglect the development of such magnificent resources, placed within the borders of the United States.

Next in importance, after the iron, is the copper of the Superior country. The region where that metal is found, along the southern shore of the lake, is described, as follows, by Messrs. Foster and Whitney, United States geologists: "The examination of a great number of localities has demonstrated that the veins of copper, and its ores, in the sandstone and conglomerate, are not to be relied on, and that when worked, even to an inconsiderable depth, they give out. Although copper is found at short intervals, from the Pictured Rocks to the Montreal River, in this rock, yet we have designated no tract in it as mineral land. As all the productive lodes are confined to the ranges of trap, all of the mineral tracts designated lie within those ranges. What is generally known as the trap-range, consists of a belt of igneous rocks, composed for the most part of hornblende and feldspar, which in places have broken through the sandstones, tilting them up at high angles; but oftener are found in alternating beds, having the same dip as the detrital rocks. The trap range extends from Montreal River—the western boundary of the district—and disappears in the lake at the extremity of Keweenaw Point. Its general course is a little north of east, preserving a pretty uniform parallelism with the southern coast of Lake Superior. Its width varies from two miles to twelve. Throughout this range—nearly one hundred and fifty miles in extent—copper, mostly native, is disseminated, but more profusely in some places than others. In fact, there may be said to exist two centers of metallic riches, around each of which copper has been accumulated in considerable quantity, but under circumstances somewhat different. The one may be designated as the Keweenaw Point center, which has a system of veins cutting across the trap-range. The other may be designated as the Ontonagon center; and here the veins preserve a certain parallelism with the ranges, or run with the formation."

The red sandstone and conglomerate rocks of Keweenaw Point undoubtedly existed long before the trap-rocks were pushed up through them, and were produced by the deposition of fine sand and pebbles in water; for the ripple marks are well preserved, and record this fact in the most absolute and positive manner. It is supposed that, by pressure and heat, the materials of a loose, shifting sand, became converted into a solid sandstone, the layers of sand forming the different strata. Previous to the action of the disturbing forces from beneath, the sandstone must have been composed in horizontal layers, as water necessarily deposits a mechanical sediment in that manner. But the sandstone has been broken through by the trap-rocks, and elevated at considerable angles along the line of its disruption. It is plain, that the forcing of a melted mass of rocks up through such a sedimentary strata must have exerted a powerful influence upon the sediment itself. Accordingly, it is found, at Keweenaw Point, that a chemical combination took place, of the material of the sandstone with the material of the trap rocks, along the line of junction, resulting in the formation of an amygdaloid rock. And between the sandstone and the trap is found a mass of broken, indurated sandstone, scoria of fused trap and sandstone, amygdaloidal and compact trap, and porphyry; which together form, when re-cemented by heat, a rock known as trap-tuff or breccia. Near Eagle River, the trap breccias occupy a considerable space between the sandstone and the amygdaloid; and some have mistaken them for a conglomerate of the sandstones in that vicinity. And when the trap rocks conjoin with the sandstone, the former is found to be amygdaloidal, and the cavities generally filled with chlorite, in particles varying in size from a pea to a walnut. In one portion, it has been noticed that, whenever a cavity is filled with chlorite, a granule of copper will be found concealed in its center; but nearer the copper veins the cavities are oftener filled with pure copper or silver, or with both these metals. One of the most surprising features of the trap region of Lake Superior is the occurrence of veins of solid metallic copper, admixed with native silver, and yet not alloyed with it. Two veins occurring in a stratified rock generally traverse the strata at a considerable angle, and are more regular than those which run parallel to the layers, possessing well-defined walls, and often incrusted with vein-stone, prehnite, quartz, and calcareous spar. The rocky fissure is filled with vein-stones of different kinds, which, together with the accompanying minerals, constitute the lode. Sometimes the veins, at the surface, are composed entirely of prehnite, and contain only minute specks of copper inclosed in the crystals, or sparsely scattered throughout the mass. Beneath this covering of vein-stones is found the solid metallic copper of Lake Superior.

The rocks of the copper region have been elevated to an angle of about forty degrees, inclining to the northwest, by the terrific forces that injected the molten copper throughout their cracks and crevices. Along the hill-sides, where, by reason of this angular elevation, the rocks are made to out-crop the superincumbent masses of decayed rock, and other accumulations, have been washed away by the action of torrents; and the metal, in some places, appears at the surface. Some of those points, where the copper is thus exposed, would seem to have attracted the attention of the Indians, long before any white man ever trod the bleak and sterile shores of Lake Superior. Along the banks of the Ontonagon River have been found the ancient mines, to which the tribes must have resorted for a supply of copper for the manufacture of tools and ornaments. The metal was very highly prized by them; and pieces of native copper were treasured up with great care, and used as an article of traffic. It is evident that the aboriginal miners were not more advanced toward civilization than the Indians generally; because the mining and other implements, found on the Ontonagon in the ancient excavations, are precisely similar to those which are known to have been in use among the tribes of the Atlantic coast. The stone-hammers, made of oval pebbles, groved about the middle, for withes, which formed the handles, were the native instruments for breaking out pieces of copper, on Lake Superior, and for breaking the hard rocks of Moosehead Lake for the arrow and spear-heads of the eastern Indians. Such hammers, together with half-finished stone scalping-knives, have been found both at Ontonagon and at Eagle River. The Indian miner also assisted the operation of breaking the rocks by kindling fires upon them; and hence the origir of the charred brands and coal that have been found around the battered and beaten projections of copper.

The Lake Superior was greatly reverenced by the Indians inhabiting its shores at the time of the early explorations of the Jesuit missionaries. Claude Allouez says, respecting this superstition: "The savages respect this lake as a divinity, and make sacrifices to it; on account perhaps, of its magnitude, for it is two hundred leagues long and eighty wide; or on account of its goodness in furnishing them with fishes, which nourish all these people, where there is but little game. There are often found, beneath the water, pieces of copper, all formed, and of the weight of ten and twenty pounds. I have seen them many times in the hands of the savages; and as they are superstitious, they keep them as so many divinities, or as presents from the gods beneath the water, who have given them as pledges of good fortune. On that account, they keep the pieces of copper enveloped among their most precious furniture. There are some who have preserved them for more than fifty years, and others who have had them in their families from time immemorial, and cherish them as household gods."

The first Englishman that ever visited the copper region was Alexander Henry, who, after having his hair almost started out of his head at the frightful massacre of Michilimackinac, continued in the Superior country for several years, poking about among its ravines and precipices with a most refreshing indifference to danger. One or two extracts from his journal will show what he saw there.

"On the 19th of August, 1765, we reached the mouth of the Ontonagon River, one of the largest on the south side of the lake. At the mouth was an Indian village; and three leagues above, a fall, at the foot of which sturgeon, at this season, were obtained so abundant, that a month's subsistence for a regiment could have been taken in a few hours. But I found this river chiefly remarkable for the abundance of virgin copper which is on its banks and in its neighborhood.

"On my way back to Michilimackinac, I encamped a second time at the mouth of the Ontonagon River, and now took the opportunity of going ten miles up the river with Indian guides. The object for which I most expressly went, and to which I had the satisfaction of being led, was a mass of copper of the weight, according to my estimate, of no less than five tons. Such was its pure and malleable state, that, with an ax, I was able to cut off a portion weighing a hundred pounds. On viewing the surrounding surface, I conjectured that the mass, at some period or other, had rolled down the side of a lofty hill which rises at its back." This copper rock has been removed to Washington, and may now be seen lying on the ground near the War Department.

That same enterprising explorer was also the first to organize a Lake Superior Mining Company. In 1770, Messrs. Baxter, Bostwick, and Henry built a barge at Point aux Pius, and laid the keel of a sloop of forty tons. They were in search of gold and silver, and expected to make their fortunes. The other partners in England were "His Royal Highness, the Duke of Gloucester; Mr. Secretary Townshend; Sir Samuel Tuchet, Bart.; Mr. Baxter, consul of the Empress of Russia; and Mr. Cruikshank: in America, Sir William Johnson, Bart.; Mr. Bostwick; Mr Baxter, and myself. A charter had been petitioned for, and obtained; but, owing to our ill success, it was never taken from the seal-office." Mr. Baxter sold the sloop and other effects of the company, and paid its debts, which certainly was a most commendable feature of their operations. Lake Superior seems then to have been abandoned, and its mineral resources forgotten.

Since 1845, public attention has been again drawn toward the Superior country. Its mineral lands have been surveyed, affording tolerably accurate information of the localities where the ores of copper, and iron, and silver abound. A large number of mining companies have been organized, and some of them have gone into successful operation. It has been stated that there are forty-one companies carrying on mining operations at Keweenaw Point alone, among which are the following: Northwest, Siskowit, Algonquin, Piscataqua, Ontonagon, Bohemia, Chesapeake, and Cape — eight, having their offices in Philadelphia; the Pittsburg and Boston, Northwestern, North American, Iron City, Eureka, Ohio Trap Rock, Colling, Ohio, Aztec, Adventure, Ridge, and Fire-Steel — twelve, having their offices at Pittsburg; the Minesota, Norwich, Wheal Kate, Albion, and Forest — five, with their offices in New York; the Copper Falls, Phœnix, Winthrop, Dana, Douglass Houghton, Quincey, Alcomah, Farm, and Toltec — nine, with their offices in Boston.

The belt of the trap rocks on Keweenaw Point is three miles in width, in its narrowest part, and seven miles in its widest. It underlies seven townships, or, more exactly, two hundred and seventeen sections of land, between Portage Lake and the extremity of the promontory. It is exceedingly rich in copper and silver. The country is broken, hilly, and irregular, and very much cut up by the streams. The soil is represented to be of an excellent quality — warm and fertile, as trappean soils generally are; and is covered with a heavy growth of hard-wood forest-trees, with some soft-wood. The forests are more open than those on the adjacent sandstone rocks, and the timber is more thrifty. The appearance of the trap-rock is quite singular; for the melted mass, when it was forced up from below, did not burst out in circular spaces, or through cylindrical chimneys, like lava eruptions of modern times; but intruded itself through chasms and fractures of the superincumbent rocks, frequently overflowing them, and spreading out between the strata, and existing as intervening masses, or beds.

At the Lake Superior Company's mines, shaft number two, passing into the western side of the vein, was very rich in copper and silver at the surface, where it immediately bordered upon the leader, and impoverished as it left it in descending. So, after working downward, for a time, through barren rock, "the miners sent off a level toward the river, with the intention of striking the vein under the stream; but, to their great surprise, opened into a deep and wide ravine, or ancient channel of the river, filled with great masses of copper, lumps of copper and silver mixed, small globules of pure silver—all rounded and worn by the action of running water, and mixed with sand, gravel, and pebbles. A single mass of silver was obtained from this ravine, which weighed more than six pounds, and was worth one hundred and thirty dollars." That lump of silver is now in the cabinet of the United States Mint, at Philadelphia. Masses of copper were also found in that ravine, weighing a thousand pounds. These were exported to France.

The Cliff Mine, belonging to the Boston and Pittsburg Mining Company, is situated on the south-west branch of Eagle River, three miles from the office of the Lake Superior Company. "The Cliff Mine," says Mr. Jackson, United States geologist, "is one of the most remarkable known, for the enormous masses of native copper it contains. One of the masses, now got out, is estimated at fifty tons weight. It is cut by means of steel chisels, driven by blows of a heavy sledge-hammer—one man holding the chisel, while the other strikes with the sledge; a groove is mortised out across the mass of copper; and then a series of ribbons of it, about a quarter of an inch in thickness, are cut out, until the channel thus mortised divides the mass. The copper is perfectly mal leable and ductile, and is very tough. The masses of solid copper are very pure, and ought to yield more than ninety per cent. of refined metal."

To get out such huge masses of copper, a place is sought in the shaft where a hole may be bored into the rock, and then firing a heavy blast. This starts the copper from the wall of rock, and sometimes removes it entirely. It is then cut up with chisels. This vein varies from two to four feet in width, and increases in width and richness as it descends in the rock. The hight of the cliff in which this vein is seen, is nearly three hundred feet, and the upper exposure of the veins, two hundred and thirteen feet. The top of the cliff is seven hundred feet above Lake Superior.

At the Copper Falls mines, about two hundred feet above the level of the lake, the shafts descend perpendicularly into the rock nearly to that depth. There is a vein of solid copper. The sheets of copper are of amazing dimensions. Mr. Jackson says: "One of the masses of copper got out was twenty feet long, nine feet wide, and from four to six inches thick, and weighed, by estimation, ten tons." The Copper Falls mines are exceedingly rich in silver. In many parts of the vein, from twenty-five to one hundred dollars' worth of silver is contained in an hundred weight of rock. Mr. Jackson analyzed a rich specimen, which yielded five ounces of silver to six pounds of veinstone.

The largest mass of copper that has yet been removed, was at the bottom of the Cliff Mine, and was estimated to weigh eighty tons. It was pure copper, having a den-

EAGLE HARBOR — LAKE SUPERIOR.

sity equal to that of the hammered copper of commerce, and much tougher than that which is obtained by artificial smelting.

The great national value of the copper mines of Lake Superior will be seen by comparing their capability for the production of metal with the other copper mines in different parts of the earth. The following table exhibits the foreign mines, together with the annual yield of metal.

Sweden,	1,000 tons.
Russia,	2,000 "
Hungary,	2,000 "
Hartz Mountains,	212 "
East Germany,	143 "
Hesse,	500 "
Norway,	7,200 "
United Kingdom of Great Britain,	14.465 "
Mexico,	200 "

The principal landing-place on Keweenaw Point, to get access to the mines, is Eagle Harbor. The village occupies a beautiful site. The houses are built on the rising ground, in a magnificent grove of Norwegian pines. The harbor is a fraction less than a mile wide; the greatest depth of water, one hundred feet; depth on the bar, ten feet; and there it can be easily deepened to sixteen feet, by blasting away the rocks. This ought to be done for the safety of loaded steamboats, which frequently take shelter in the bay.

The Superior country is quite destitute of game; but the waters abound in fish of the choicest kinds. The streams throughout the iron region are alive with speckled trout. The lake fisheries will one day rival those of the ocean, both in extent and value. Isle Royale is a favorite place of resort for fishermen, who take there great numbers of the siskowit—the fattest and finest variety of the lake-trout family; also, lake-trout and whitefish. The siskowit has been known to attain to the weight of twenty-five pounds; and the lake trout, fifty pounds. The siskowit has only to become introduced into the eastern market, to take the place of all other fish, as a delicacy for the table of the epicure. The capability of the fisheries of the Superior country may be estimated by the quantities taken at one place, near Mackinaw, at which ten thousand barrels are packed annually. The preparations for packing are very simple. After being cleaned, the fish are laid, with the scales on, upon broad benches, and salted; then thrown into a box, or crate, with a grating at the bottom, to drain. Sometimes a common wagon-wheel is used, suspended by a rod passing through the hub; the water passes off from the fish, between the spokes. After draining, the packing commences. Fish are an important article of food at the mines, and will continue to become more valuable as the business of mining increases.

The Superior country is a healthy country; but the climate is too cold and forbidding, and the winters too long, to attract emigrants, who prefer to cultivate the soil. In July, the days are very warm; the nights, however, are cool. The changes in the temperature are very sudden and very great. It is no uncommon thing for the thermometer, to fall forty degrees in twenty-four hours. Frosts occur about the tenth of September, sufficient to kill all vegetation. The snows attain to the depth of six feet, and remain to the last of May. Winter sets in early in October. During the fall months there are frequent and terrible gales of wind, and storms of rain and snow.

The Superior country will one day be erected into a territory by itself, or admitted as a state. It will be, for all time, not only a mine of wealth to the Union, but also a nursery of a tough, hardy, and energetic race of men. The full development of its vast resources would require a population that will make it the great northern hive of America.

CHAPTER XVIII.

KANSAS AND NEBRASKA.

Boundary of Kansas — Best lands open for settlement — Valleys of the tributaries of the Arkansas River, and of the Smoky Hill Fork of the Kansas — Pasturage — The land between the desert hills and the Rocky Mountains — The Kansas River — Valley of the Grand River — Timber — Coal — Springs — Council Grove — The Grand Prairie — The Upper Arkansas — Pawnee Rock — The *mirage* — Table of distances from Independence City to Pawnee Rock — The Santa Fé trade — Southern Kansas ores — Settlements of Eastern Kansas — Kansas laws for the recognition of land claims — Indians of Kansas — "First right" — Table of distances from Fort Riley to Missouri border — Military roads — Climate of Kansas — Nebraska.

KANSAS Territory lies spread out between the thirty-seventh and the fortieth parallels of north latitude, and from the border of Missouri clear over the Rocky Mountains. The northern boundary consists of a straight line, running due east and west. The southern boundary is directly west along the line of the Indian Territory, and of Texas to New Mexico; thence, ascending northward one degree, it again turns away westward. The eastern portion, therefore, is considerably wider than the western. The territory comprises an area of nearly one hundred and fifteen thousand square miles. It has been suggested, that "ultimately, the State of Kansas will probably be restricted, by cutting off the western portion to form a new state or states, so as to leave this about three hundred miles long, from east to west, and two hundred wide, from north to south." The eastern boundary, for more than one hundred miles, is formed by the Missouri River, between the mouth of the Kansas and the southern border of Nebraska.

The eastern and the western extremities of the territory comprise the best lands in Kansas; the middle regions being quite indifferent, and in some places absolutely barren. The finest portions now open for settlement are comprised in the strip which extends across the territory contiguous to the Missouri boundary, varying in width from seventy-five to one hundred and eighty miles. This tract of land has a limestone basis; and the soil, consisting of a dark vegetable mold far superior to the ordinary prairie soil, is exceedingly fertile, and of great depth. The soil, throughout the entire region, is represented as having an average depth of four feet, which, with its calcareous quality, and freedom from stone, makes it most desirable for agricultural purposes. The bottom-lands along the borders of the rivers are equal to any in the world. The upland is composed of a continual succession of ridges and valleys, rising and falling with the regularity of ocean waves. The general direction of the ridges is north and south, except where their uniformity is broken by the courses of the streams. The rivers are belted with timber; but the forests are not so thick, nor the trees so large as those which originally grew in New York and Ohio. The woods have not a sufficient supply of timber for a dense population; but it is presumed to be sufficient for the purposes of settlement, until hedges can be raised, and the fires shut out from the plains, permitting a growth of trees to spring up where now every twig is consumed. The effect of narrowing the limits of the autumnal fires will, no doubt, be the same in Kansas that it has been in Missouri, converting prairie into thrifty timbered lands. The upland country, diversified with hills and valleys, is rendered picturesque by groves, scattered unevenly and irregularly over the surface, sometimes on the hillsides, but oftener in the valleys, consisting, in the former case, of the stately cottonwoods, and in the latter, of elms. Clumps of oak are found in some places. The timber of the bottom-lands consists of oak, ash, elm, white and sugar-maple, and hickory. This eastern tract is known among the overland travelers to Oregon and California as the region of "tall grass." The blade is coarse and rough at the edges, like the grass of Illinois. It ordinarily attains to the hight of three feet, toward the close of summer; but where the land is moist it grows more luxuriantly, and is said to become "tall enough to hide from view horse and rider." In June, those rolling prairie lands are covered with gaudy flowers. The small streams are quite numerous, having their sources in springs; and though they may not entirely dry up, they are, nevertheless, "dry-weather streams," showing little more in September than pebbly beds, but swelled full, muddy and turbulent, in the spring. These streams have cut their channels down deep in the soil, forming ravines difficult to cross; but with their borders fringed with timber, and winding through the country in all directions, they add very much to the beauty of the landscape.

Immediately contiguous to the fertile plains of eastern Kansas is a narrow belt, averaging twenty miles in width, of an entirely different character, having a sandstone basis. The country is not so rolling. Spring-water is rarely found; but there are many large rivers, together with their head streams, which flow through this tract. As a general thing, the soil would be considered too light and sandy for profitable cultivation. The traveler will observe that the hickory timber has entirely disappeared, and the few trees which he will find "are mostly the black-jack, elm, cottonwood, ash, and willow." This region, however, is said to possess some attractions for the tourist.

It has been thus described: "Here the finest patches of buffalo grass intermingle with stinted meads of tall grass, and beds of pale-green moss, long and slender; which, with the oxlip, blue and white violet, and, near the streams, a sensitive plant of yellow-cup dotted with jet, and many another of the floral sisterhood, fragile and aromatic as the field-flowers of the Atlantic, all blooming in the lively green of the vernal season, form a mosaic, as agreeably contrasted as any garden of art."

Further to the westward is a region which possesses considerable interest, and affords some advantages for keeping flocks and herds. It is not a belt of country stretching like the other two across the territory, but consists rather of long reaches of fertile and well-watered land, lying upon the banks of the tributaries of the Arkansas River, and of the Smoky Hill Fork of the Kansas. The valleys of these streams are much depressed below the level of the surrounding and intervening plains. The river bluffs often sweep away from the banks in semicircular walls, to a distance of three and four miles, inclosing narrow sections of fertile bottom-lands, covered with vegetable mold to the depth of many feet. These are studded with groves of willow and cottonwood, and sometimes of ash, and, along the Arkansas, but rarely, groups of oak, and mezquit. These alluvial lands are highly productive; but the plains are supposed to be worthless for cultivation, though finely adapted to pasturage, being covered with the buffalo grass, "which has been described" as "a soft, slender, and very nutritious blade, seven inches high when in perfection, but nearly every where so cropped down by herds of buffalo and antelope as to look like a lawn over which the scythe has lately passed."

Beyond this is the vast tract known as the American Desert, extending from Nebraska through Kansas into

Texas and New Mexico. There are no small streams, and but few rivers, flowing through this desolate region. The surface is almost a dead, uniform level, sweeping in every direction to the horizon, and is composed of a heavy gray and yellow clay, destitute of rocks and stone, with not a single tree, only here and there a grease-bush, or knob of cactus, and a few juiceless blades of bitter, unpalatable grass. The desert terminates to the westward in a range of hills composed of marl and limestone, which rise abruptly from the plain, and have precipitous sides and flat tops. This narrow belt of hill-country is known as the range of "*buttes.*"

From the desert-hills to the Rocky Mountains is a beautiful, fertile country, resembling, in many respects, eastern Kansas, but more broken, with an abundance of timber, and innumerable rivulets. The soil is rich and warm. The country is filled with sheltered valleys. The scenery is represented as exceedingly beautiful and various—a mixture of mountains, valleys, streams, waterfalls, natural meadows, and groves of cedar, walnut, and oak. But few persons have visited that distant region, and little is known concerning it, except this, that all agree in saying that it is very attractive, and appears to possess a good soil, with plenty of wood-land, and a mild, salubrious climate.

Probably the choicest lands, and the most easily accessible, within the borders of Kansas, are those which lie along the river from which the territory has taken its name. Mr. Greene, in his interesting book on the Kansas Region, gives the following description of the river: "The Kansas River at its delta is six hundred yards wide; and, for the first hundred miles above, its average width is nearly the same; from Pottawatomie to Big Blue it is four hundred yards; and, from that to Fort Riley, two hundred yards. This river is turbid like the lower Mississippi. For one hundred and twenty-five miles from the mouth, it is quite straight—above that it is crooked as the mad Missouri; but the current is less rapid, there are fewer snags, the banks are firmer, and not so often cut away for new channels. It is a good navigable stream, for three months in the year, and in very wet seasons, for as many as five months. Ascending fifteen miles, to the entrance of Delaware creek, the river is bordered with wood-land and prairie; and from thence to Fort Riley, both banks are heavily timbered, with here and there a high bottom of dry, rich alluvion. Along every few miles of this region, fine arable bluffs project boldly into, or swell out gently from the rippling waters that float dreamily by, or glide on with arrowy sweep. On the north side there is a mound of remarkable beauty; from the western curve of which a brook, poetically named The Stranger, pours in its pellucid tribute; and immediately above, there is a great horseshoe bend, where a tract of excellent bottom-land, high and dry, might, with much saving of labor, be inclosed by a fence of a few rods across the neck. Opposite, there is a gradually-rising grass-plat, ornamented with groups of trees, and rolling up into a bold and broad prairie. Still passing up the Kansas, from the foot of a low bluff on the north, Sugar creek comes in, under spread of a grape thicket of several thousand acres, alternated with a rich walnut bottom. Near by, an abundance of coal is found; and an undulating eminence, diversified with grove and prairie, affords an eligible site for a flourishing city. On the south, the Wakaroosa flows in, near the western limit of the Shawnee Reserve. The Wakaroosa, like most other western streams, is in some places deeply indented, clearing its banks canal-like, and revealing a fat, black loam, five feet in depth. Studding the banks of the rivulets, and in clumps on the prairie, are several varieties of plum, wild cherry, the delicious pawpaw, persimmon, hazel-nut, and hickory, white and black walnut, coffee-bean, butternut, gooseberry, haw, and, of all nuts, the unapproachable pecan. The soil is well adapted to the culture of the apple, peach, pear, and currant, and produces exuberant crops of wheat, hemp, corn, buckwheat, oats, rye, potatoes, tobacco, and all the vegetables of the eastern states. Proceeding up the Kansas, the next region of mark is that adjacent to Grasshopper creek. Here is a bluff of more than ordinary beauty, commanding a wide and pleasant prospect. From this to Mud creek, a prairie-bottom spreads out its lap of natural treasures, alluring the industrious emigrant to pause and make himself a home. At the Hundred Mile Point, on the north side, rises a lofty, handsome bluff, like an island, from out a sea of timber; its summit decorated with inwoven foliage of the oak and walnut; while afar, the thick rolls of prairie surge off to the horizon, with its narrow curtain of haze separating the bright-green from the brighter blue. Along the left bank, the prairie dips smooth and velvety to the river's rim. Pursuing the westward route, there is a rapid alternation of meadow and grove, affording the largest facilities for farming. Next we have Uniontown, a village of log cabins, a mile to the south of the river. Twenty-five miles above, the Vermilion River disgorges; with its umbrageous binding of timber, like a dark serpent, trailing out to the north. This stream is marked with many available mill-sites. And, in fact, it is upon the northern tributaries of the Kansas, deeply indented, and of descending volume, that the most frequent and valuable water-power of the territory is to be found; a short distance above, the Big Blue pours in its affluence of waters from the hills of Nebraska. From this point, the southern acclivity of the Kansas Valley presses against the channel every four or five miles, inlocking intervals of enticing loveliness, and snug little coves for tranquil neighborhoods; while on the northern bank, there is a continuous bottom, five miles broad, stretching down-stream for fifty miles; not so extensive, but in richness rivaling the American Bottom south of St. Louis, and more elevated and healthier, blessed with a salubrious atmosphere, and not subject, like that, to inundation. Immediately west of the Blue, a fine prairie slopes northward further than the eye can follow; and a lawn of several thousand acres is inclosed by a river-bend, with an isthmus of about a half a mile. While from an adjacent bluff, ledges of building-stone crop out."

The valley of the Grand River—a branch of the Arkansas—possesses a great many attractions for agriculturists. Commencing south of Fort Riley, the valley extends south-easterly, almost to the boundary of the territory. Indeed, the advantages offered to the emigrant in the regions upon the Grand and Osage rivers are fully equal to any in Kansas. The country is beautifully rolling, and inclines greatly toward the south. In addition to the richness and depth of the soil, every acre of land is suitable for cultivation, being entirely free from swamps and bluffs. The timber is the best and most abundant in the territory, consisting of a large growth of hickory, oak, elm, sycamore, mulberry, and sassafras, with numerous groves of maple, and here and there a clump of beeches. In both valleys there are quarries of excellent limestone, and apparently inexhaustible. Bituminous coal has been found in several localities, leading to the supposition that a coal-field underlies all that part of the territory. The valley of the Grand River is well known for its numerous springs of pure and sparkling water—wells have to be sunk only some twelve feet to obtain an unfailing supply. In the vicinity of Council Grove, and, indeed, in most parts of Kansas, the soil rests upon a regular substratum of hard pan, and is thus enabled to retain a supply of moisture for the nourishment of crops in the severest droughts. The clay is very compact, and dries readily into *adobe,* or sun-made brick,. such as is commonly used in Mexican structures. Council Grove takes its name from a grove, or forest rather, three miles in width and fifteen miles long, consisting, in most part, of gigantic walnuts, hickories, and oaks. And there, in 1825, a treaty was ratified between the United States and the Indians, granting a right of way from Missouri to Texas. And in the early Santa Fé trade, it was customary for parties to assemble at the grove, and organize their caravans, by appointing officers, and adopting a code of laws. From thence to Santa Fé, timber is not to be had, and caravans always carried a sufficient quantity with them for repairs. For that purpose, logs were lashed underneath the wagons, and sometimes were carried to Santa Fé and back again. On the road, further westward, the undulations of the land gradually subside into one uniform level, known as the Grand Prairie, which is of an average width of five hundred miles; and at the base of the Rocky Mountains, that prairie is said to be a thousand miles wide. The Grand Prairie is the great buffalo pasture of the West. As Mr. Green says: "The commercial value to Kansas of the prairie cattle, may be inferred from the simple statement of the item, that one hundred thousand buffalo rugs are now exported annually."

The Santa Fé road strikes the Arkansas at the Big Bend. The river is there about a quarter of a mile broad The Upper Arkansas has been thus described: "From the adjacent hights the ledges of wave-like yellow sand, along the southern bank, look like wind-driven piles of wheat, beneath which, through a low and wide trench, the majestic waters sweep placid as 'the river of a dream.' *Rio Napesté*, as the Mexicans name it, will probably measure two thousand miles in length from its sources to the frontiers of Arkansas. The channel is wide and shallow, with banks in many places not five feet above low-water-mark. It varies from a quarter to three-quarters of a mile in width, and at certain points can be forded, except in time of freshet; but care is requisite to avoid quicksands; and the current has a velocity and coolness that would not be anticipated from the smoothness of the surface." It has been suggested, that, without very great expense, the Arkansas might be made navigable for small steamboats, to the mountains. If so, it would furnish an immense channel of inland communication for the rising territory. One of its branches, the Grand River, is navigable to as great a distance as the Hudson. With the seat of empire steadily removing westward, the time may come when steam navigation on the Arkansas shall reach from the Mississippi to the Rocky Mountains, a distance twice the length of the Ohio River.

Beyond Walnut creek, a tributary of the Arkansas, at the head of a prairie-slope, which rises from the very edge of the water, stands the Pawnee Rock, five miles from the river, celebrated in Indian story, overlooking a boundless expanse of country—its front and sides of highly ferruginous sandstone, covered over with the names and memorials of prairie voyagers. The atmosphere is dry. There are no marshes in the valley of the river, and no fogs arising from the stream. The *mirage* is astonishing, and ofttimes ludicrous enough. A facetious traveler, having encamped at the foot of the rock, "saw the elephant" himself, and thus describes it: "Our party were amused with a series of these grotesque transformations on the part of a buffalo, intent upon having a drink from the Arkansas. As the staid fellow unwittingly plodded along, his hump shot into a pyramid; then jauntily cocking it one side, like the beaver of a lop-eared dandy, and descending a knowl, he turned a flip-flap somerset, swallowed himself, and came out a very elegant giraffe, which shortly settled into a brown and shapeless heap; and in another second, reassumed its ancient buffalonian aspect, only to undergo momentary changes as ludicrous as before."

The Upper Arkansas Valley is said to possess a warm, quick soil, composed of vegetable mold, rather sandy, adapted to gardening, and capable of yielding support to a pastoral community. The waters of this region are frequented by the American crane—a very large bird—twice the size of the eagle. This crane is represented as "superbly white," except the tips of the wings, which are raven-black. The frogs of the Arkansas attain to an enormous size, and mingle their hoarse croaking with the doleful howling of the wolves. The atmosphere is peculiarly sweet and wholesome, and those who have breathed it pronounce it astonishingly invigorating.

The following table of distances may be useful to those who design looking in the southern part of Kansas for locations. It commences from Independence City, in Missouri, because that is, or was, the old frontier town, the port for fitting out for the wilderness and Santa Fé. The route lies through some of the most delightful regions of Kansas, on the head-waters of the Osage and Grand rivers, where settlements are springing up and growing with unexampled rapidity.

Independence City to—	Miles.	Aggregate.
Kansas boundary, ...	22	22
Love Elm, ...	7	29
Round Grove, ...	6	35
The Narrows, ...	30	65
Black Jack, ...	3	68
One-hundred-and-ten-mile Creek, .	32	100
(Council City,) Switzler's Creek, .	9	109
Dragoon Creek, ...	5	114
(Council Grove,) Big John Spring,	35	149
Kansas Village, ...	1	150
Sylvan Camp, ...	2	152
Willow Spring, ...	6	158
Diamond Spring, ...	13	171
Lost Spring, ...	16	187
Cottonwood Fork of Grand River, .	12	199
Turkey Creek, ...	29	228
Mud Creek, ...	19	247
Little Arkansas, ...	3	250
Cow Creek, ...	20	270
Plum Buttes, ...	14	284
Great Bend of the Arkansas, . .	2	286
Walnut Creek, ...	7	293
Pawnee Rock, ...	14	307

The Santa Fé trade is quite an item in estimating the advantages which Kansas offers to the enterprising settler. The following statement, compiled by Mr. Greene, will show the development of that trade:

"The growth and fluctuations of business, from 1822 to this period, may be inferred from this condensed statement; which, if not entirely accurate, is sufficiently so for our purpose, having been derived from the best authorities, and conversations with intelligent gentlemen in the trade.

"In 1822, fifteen thousand dollars' worth of merchandise were transported, pack animals solely being used; and fifteen men were employed besides the sixty interested proprietors. In 1824, twenty-six wagons, in addition to the beasts of burden, were brought into service; and twenty-five thousand dollars' worth of goods were carried over. In 1826, our exports equaled one hundred thousand dollars; there were seventy proprietors, and one hundred men employed. Thenceforth, wagons only were used. In 1828, there were one hundred and fifty thousand dollars' worth of merchandise transported; there were one hundred wagons in requisition; eighty proprietors engaged; giving employment to two hundred men. In the year 1830, oxen were first used; which have never been brought into successful competition with mules. In 1831, the transports were to the amount of two hundred and fifty thousand dollars; there were eighty owners; one hundred and twenty-five wagons; and three hundred men. In 1832, one hundred and fifty thousand dollars; seventy wagons; one hundred and fifty men; and forty owners. In 1839, two hundred and fifty thousand dollars; one hundred and twenty-five wagons; two hundred and fifty men; and forty proprietors. And in 1843, the transports amounted to half a million of dollars; there were two hundred and fifty wagons, and four hundred men employed; while the proprietorship had dwindled into the hands of thirty capitalists. The reopening of the next year tempted fewer owners into the field; yet our aggregate of exports amounted to two hundred thousand dollars; in the conveyance of which, one hundred wagons and two hundred men were employed. For ten years antecedent, a heavy proportion of all merchandise had been carried by Missouri freighters, from Independence to Santa Fé, at rates varying from ten to twelve cents a pound; as late as 1850, the price was nine cents.

"Of course, the statement of value of goods are at United States costs. In the earliest history of the traffic, the advanced price of sales was immensely more; but from 1830 to 1843 witnessed considerable diminution; the rates at the latter period scarcely averaging one hundred per cent. over original costs—calicoes selling at from twenty-five to fifty cents, that had, in 1825, commanded two and three dollars.

"Since our war with Mexico, and its consequent revolution, entrance to the ports is unimpeded by the oppressive *arancel* formerly interposed by the Mexican executive; and as a consequence, I am informed by Mr. Aubrey and other reliable gentlemen, that, from 1850 to the present date, our annual exports range from two to three million of dollars; much of which has been freighted into Chihuahua, at charges varying from six to eight cents a pound.

"The big prices have gone down, yet the palmy days of the Santa Fé trade are not ended. Its story in the future can not be so romantic, for the hazardous element is disappearing, and the interests merged are gradually equalizing, as the route to be traversed is shortened, and the supply and demand are more accurately fitting into each other. In after time, its records will be rather statistical than biographical, and more magnificent with wealth achieved, than lustrous with heraldry of high-hearted men.

"That town of Kansas will be fortunate which shall be destined as the *entrepôt* of this prairie commerce; and trebly fortunate will it be, if it converge other interests, and become the emporium of all the traffic with the plains and distant mountains; and the outfitting mart and place of transhipment for the trappers who range the vast region beyond." U

In the southern part of Kansas, in the region of the Cimarron River, iron, lead, copper, and silver ores, have been found, sufficiently rich to make mining profitable when the country shall have become inhabited. There are many indications of the existence of an immense bed of salt; the smaller streams soon become strongly impregnated, and numerous springs boil up in brine, within pot-shaped fountains formed of calcareous and saline concretions. In some places, the prairie is covered with crystallized salt, white as a marble floor. "This salt-plain is near the mouth of the Cimarron, and extends for miles without the slightest irregularity of surface, being so low and level that the bordering streams sometimes overflow it." Adjacent to this saline tract, the river-bluffs are largely composed of gypsum.

Settlements are progressing rapidly throughout eastern Kansas. Emigrants are flocking thither from all parts of the United States. Villages are springing up as if by magic. Lawrence is located in a most delightful region, and so strong is the tide flowing into that vicinity, that, it is said, claims have been taken up in every direction for fifteen miles. Pawnee is situated about a mile below the junction of the Republican and Chetolah rivers. Many of the buildings are of stone. Claims have been taken up on Clark's creek for six or seven miles; on the Republican Fork, near ten miles; and on the Chetolah, or Smoky Hill Fork, over fourteen miles. Kenilworth is destined to be a manufacturing village. A company is engaged in constructing mills at this place, which is situated on the east bank of the Republican Fork, fifteen miles above its mouth. The soil is equal to that of Illinois. The country is watered by numerous springs, and forests of good timber are in the immediate vicinity. Topeka is situated on the Kansas River, below Pawnee. It is settled chiefly by Pennsylvanians. Bituminous coal has been found, of the best quality, within two miles of this thriving settlement. On Sugar creek, some fifty miles south of Council City, is a settlement of anti-slavery Missourians. Rock City, on the military road, ninety miles west of the Missouri River, is situated in a region of heavy timber. It is impossible to enumerate the settlements of Kansas, or to give their respective populations; for, where yesterday the silence of nature brooded over the prairie, to-day the hammer of the builder is heard, and the voices of civilization.

The lands of Kansas have not been surveyed, and will not be for some years. All the settlers, therefore, are "squatters." Now, squatting is an American "institution," indispensable to the growth of the West, working wonders in the way of transforming the wilderness into cultivated fields. Squatting, although lawless, has regulations of its own; it has been reduced into system; and "claims" are not only respected but protected. In August, 1854, the Mutual Settlers' Association of Kansas Territory agreed to the following laws for the recognition of land-claims, viz.:

"1. Recognizing the right of every citizen to a claim of two hundred and forty acres, eighty of timber, and one hundred and sixty of prairie-land; the claim to be secured by improvement and residence, which must commence within sixty days from the entry of the claim, on either the prairie or timber-land, which is to secure the claim to both.

"2. Single persons and females allowed to secure their claims by residing in the territory, without residing on their claims. Persons allowed a day additional to the time provided above for every five miles they may have to travel to reach their families.

"3. No person to hold, directly or indirectly, more than one claim.

"4. No person allowed to enter any previously marked claim.

"5. Persons neglecting to improve within the specified time, to forfeit their claims, which can then be taken up by any other citizen.

"6. Any person to point out the extent of his claim whenever another may wish to ascertain it.

"7. Claimant to make oath that his claim does not infringe on that of any other person.

"8. Form of application for registry to describe the claim, and date of its selection.

"9. On the survey of the territory, the settlers to deed and redeed to each other, so as to secure to each the amount of land specified as the amount of claim.

"10 to 13, inclusive, provide for the appointment of a chief justice, a register, and marshal, and a treasurer, and define their duties.

"14. The limits of the association to be the waters of the Wakaroosa and Kansas rivers, and the territory between the same, from the mouth of the Wakaroosa up to the Shawnee purchase.

"15 to 21 provide for the election and removal of officers by a majority of members, and other incidental regulations."

And such is presumed to be the method of securing a recognition of land-claims throughout the territory.

The aboriginal Indians, with the exception of the Pawnees, are still in possession of the central and western districts of Kansas. The Pawnees, once the most powerful of the prairie tribes, have been reduced by war and disease to utter insignificance as to numbers, wealth, and valor. Twenty-five years ago, the small-pox swept away one-half their numbers; and, since that time, other tribes, once held in subjection, becoming relatively stronger, have been wiping out the remembrance of traditional wrongs. The Pawnees were located, for a time, north of the Nebraska River, and west of the Missouri—the feeble remnant of a nation that, fifty years ago, spread terror from the sources of the Missouri to the mountains of Mexico; but becoming disheartened under the attacks of the Blackfeet and Sioux, the Pawnees have again migrated south, near the Ottoes and Omahas, and exist in a most wretched condition.

The Arapahoes roam over the western part of Kansas. They profess to be friendly to the whites; but the safer policy is to give them a wide berth. The Cheyennes are in alliance with the Arapahoes, professing friendship, but treacherous to a proverb. These tribes have control of the Grand Prairie; and they are said to hold there, what in Europe would be called, "the balance of power." These tribes are known to be very numerous—for it is quite common to stumble upon three or four thousand of them, collected in a single hunting-camp. The other aboriginal tribes are the Osages, Kansas, and Arkansas, numbering about nine thousand. The hunting-grounds of the Kansas lie around the confluence of the Smoky Hill and Republican Forks. "The name of this tribe is variously spelled—Kanzas, Kansas, Cansas, Konzas, and Consas—and, to cap all with absurdity, they scarcely know themselves by any other word than Kaws." Since we have "Hoosiers," and "Suckers," and "Pukes," in the older states, it may be questioned whether we shall not have "Kaws" in Kansas.

The whole Indian population of the territory has been estimated at twenty-five thousand. The Kickapoos, Wyandots, Sacs and Foxes, Munsers, Weas, Piankashaws, Peorias, Kaskaskias, Pottawatomies, Chippewas, Delawares, and Shawnees have reservations in Kansas. But those who are instructed in these matters say, that a person may safely squat where it pleases him best; that if he should intrude upon an Indian reservation, a small fee of ten dollars will propitiate the owning tribe. The lands of the territory can not, probably, be brought into market under three or four years; and when it shall be exposed for sale, the squatter is entitled to the first bid. And whenever a stranger trespasses upon a regular claim, an arrow, placed over the cabin door, will signify to the intruder that "first right" must be respected.

Fort Riley stands near the confluence of the Smoky Hill and Republican Forks, at the head of the Kansas River. This fort was built in 1854, for the purpose of holding the Indians more completely in check, and furthering intercourse between frontier posts. It is said to be a handsome pile of buildings, constructed of limestone taken from the neighboring bluffs. The following table will show the probable distances, by the river route, from Fort Riley to the Missouri border:

	Miles.	Aggregate.
Fort Riley to —		
Wild Cat,	12	12
Big Blue,	7	19
Sargent's Creek,	3	22
Rock Creek,	14	36
Vermilion,	4	40
Lost Creek,	5	45
Catholic Mission,	7	52
Soldier Creek,	20	72
Grasshopper Creek,	20	92
Hickory Point,	10	102
Stranger Creek,	12	114
Salt Creek,	9	123
Missouri State Line,	4	127

Congress, in 1855, made two appropriations for military roads in Kansas—one of fifty thousand dollars, for the construction of a road from Fort Riley to such point on the Arkansas River as may, in the opinion of the secretary of war, be most expedient for military purposes; and the further sum of fifty thousand dollars for the construction of a road from Fort Riley to Bridger's Pass, in the Rocky Mountains.

The climate of Kansas is very nearly that of Virginia; but it is less sultry. In the warmest days, a gentle breeze is blowing from the mountains. Spring is attended with much rain from March till June. The rivers become swollen; the roads miry—but not hub-deep, as in Indiana. It is supposed that plank-roads will never be needed in Kansas, for the soil does not soften into mud. Vegetation is early and exuberant. Plowing commences in January. December is frequently warm enough for shirt-sleeves and calico. But there are also terribly bleak days, when the north wind sweeps like a scythe across the prairies. The average depth of snow is said not to exceed three inches. The weather during the months of August, September, and October, is dry; and the Indian summer lingers far into the season of winter. It is claimed for Kansas, that the climate is "decidedly superior to that of Wisconsin, Iowa, and Michigan." The western plains are noted for the frequent and terrific thunder-storms that sweep over them. The lands of Kansas lie high and dry, far above the swamps and fogs of the Mississippi Valley. One great blessing which the settlers of this new territory will enjoy over those in other parts is graphically described by an old squatter, thus: "'sketers is scuss." It would seem that the tiny insects dry up and blow away. The salubrity of the climate is unquestionable.

Nebraska is divided into nine counties, viz.: Douglass, Ottoe, Richardson, Dodge, Dacotah, Burt, Cass, Nemaha, and Washington. The whole white population numbers about six thousand souls. Nebraska has a less quantity of valuable timbered land than Kansas. The south-western part is said to resemble the prairies and openings of Iowa, and to possess a deep and fertile soil. The eastern boundary is formed by the Missouri River for about twelve hundred miles. The Platte River is the principal stream in the southern part of the territory. There are groves of timber on the banks of the Platte, and the bottom-lands are represented as strong, and capable of sustaining a long succession of crops. The soil is found to have a limestone basis. It is reported that coal has been discovered in the territory, and other minerals; but it is certain that Nebraska will become an agricultural region. The climate is warmer than in the same latitude east of the lakes. Owing to the vast extent of prairie surface, the changes of temperature are very sudden and very great; and the winds from the north and west have a wide sweep over the plains. "Squatter law" prevails there as well as in Kansas; and the "general principles" are the same as those recognized in the neighboring territory.

Congress has appropriated fifty thousand dollars for the purpose of constructing a territorial road from opposite Council Bluffs to New Fort Kearney, which, when completed, will greatly facilitate settlements in Nebraska. Also, Congress has appropriated thirty thousand dollars for the construction of a military road from the Great Falls of the Missouri River, to intersect the military road from Walla Walla to Puget's Sound; which will open a safe thoroughfare for emigrants through central and north-western Nebraska.

CHAPTER XIX.

KANSAS—ITS HISTORY AND POLITICS.

THE extensive region included within the territories of Kansas and Nebraska was annexed to the United States, by virtue of a treaty with France, concluded at Paris, on the thirtieth day of April, 1803. It formed a portion of the vast tract of country known as the "Louisiana Purchase." That purchase embraced all the lands within the limits of the following states and territories, viz.: Louisiana, Arkansas, Missouri, and Iowa; Indian Territory, Kansas, Nebraska, and Minesota, west of the Mississippi River.

In December, 1818, the legislature of Missouri Territory petitioned Congress for admission into the Union as an independent state. A bill, embodying the views of the petitioners, having been accordingly framed, on the nineteenth day of February following, an amendment, prohibiting the further introduction of slavery, or involuntary servitude, was adopted by a vote of eighty-seven to seventy-six, in the House of Representatives. Also, on the fifteenth day of March, another amendment, providing that all children born within said state after its admission should be free at the age of twenty-five years, was adopted in the House, by a vote of seventy-nine to sixty-seven. The Senate of the United States, however, refused to concur in these two amendments, and the House, insisting upon them, the bill did not pass at that session. But during the next session of Congress, when the Missouri bill came again under consideration, in order to free the measure from the embarrassment resulting from the disagreement of the two houses, a compromise was effected, by which Missouri was to be admitted as a slave state, without any restriction or limitation whatever, as to the existence of slavery, on the express condition, that slavery should be forever prohibited in all the territory of the United States north of the line of thirty-six degrees and thirty minutes north latitude. For that purpose, both houses concurred in an amendment to the bill, by which it was enacted, "That in all that territory ceded by France to the United States under the name of Louisiana, which lies north of thirty-six degrees and thirty minutes north latitude, excepting only such part thereof as is included within the limits of the state contemplated by this act, slavery and involuntary servitude, otherwise than in the punishment of crimes, whereof the party shall have been duly convicted, shall be, and is hereby forever prohibited; provided always, that any person escaping into the same, from whom labor or service is lawfully claimed in any state or territory of the United States, such fugitive may be lawfully reclaimed, and conveyed to the person claiming his or her labor or service as aforesaid." After the incorporation of that amendment, the bill admitting Missouri into the Union was passed early in March, 1820. That amendment constituted the celebrated compromise of 1820.

The principle of that compromise has twice been solemnly recognized and reaffirmed. First, upon the admission of Texas, in 1845, the joint resolution of March the first provides that such states as may be formed out of that portion of the territory of Texas which lies south of thirty-six degrees and thirty minutes north latitude, commonly known as the Missouri Compromise Line, shall be admitted, with or without slavery, as the people of each state asking admission may desire; and in states formed north of that line, slavery shall be prohibited. And second, in 1848, when the admission of Oregon was under consideration, Mr. Douglass, in the Senate, moved an amendment, by which the Missouri Compromise Line was extended to the Pacific Ocean; but as the House of Representatives did not concur in the amendment, the Senate receded, and substituted a clause prohibiting slavery.

Other measures, also, of the federal government, running through a period of more than thirty years, have in some instances sanctioned that compromise; in others, recognized it as binding and obligatory upon the government and people. The principle of sustaining that compromise is embraced in the following solemn compacts among the people of the United States:

1st. The admission of Missouri as a slave state.

2d. The admission of Texas into the Union.

3d. The organization of the Territory of Oregon.

4th. The establishment of the Texan boundary.

5th. The organization of the Territory of New Mexico.

6th. The organization of the Territory of Utah.

7th. The admission of California.

8th. The fugitive slave act.

9th. The suppression of the slave-trade in the District of Columbia.

Yet, notwithstanding the course of federal legislation for thirty years, the act providing a territorial organization for the territories of Kansas and Nebraska, approved the twenty-seventh day of May, 1854, repeals the restriction upon the existence of slavery north of the line of thirty-six degrees and thirty minutes north latitude, and leaves the character of the institutions of the states in contemplation there, with respect of freedom or slavery, to be determined by a contest upon the soil. From thence have followed a most terrible excitement throughout the entire Union, and all the scenes of anarchy and blood that have been enacted within those territories. For the question, once supposed to have been finally disposed of, is made again an open question to be settled by political and by physical force, whether the new states shall be free states or slave states. Every inhabitant of those territories has a direct personal interest, and every citizen of the United States a political interest, in the settlement of that vexed question. As the controversy has now got to be decided within the territories themselves, the advocates and the enemies of slavery are alike hastening thither to secure the necessary majorities, to sanction or to prohibit the existence of slavery.

Hon. A. H. Reeder, of Pennsylvania, was appointed Governor of Kansas Territory; and Daniel Woodson, of Arkansas, secretary. The first election of delegate to Congress was fixed to take place on the twenty-ninth day of November, 1854. Governor Reeder had appointed election judges, and had instructed them to administer the oaths to every person suspected of residing in another state or territory. It would seem to have been determined upon by a large number of persons, inhabitants of the State of Missouri, to vote at the approaching Kansas election. A few days before the polls were to be opened, a great crowd assembled at St. Joseph, in Missouri, and were addressed by General Stringfellow, with reference to the election soon to be held in the adjacent territory. In the course of that speech, he said: "I tell you to mark every scoundrel among you that is the least tainted with free-soilism, and exterminate him. Neither give nor take quarter from the d—d rascals. To those who have qualms of conscience, as to violating laws—state or national — the time has come when such impositions must be disregarded; and I advise you, one and all, to enter every election district in Kansas, in defiance of Reeder and his vile myrmidons, and vote at the point of the bowie-knife and revolver. What right has Governor Reeder to rule Missourians in Kansas? His proclamation and prescribed oath must be repudiated."

Similar gatherings took place at other points within the Missouri border. On the day of the election, the Missourians, having crossed over into Kansas, forcibly took possession of the polls in several election districts, and deposited their votes in such numbers as they pleased. In reference to those transactions, the people of Kansas in their representation, say: "The first ballot-box that was opened upon our soil was closed to us by overpowering numbers and impending force. So bold and reckless were our invaders, that they cared not to conceal their attack. They came upon us, not in the guise of voters, to steal away our franchise, but openly, to snatch it with a strong hand. They came directly from their own homes, and in compact and organized bands, with arms in hand, and provisions for the expedition, marched to our polls; and when the work was done, returned whence they came. It is enough to say, that in three districts — in which, by the most irrefragable evidence, there were not one hundred and fifty voters, most of whom refused to participate in the mockery of the elective franchise — these invaders polled over a thousand votes." It is alleged that, in consequence of this violation of the elective franchise, Whitfield was elected over his competitors, as the delegate for Kansas to the Congress of the United States.

In the spring following, on the thirteenth day of March, at the election of members of the territorial legislature,

Kansas was again invaded by persons foreign to its territory, and similar scenes were reënacted on a grander scale of violence and outrage. Concerning the proceedings of the Missourians on the day of that election, the people of Kansas, in their representation, make the following statement: "They (the Missourians) arrived at their several destinations the night before the election, and having pitched their camps, and placed their sentries, waited for the coming day. Baggage wagons were there, with arms and ammunition enough for a protracted fight, and among them two brass field-pieces, ready charged. They came with drums beating, and flags flying, and their leaders were of the most prominent and conspicuous men of their respective states. In the morning, they surrounded the polls, armed with guns, bowie-knives, and revolvers, and declared their determination to vote at all hazards, and in spite of all consequences. If the judges could be made to subserve their purposes, and receive their votes, and if no obstacle was cast in their way, their leaders exerted themselves to preserve peace and order in the conduct of the election; but, at the same time, did not hesitate to declare that, if not allowed to vote, they would proceed to any extremity in destruction of property and life. If the control of the polls could not be had otherwise, the judges were, by intimidation, and, if necessary, by violence, prevented from performing their duty, or, if unyielding in this respect, were driven from their post, and the vacancy filled in form by the persons on the ground; and whenever, by any means, they had obtained the control of the board, the foreign vote was promiscuously poured in, without discrimination or reserve, or the slightest care to conceal its nefarious illegality. At one of the polls, two of the judges having stood up in the face of an armed mob, and declared they would do their duty, one portion of the mob commenced to tear down the house, another proceeded to break in the door of the judge's room, while others, with drawn knives, posted themselves at the window, with the proclaimed purpose of killing any voter who would allow himself to be sworn Voters were dragged from the window, because they would not show their tickets, or vote at the dictation of the mob; and the invaders declared openly, at the polls, that they would cut the throats of the judges, if they did not receive their votes without requiring an oath as to their residence. The room was finally forced, and the judges, surrounded by an armed and excited crowd, were offered the alternative of resignation or death, and five minutes were allowed for their decision. The ballot-box was seized, and, amid shouts of 'hurrah for Missouri,' was carried into the mob. The two menaced judges then left the ground, together with all the resident citizens, except a few who acted in the outrage, because the result expected from it corresponded to their own views

"When an excess of the foreign force was found to be had at one poll, detachments were sent to the others. . . . . A minister of the gospel, who refused to accede to the demands of a similar mob of some four hundred armed and organized men, was driven by violence from his post, and the vacancy filled by themselves. . . . . Another clergyman, for the expression of his opinion, was assaulted and beaten. . . . . The inhabitants of the district — powerless to resist the abundant supply of arms and ammunition, organized preparation, and overwhelming numbers of the foreigners — left the polls without voting. . . . . In the Lawrence district, one voter was fired at, as he was driven from the election ground. . . . . Finding they had a greater force than was necessary for that poll, some two hundred men were drafted from the number, and sent off, under the proper officers, to another district; after which they still polled from this camp seven hundred votes. . . . . In the fourth and seventh districts, the invaders came together in an armed and organized body, with trains of fifty wagons, besides horsemen; and the night before election, pitched their camps in the vicinity of the polls; and having appointed their own judges, in place of those who, from intimidation or otherwise, failed to attend, they voted without any proof of residence. In these two election districts, where the census shows one hundred voters, there were polled three hundred and fourteen votes; and last fall, seven hundred and sixty-five votes, although a large part of the actual residents did not vote on either occasion. . . . . From a careful examination of the returns, we are satisfied that over three thousand votes were thus cast by the citizens and residents of the states."

A legislature, so elected, was altogether pro-slavery, and no more represented the people of Kansas than it did the man in the moon. Some of its members were not, at the time of its assembling, in July, and never had been, residents of the territory, but were living in the State of Missouri, while legislating for Kansas. One of the acts of the legislature provides a very cheap method of obtaining the right to vote at any election in the territory, without requiring a residence within its borders for a single day. It opens the ballot-boxes for a dollar a head to all citizens from Maine to California, no matter where they may reside. The enactment is as follows: "That every free white male above the age of twenty-one years, who shall pay to the proper officer in Kansas Territory the sum of one dollar as a poll-tax, and shall produce to the judges of any election within and for the territory of Kansas, a receipt showing the paying of said poll-tax, shall be deemed a legal voter, and shall be entitled to vote at any election in said territory during the year for which the same shall have been paid." This is the first time the elective franchise has ever been put up for sale within the United States.

That legislature then proceeded to a wholesale and an indiscriminate adoption of the statute laws of Missouri; and then, to conceal the evidences of indecent haste, subsequently enacted that wherever the word "state" occurred in those statutes, the word "territory" should be substituted.

The following statutes were also passed, for the protection of slave property, which are here inserted in full for the benefit of those who design settling in Kansas:

AN ACT TO PUNISH OFFENSES AGAINST SLAVE PROPERTY.

§ 1. *Be it enacted by the Governor and Legislative Assembly of the Territory of Kansas,* That every person, bond or free, who shall be convicted of actually raising a rebellion or insurrection of slaves, free negroes, or mulattoes, in this territory, shall suffer death.

§ 2. Every free person who shall aid or assist in any rebellion or insurrection of slaves, free negroes, or mulattoes, or shall furnish arms, or do any overt act in furtherance of such rebellion or insurrection, shall suffer death

§ 3. If any free person shall, by speaking, writing, or printing, advise, persuade, or induce any slave to rebel, conspire against, or murder any citizen of the territory, or shall bring into, print, write, publish, or circulate, or cause to be brought into, printed, written, published or circulated, or shall knowingly aid or assist in the bringing into, printing, writing, publishing, or circulating, in this territory, any book, paper, magazine, pamphlet, or circular, for the purpose of exciting insurrection, rebellion, revolt, or conspiracy on the part of the slaves, free negroes, or mulattoes against the citizens of the territory, or any part of them, such person shall be guilty of felony, and suffer death.

§ 4. If any person shall entice, decoy, or carry away out of this territory any slave belonging to another, with the intent to deprive the owner thereof of the services of such slave, or with intent to effect or procure the freedom of such slave, he shall be adjudged guilty of grand larceny, and, on conviction thereof, shall suffer death, or be imprisoned at hard labor for not less than ten years.

§ 5. If any person aid or assist in enticing, decoying, or persuading, or carrying away, or sending out of this territory, any slave belonging to another, with intent to procure or effect the freedom of such slave, or with intent to deprive the owner thereof of the services of such slave, he shall be adjudged guilty of grand larceny, and on conviction thereof shall suffer death, or be imprisoned at hard labor for not less than ten years.

§ 6. If any person shall entice, decoy, or carry away, out of any state or other territory of the United States, any slave belonging to another, with intent to procure or effect the freedom of such slave, or to deprive the owner thereof of the services of such slave, and shall bring such slave into this territory, he shall be adjudged guilty of grand larceny, in the same manner as if such slave had been enticed, decoyed, or carried away out of this territory; and in such case the larceny may be charged to have been committed in any county of this territory, into or through which such slave shall have been brought by such person; and on conviction thereof, the person offending shall suffer death, or be imprisoned at hard labor for not less than ten years.

§ 7. If any person shall entice, persuade, or induce any slave to escape from the service of his master or owner in this territory, or shall aid or assist any slave in escap ing from the service of his master or owner, or shall assist, harbor, or conceal any slave who may have escaped from the service of his master or owner, he shall be deemed guilty of felony, and punished by imprisonment at hard labor for a term of not less than five years.

§ 8. If any person in this territory shall aid or assist, harbor or conceal, any slave who has escaped from the service of his master or owner in another state or territory, such persons shall be punished in like manner as if such slave had escaped from the service of his master or owner in this territory.

§ 9. If any person shall resist any officer while attempting to arrest any slave that may have escaped from the service of his master or owner, or shall rescue such slave when in custody of any officer or other person, or shall entice, persuade, aid, or assist such slave to escape from the custody of any officer or other person who may have such slave in custody, whether such slave may have escaped from the service of his master or owner in this territory, or in any other state or territory, the person so offending shall be guilty of felony, and punished by imprisonment at hard labor for a term of not less than two years.

§ 10. If any marshal, sheriff, or constable, or the deputy of any such officer, shall, when required by any person, refuse to aid or assist in the arrest and capture of any slave that may have escaped from the service of his master or owner, whether such slave shall have escaped from his master or owner in this territory, or any state or other territory, such officer shall be fined in a sum of not less than one hundred, or more than five hundred dollars.

§ 11. If any person print, write, introduce into, publish, or circulate, or cause to be brought into, printed, written, published, or circulated, or shall knowingly aid or assist in bringing into, printing, publishing, or circulating, within this territory, any book, paper, pamphlet, magazine, hand-bill, or circular, containing any statements, arguments, opinion, sentiment, doctrine, advice, or inuendo, calculated to produce a disorderly, dangerous, or rebellious disaffection among the slaves in this territory, or to induce such slaves to escape from the service of their masters, or to resist their authority, he shall be guilty of felony, and be punished by imprisonment at hard labor for a term not less than five years.

§ 12. If any free person, by speaking or writing, assert or maintain that persons have not the right to hold slaves in this territory, or shall introduce into this territory, print, publish, write, circulate, or cause to be introduced into this territory, written, printed, published or circulated in this territory, any book, paper, magazine, pamphlet, or circular, containing any denial of the right of persons to hold slaves in this territory, such person shall be deemed guilty of felony, and punished by imprisonment at hard labor for a term of not less than two years.

§ 13. No person who is conscientiously opposed to holding slaves, or who does not admit the right to hold slaves in this territory, shall sit as a juror on the trial of any prosecution, for any violation of any of the sections of this act.

AN ACT TO PUNISH PERSONS DECOYING SLAVES FROM THEIR MASTERS.

§1. *Be it enacted by the Governor and Legislative Assembly of Kansas Territory:* If any person shall entice, decoy, or carry away out of this territory, any slave belonging to another, with intent to deprive the owner thereof of the services of such slave, or with intent to effect or procure the freedom of such slaves, he shall be adjudged guilty of grand larceny, and on conviction thereof, shall suffer death.

§2. If any person shall aid or assist in enticing, decoying, or persuading, or carrying away, or sending out of this territory, any slave belonging to another, with intent to procure or effect the freedom of such slave, or with intent to deprive the owner thereof of the services of such slave, he shall be adjudged guilty of grand larceny, and on conviction thereof, shall suffer death.

§3. If any person shall entice, decoy, or carry away out of any state or other territory of the United States, any slave belonging to another, with intent to procure or effect the freedom of such slave, or to deprive the owner thereof of the services of such slave, and shall bring such slave into this territory, he shall be adjudged guilty of grand larceny, in the same manner as if such slave had been enticed, decoyed, or carried sway out of this territory; in such case the larceny may be charged to have been committed in any county of this territory into or through which such slave shall have been brought by such person, and, on conviction thereof, the person offending shall suffer death.

The sober and well-intended residents of the territory seem at once to have repudiated the action of the territorial legislature. They regarded it as an assemblage that had been forced upon them. They determined not to submit to the control of a body—many of whose members were non-residents, and all of whom had been elected to office by non-resident voters over the heads of voters of the territory. On the fifth day of September, 1855, a convention representing the people of Kansas was held at Big Springs, numbering in all one hundred delegates. That convention resolved to repudiate all the acts of the territorial legislature; to take no part in the election of a delegate, which that body had appointed to be held; but to appoint an election to be held one week after that one

Ex-Governor Reeder, who had been removed by the President, and Governor Shannon appointed in his place, was agreed upon as candidate for delegate. It was expected that he would be elected without much opposition; and that, as Mr. Whitfield would be again elected by the Missourians, the effect would be to bring the question of popular rights in Kansas before the House of Representatives at Washington. A committee of the House was sent, in April last, 1856, to Kansas, for the purpose of investigating the character of these elections.

Another convention, on the nineteenth day of September, assembled at Topeka, and adopted a resolution, "by the people of Kansas Territory, in delegate convention assembled," authorizing the holding of an election on the second Tuesday of October, for members of a convention to form a state constitution, preparatory to application for admission into the Union. The number of delegates was fixed at fifty-two, and the convention was authorized to be held at Topeka on the fourth Tuesday of October. The election was accordingly held at the appointed time. No non-resident was permitted to vote, and no resident who had not been such for at least thirty days. The constitutional convention assembled, and adopted a constitution for the State of Kansas, eminently republican in its character, and commending itself to the people of the territory, by whom it was ratified, and who, soon afterward, proceeded to the election of state officers to carry the new government into effect. That, in brief, is the political position of the people of Kansas, who are now awaiting the action of the federal government to recognise them as a free and independent state. Charles Robinson was elected governor.

CHAPTER XX.

AID SOCIETIES AND PREËMPTIONS.

SEVERAL societies have been organized in the eastern and middle states, to facilitate emigration to Kansas; and through them such arrangements have been made with the different railroad and steamboat lines as lessens very materially the expense of removing to those distant regions. Under these arrangements, the following tables will show the routes, distances, time, and fares, from New York to St. Louis.

From New York, viâ the New York and Erie Railroad, Lake Shore Railroad, and Chicago and Mississippi Railroad, to St. Louis; fare, twenty-eight dollars — meals and state-rooms extra.

To Dunkirk, ...	460 miles.
Thence to Toledo, ...	254 "
" Chicago, ...	243 "
" Alton, ...	290 "
" St. Louis, ...	25 "
" Kansas, ...	450 "
From New York to Kansas, . . .	1,722 miles.

From New York, viâ Hudson River Railroad, New York Central Railroad, Southern Michigan Railroad, and Chicago and Mississippi Railroad, to St. Louis; fare to St. Louis, twenty-six dollars; whole distance, 1,760 miles.

Upon the same route, but from Buffalo to Chicago by the Michigan Central Railroad, the fare is the same and distance the same.

Upon the same route, but by Hudson River steamboats, and through Canada by the Great Western Railway; fare, twenty-eight dollars; distance, 1,736 miles.

From Pittsburg to St. Louis, by steamboat — fare, generally, about ten dollars, meals and state-rooms included.

Down the Ohio River, ...	1,006 miles.
To St. Louis, ...	177 "
St. Louis to Kansas, ...	450 "
Pittsburg to Kansas, ...	1,633 miles.

Fare, from St. Louis to Kansas, from eight to ten dollars.

The average time from New York to Kansas is about twelve days.

There can be no doubt that Kansas, with its fertile soil, and genial climate, and the strong political motives just now operating to encourage settlement, will speedily fill up with inhabitants coming from all parts of the Union. None need be disappointed in their expectations. The state of the controversy respecting the existence of slavery in the territory is well known. Those who would prefer a home where politics are undisturbed by any stong element of agitation had better go into the more northern territory. Nebraska will furnish room for immigrants for many years to come.

The expense of removing to the West, and the hardships that have to be endured, are exceedingly discouraging to persons of very limited means; and, although Congress has not authorized the sale of the public lands upon credit, yet provision has been made by which the settler has allowed him a certain period, within which "to turn himself," and make his payments. The following is the preëmption act of 1841:

"§ 10. *And be it further enacted*, that from and after the passage of this act, every person, being the head of a family, or widow, or single man over the age of twenty-one years, and being a citizen of the United States, or having filed his declaration of intention to become a citizen, as required by the naturalization laws, who, since the first day of June, Anno Domini eighteen hundred and forty, has made, or shall hereafter make, a settlement, in person, on the public lands, to which the Indian title has been at the time of such settlement extinguished, and which has been, or shall have been, surveyed prior thereto, and who shall inhabit and improve the same, and who has or shall erect a dwelling-house thereon, shall be, and is hereby authorized to enter with the register of the land-office for the district in which such lands may be, by legal subdivisions, any number of acres not exceeding one hundred and sixty, or a quarter-section of land, to include the residence of such claimant, upon paying to the United States the minimum price of such land; subject, however, to the following limitations and exceptions: No person shall be entitled to more than one preëmptive right by virtue of this act; no person who is the proprietor of three hundred and twenty acres of land in any state or territory of the United States, and no person who shall quit or abandon his residence on his own land to reside on the public land in the same state or territory, shall acquire any right of preëmption under this act:

"§ 11. *And be it further enacted*, That, when two or more persons shall have settled on the same quarter-section of land, the right of preëmption shall be in him or her who made the first settlement, provided such persons shall conform to the other provisions of this act: and all question as to the right of preëmption, arising between different settlers, shall be settled by the register and receiver of the district within which the land is situated, subject to an appeal to, and a reversion by, the secretary of the treasury of the United States.

"§ 12. *And be it further enacted,* That, prior to any entries being made under and by virtue of the provisions of this act, proof of the settlement and improvement thereby acquired shall be made to the satisfaction of the register and receiver of the land district in which such lands may lie, agreeable to such rules as shall be prescribed by the secretary of the treasury, who shall each be entitled to receive fifty cents from each applicant for his service, to be rendered as aforesaid: and all assignments and transfers of the right hereby secured, prior to the issuing of the patent, shall be null and void.

"§ 13. *And be it further enacted,* That, before any person claiming the benefit of this act shall be allowed to enter such lands, he or she shall make oath, before the receiver or register of the land district in which the land is situated, who are hereby authorized to administer the same, that he or she has never had the benefit of any right of preëmption under this act: that he or she is not the owner of three hundred and twenty acres of land in any state or territory of the United States, nor hath he or she settled upon or improved said land to sell the same on speculation, but in good faith to appropriate it to his or her own exclusive use and benefit, and that he or she has not directly or indirectly made any agreement or contract, in any way or manner, with any person or persons whatsoever, by which the title, which he or she might acquire from the government of United States, should insure, in whole or in part, to the benefit of any person except himself or herself; and if any person taking such oath shall swear falsely in the premises, he or she shall be subjected to all the pains and penalties of perjury, and shall forfeit the money which he or she may have paid for said land, and all right and title to the same: and any grant or conveyance which he or she may have made, except in the hands of *bona-fide* purchasers for a valuable consideration, shall be null and void; and it shall be the duty of the officer administering such oath to file a certificate thereof in the public land-office of such district, and to transmit a duplicate copy to the General Land Office, either of which shall be good and sufficient evidence that such oath was administered according to law.

"§ 14. *And be it further enacted*, That, this act shall not delay the sale of any of the public lands of the United States, beyond the time which has been, or may be appointed by the proclamation of the President, nor shall the provisions of this act be available to any person or persons who shall fail to make the proof and payment, and file the affidavit required, before the day appointed for the commencement of the sales aforesaid.

"§ 15. *And be it further enacted*, That, whenever any person has settled or shall settle and improve a tract of land subject at the time of settlement to private entry, and shall intend to purchase the same under the provisions of this act, such person shall in the first case, within three month after passage of the same, and in the last within thirty days next after the date of each settlement, file with the register of the proper district a written statement, describing the land settled upon, and declaring the intention of such person to claim the same under the provisions of this act; and shall, where such settlement is already made, within twelve months after passage of this act, and where it shall hereafter be made within the same period after the date of such settlement, make the proof, affidavit, and payment herein required.

"*Approved Sept. 4th.*, 1841."

In 1854, further provision respecting preëmptions was made by the act providing for the graduation in the price of the public lands. The first section provides, in substance, that the lands which have been in market ten years shall be subject to entry at one dollar per acre; fifteen years, at seventy-five cents per acre: falling in price twenty-five cents on an acre every five years, until the lands shall have fallen to twelve and one-half cents per acre.

The second section provides, "That upon every reduction in price, under the provisions of this act, the occupant and settler upon the lands shall have the right of preëmption, at such graduated price, upon the same terms, conditions, restrictions, and limitations, upon which the public lands of the United States are now subject to the right of preëmption, until within thirty days preceding the next graduation or reduction that shall take place; and if not so purchased, shall again be subject to the right of preëmption for eleven months, as before:" and so on, from time to time, as reductions shall take place.

The oath and proof required by this act are similar to the Act of 1841, and are to be made before the register and receiver, who are entitled to a fee of fifty cents each for their services.

The provisions of the preëmption laws are all very well so far as they go; but another step will undoubtedly be taken, and the hardy settler, battling with privation and toil, remote from civilization, redeeming the wilderness, and peopling the waste, will be rewarded, under suitable restrictions, with the fee of one hundred and sixty acres of land for his pains.

From the survey which has been taken of the states and territories of the Great West, it is evident, that the seat of empire on the continent of North America is being removed to the regions around the lakes and upon the upper tributaries of the Mississippi. The people inhabiting these are profoundly interested in the continuance, the peace, and the prosperity of the whole Union. They grasp the east by means of the lakes; they grasp the south by means of the Mississippi. The people of the West will not dissolve the Union themselves; and they will not permit any body else to do it. Their watchword is "Liberty and union, now and forever, one and inseparable!"

TABLE OF DISTANCES

VIÂ THE

PRINCIPAL THOROUGHFARES TO THE GREAT WEST.

From Boston to New York.

Place	Miles
Boston to	
Worcester	44
Clappville	53
Charlton	57
Spencer	62
East Brookfield	64
Brookfield	67
West Brookfield	69
Warren	73
Brimfield	
Palmer	83
Indian Orchard	92
Springfield	98
West Springfield	100
Westfield	108
Russell	116
Huntington	119
Chester Factory	126
Middlefield	
Becket	135
Washington	138
Hinsdale	143
Dalton	146
Pittsfield	151
Shaker Village	154
Richmond	159
State Line	162
Canaan	167
East Chatham	172
Chatham Four-Corners	177
Chatham Center	181
Kinderhook	184
Schodack	192
Greenbush	199
Albany	200
New York	344

New York to Albany.

Place	Miles
New York, Chambers street, to	
Thirty-first street	3
Manhattan	8
Yonkers	17
Hastings	21
Dobbs Ferry	22
Irvington	25
Tarrytown	27
Sing Sing	32
Crugers	36
Peekskill	43
Garrison's	51
Cold Spring	54
Fishkill	60
New Hamburg	66
Poughkeepsie	75
Hyde Park	81
Staatsburg	85
Rhinebeck	91
Barrytown	
Tivoli	100
Germantown	105
Oak Hill	110
Hudson	116
Stockport	120
Coxsackie	123
Stuyvesant	126
Schodack	133
Castleton	136
East Albany	144

Albany to Buffalo.

Place	Miles
Albany to	
Troy	
Schenectady	17
Hoffman's	26
Crane's Village	30
Amsterdam	33
Tribe's Hill	39
Fonda	44
Yost's	49
Spraker's	52
Palatine Bridge	55
Port Plain	58
St. Johnsville	64
Little Falls	74
Herkimer	81
Ilion	83
Frankfort	86
Utica	95
Whitesboro'	99
Oriskany	102
Rome	109
Green's Corners	114
Verona	118
Oneida	122
Wampsville	125
Canastota	127
Canasaraga	131
Chittenango	133
Kirkville	137
Manlius	140
Syracuse	148
Warner's	157
Canton	159
Jordan	165
Weedsport	169
Port Byron	172
Savannah	179
Clyde	186
Lyons	193
Newark	198
Palmyra	206
Macedon	210
Fairport	219
Rochester	229
Cold Water	235
Chili	239
Churchville	244
Bergen	247
West Bergen	251
Byron	254
Batavia	261
Croft's	268
Pembroke	272
Alden	277

Wende 279
Town Line 282
Lancaster 287
Forks 289
Buffalo 298

Rochester to Suspension Bridge.

Rochester to
Gates 5
Spencerport 10
Adam's Basin 12
Brockport 17
Holley 22
Murray 25
Albion 30
Medina 40
Middleport 45
Gasport 51
Lockport 56
Pekin 66
Suspension Bridge 74
Connects with Great Western Railway.

Buffalo to Suspension Bridge.

Buffalo to
Black Rock 4
Tonawanda 11
La Salle 17
Niagara Falls 22
Suspension Bridge 24

New York to Dunkirk, viâ New York and Erie R. R.

New York to
Jersey City 1
Bergen 3
Hackensack Bridge 7
Boiling Spring 9
Passaic Bridge 12
Huyler's 13
Paterson 17
Godwinville 22
Hohokus 24
Allendale 26
Ramsey's 28
Suffern's 33
Ramapo 34
Sloatsburg 36
Southfields 43
Greenwood 45
Turner's 48
Monroe 50
Oxford 53
Junction 55
Chester 56
Goshen 60
Hampton 64
Middletown 68
Howell's 72
Otisville 76
Port Jervis 89
Shohola 108
Lackawaxen 112
Mast Hope 117
Narrowsburg 123
Cochecton 132
Callicoon 137
Hankin's 144
Lordville 154
Stockport 160
Hancock 165
Hale's Eddy 173
Deposit 178
Susquehanna 193
Great Bend 201
Kirkwood 207
Binghamton 216
Union 224
Campville 231
Owego 238
Tioga 243
Smithboro' 247
Barton 250
Waverly 257
Chemung 261
Wellsburg 267
Elmira 274
Junction Elmira, Canandaigua, and Niagara Falls Railroad 278
Big Flats 284
Corning 292
Painted Post 293
Addison 303
Rathboneville 308
Cameron 315
Crosbyville 324
Canisteo 329
Hornelsville 333
[See table from Hornelsville to Buffalo.]
Almond 338
Alfred 342
Andover 350
Genesee 359
Scio 363
Phillipsville 367
Belvidere 370
Friendship 375
Cuba 384
Hinsdale 390
Olean 396
Allegany 399
Great Valley 412
Little Valley 222
Cattaraugus 429
Dayton 439
Perrysburg 442
Smith's Mills 449
Forestville 452
Dunkirk 461

Hornelsville to Buffalo.

Hornelsville to
Burns 9
Whitney Valley 13
Swainville 17
Nunda 24
Portage 30
Castile 34
Gainesville 37
Warsaw 44
Middlebury 49
Linden 53
Attica 60
Darien City 64
Darien Center 66
Alden 71
Town Line 76
Lancaster 81
Buffalo 91

Philadelphia to Williamsport.

Philadelphia to
Port Clinton 78
Ringgold 88
Tamaqua 98
Summit 110
Mahanoy 118
Ringtown 123
Beaver 130
Maineville 138
Catawissa 146
Rupert 147
Danville 154
Mooresburg 160
Milton 170
Muncy 187
Williamsport 197

Williamsport to Elmira.

Williamsport to
McKinney's 5
Mahaffey's 7
Cogan Valley 8
Crescent 11
Trout Run 15
Field's 16
Dubois 19
Bodine's 20
Lycoming 22
Ralston 25
Canton 39
Alba 44
West Granville 48
Troy 52
Columbia Road 57
Dunning's 65
State Line 68
Elmira 78

Elmira to Suspension Bridge.

Elmira to
Junction 4
Horseheads 6
Millport 13
Havana 19
Jefferson 22
Rock Stream 28
Big Stream 30

Station	Miles
Starkey	33
Himrod's	37
Milo Center	41
Penn Yan	45
Benton	49
Bellona	51
Hall's Corners	55
Gorham	58
Hopewell	63
Canandaigua	69
East Bloomfield	77
West Bloomfield	85
Honeoye Falls	88
Genesee Valley Railroad Junction	95
Caledonia	102
Leroy	109
Stafford	113
Batavia	119
East Pembroke	125
Richville	132
Akron	135
Clarence Center	142
Transit	146
Vincent	152
Tonawanda	155
Cayuga Creek	161
Niagara Falls	166
Suspension Bridge	168

Suspension Bridge to Detroit, viâ Great Western Railway.

Suspension Bridge to

Station	Miles
Thorold	9
St. Catherines	11
Jordan	17
Beamsville	22
Grimsby	27
Ontario	32
Hamilton	43
Dundas	48
Flamboro'	52
Copetown	55
Vansickles	59
Fairchild's Creek	62
Paris	72
Princeton	79
Eastwood	86
Woodstock	91
Beachville	96
Ingersoll	100
Edwardsburg	110
London	119
Komoka	129
Mount Brydges	134
Ekfrid	139
Mosa	149
Wardsville	155
Thamesville	168
Chatham	183
Baptiste Creek	196
Rochester	210
Puce	216
Windsor	229
Detroit	230

Buffalo to Chicago, viâ Lake Shore Railroad.

Buffalo to

Station	Miles
Hamburg	10
Evans' Center	21
Irving	29
Dunkirk	40
Portland	50
Westfield	57
Quincy	65
State Line	68
North East	73
Harbor Creek	80
Erie	88
Swanville	95
Girard	103
Springfield	108
Conneaut	115
Kingsville	123
Ashtabula	129
Saybrook	133
Geneva	138
Madison	143
Perry	148
Painesville	152
Mentor	158
Willoughby	162
Wickliffe	167
Euclid	171
Cleveland	181
Rockport	187
Berea	193
Olmsted Falls	195
Ridgeville	200
Elyria	206
Amherst	212
Brownhelm	215
Vermillion	119
Berlin	227
Huron	231
Sandusky	241
Venice	244
Mixer's Point	248
Port Clinton	254
Hartford	265
Benton	271
Clay Junction	280
Toledo	288
Chicago	531

Buffalo to Chicago, via Michigan Southern Railroad.

Steamers leave Buffalo for Toledo every evening, except Sundays.

Toledo to

Station	Miles
Air Line Junction	3
Sylvania	11
Knight's	21
Blissfield	23
Palmyra	27
Adrian	33
Clayton	44
Hudson	50
Pitsford	56
Hillsdale	66
Jonesville	70
Quincy	82
Coldwater	88
Bronson	99
Burr Oak	106
Sturgis	112
White Pigeon	124
Middlebury	129
Bristol	134
Elkhart	144
Mishawaka	154
South Bend	158
Terre Coupee	169
Rolling Prairie	178
Laporte	185
Holmesville	193
Calumet	202
Bailytown	207
Miller's	214
Pine Station	221
Ainsworth	231
Junction	236
Chicago	243

Buffalo to Chicago, viâ Michigan Central Railroad.

Steamers leave Buffalo for Detroit every evening except Sundays.

Detroit to

Station	Miles
Halfway Side Track	....
Dearborn	10
Wayne	18
Ypsilanti	30
Ann Arbor	37
Dexter	47
Chelsea	54
Grass Lake	65
Jackson	75
Parma	86
Albion	95
Marengo	101
Marshall	107
Ceresco	112
Battle Creek	120
Galesburg	134
Kalamazoo	143
Oshtemo	148
Paw Paw	159
Decatur	167
Dowagiac	178
Niles	191
Buchanan	196
Terre Coupee	202
New Buffalo	218
Michigan City	228
Porter	240
Lake Station	248
Gibson's	260
Calumet	269

Station	Miles
Five Mile Side Track	
Chicago	282

Philadelphia to Pittsburg.

Philadelphia to	
Downing	32
Lancaster	68
Dillerville	70
Landisville Station	77
Mount Joy	81
Elizabethtown	87
Conewago	90
Branch Intersection	95
Middletown	96
Highspire	100
Harrisburg	106
Rockville Station	111
Cove	116
Duncannon	120
Aqueduct Station	123
Baily's	128
Newport	133
Millerstown	138
Thompsontown	143
Tuscarora	148
Mifflin	154
Narrows Station	161
Lewistown	166
Anderson's Station	173
McVeyton	178
Manayunk Station	183
North Hamilton	188
Mount Union	191
Mill Creek	197
Huntingdon	202
Petersburg	208
Spruce Creek	214
Tyrone	221
Fostoria	227
Altoona	236
Kittanning Point	242
East End of Tunnel	247
Gallitzin	249
Cresson	252
Lilly's	255
Portage	260
Willmore	262
Summerhill	264
South Fork	268
Mineral Point	270
Conemaugh	273
Johnstown	275
Dornock Point	278
Slackwater Station	281
Nineveh	285
New Florence	289
Lockport	293
Bolivar	295
Blairsville Branch	300
Hillside	304
Derry	307
Latrobe	312
Beaty's	315
Greensburg	322
Radebaugh's	324
Manor	329
Irwin's	331
Stewart's	336
Brinton's	341
Wilkinsburg	346
East Liberty	348
Outer Station	352
Pittsburg	353

Pittsburg to Fort Wayne.

Pittsburg to	
Courtney's	6
Haysville	10
Sewickley	12
Shousetown	14
Economy	17
Remington	21
Freedom	23
Rochester	25
New Brighton	28
Darlington	38
Enon	44
Palestine	49
Bull Creek	54
Columbiana	59
Franklin	65
Salem	69
Damascus	74
Smithfield	77
Alliance	82
Strasburg	88
Louisville	94
Canton	100
Massillon	108
Lawrence	115
Fairview	119
Orrville	123
Paradise	126
Wooster	134
Millbrook	140
Clinton	143
Lakeville	149
Loudonville	155
Perrysville	160
Lucas	167
Mansfield	174
Spring Mills	179
Richland	183
Crestline	187
Leesville	190
Bucyrus	199
Nevada	207
Upper Sandusky	216
Kirby	222
Forest	228
Dunkirk	234
Mount Washington	238
Johnstown	245
Lafayette	252
Lima	259
Elida	266
Delphos	273
Middle Point	279
Van Wert	286
Dixon	299
Maples	308
Fort Wayne	318

Fort Wayne to Chicago.

Fort Wayne to	
Taw-Taw	8
Coesse	14
Columbia	20
Huntsville	27
Pierceton	30
Wooster	33
Warsaw	40
Etna Green	50
Bourbon	53
Plymouth	65
Cross New Albany and Salem Railroad	95
Valparaiso	104
Hobart	117
Cross Joliet Cut-Off Railroad	120
Illinois Line	134
Chicago	147

Cleveland to Cincinnati.

Cleveland to	
Rockport	7
Berea	12
Olmstead	15
Columbia	18
Grafton	25
La Grange	29
Wellington	36
Rochester	41
New London	47
Greenwich	54
Salem	60
Shelby	67
Crestline	75
Galion	79
Iberia	85
Gilead	92
Cardington	97
Ashley	104
Eden	108
Delaware	112
Berlin	115
Orange	119
Worthinton	126
Columbus	135
Cincinnati	255

Cincinnati to Vincennes.

Cincinnati to	
Sylvania	3
Anderson's Ferry	6
Delhi	10
North Bend	15
Pike	17
Gravel Pit	18
Corn-Crib Switch	21
Junction	22
Lawrenceburg	22
Turnout	23
Aurora	25

Place	Miles
Cochran	27
Dillsborough	33
Moore's Hill	40
Milan	42
Pierceville	45
Delaware	47
Laughery Creek	49
Osgood	52
Poston	56
Holton	58
Otter Creek	61
Turnout	63
Butlerville	66
North Vernon	73
Hardenberg	80
Seymour	88

Vincennes to St. Louis.

Take steamers for all ports on the Mississippi and Missouri Rivers.

Vincennes to	
Lawrenceville	9
Sumner	19
Claremont	25
Olney	31
Noble	39
Maysville	46
Flora	53
Xenia	62
Middleton	70
Salem	79
Junction	85
Sandoval	88
Collins'	96
Carlyle	10[illegible]
Shoal Creek	110
Aviston	114
Trenton	118
Summerfield	122
Lebanon	125
O'Fallon	133
Caseyville	139
Ilinoistown	147
St. Louis	

Cleveland to Indianapolis.

Cleveland to	
Crestline	75
Galion	79
Caledonia	90
Marion	99
Bryant's	104
Larue	113
Mount Victory	121
Ridgway	124
Rushsylvania	130
Harper	133
Bellefontaine	139
De Graff	149
Pemberton	155
Sidney	162
Hardin	167
Lor. and Houston	172
Versailles	180
Dallas	188
Union	197
Harrisville	201
Winchester	207
Farmland	214
Smithfield	221
Muncie	227
Yorktown	233
Chesterfield	239
Anderson	245
Pendleton	253
Alfont	258
Fortville	261
McCord's	264
Oakland	266
Laneville	271
Delzell's	275
Indianapolis	280

Indianapolis to Terre Haute.

Indianapolis to	
Bridgeport	9
Plainfield	14
Cartersburg	17
Belleville	19
Clayton	21
Pecksburg	23
Amo	25
Cincinnatus	27
Coatsville	29
Nicholsonville	33
Greencastle	39
Putnamville	42
Hamerick's	44
Reel's Mill	48
Eaglefield's Mill	51
Croy's Creek	52
Brazil	57
Staunton	61
Cloverland	63
Wood's Mill	65
Terre Haute	73

Terre Haute to Alton, on the Mississippi, at the junction of the Missouri.

Terre Haute to	
St. Mary's	4
Sanford's	8
Paris	19
Grandview	28
Midway	32
Ashmore	37
Charleston	46
Mattoon	56
Summit	62
Windsor	68
Thornton	78
Shelbyville	80
Towerhill	88
Pana	95
Nocomis	107
Irving	117
Hillsborough	123
Litchfield	134
Clyde	139
Gillespie	144
Bunker Hill	153
Dorsey's	158
Bethalto	163
Alton	163
Junction	167
Illinoistown	187
St. Louis	

Chicago to St. Louis.

Chicago to	
Joliet	40
Elwood	49
Wilmington	56
Stewart's Grove	63
Gardner	68
Dwight	77
Odell	85
Livingston	90
Pontiac	95
Rook Creek	100
Peoria Junction	106
Lexington	113
Towanda	121
Illinois Central Railroad Junction	127
Bloomington	129
Funk's Grove	140
Atlanta	149
Lawn Dale	151
Lincoln	160
Elkhart	170
Williamsville	176
Sangamon	183
Springfield	188
Great Western Railroad Junction	190
Chatham	197
Auburn	203
Virden	210
Girard	214
Prairie Station	218
Carlinville	226
Macoupin	233
[illegible]ipman	241
Brighton	248
Monticello	255
Alton	280
St. Louis	285

Chicago to Burlington.

Chicago to	
Park Station	
Oak Ridge	8
Babcock's Grove	20
Danby	23
Wheaton's	15
Winfield	28
Junction	30
Batavia	36
Aurora	43
West Aurora	44
Montgomery	45

Oswego 47
Bristol 51
Plano 57
Newark 61
Somonauk 64
Waverly 71
Earl 77
Mendota 88
Arlington 97
Dover 104
Princeton 109
Wyanet 116
Buda 122
Neponset 128
Kewanee 136
Galvy 144
Altona 152
Wataga 160
Galesburg 168
Cameron 177
Monmouth 184
Linden 191
Oquawka Junction 202
East Burlington 210

Chicago to Madison.

Chicago to
Park Station
Oak Ridge 8
Cottage Hill 16
Babcock's Grove 20
Danby 22
Wheaton 25
Winfield 27
Aurora Junction 30
Wayne 35
Clinton 39
Elgin 42
Gilbert 50
Huntley 55
Union 62
Marengo 66
Garden Prairie 72
Belvidere 78
Caledonia 86
Roscoe 93
Beloit 98
Afton 106
Plymouth 111
Footville 114
Magnolia 118
Madison 156

Chicago to Milwaukie.

Chicago to
Chittenden 7
Evanston 12
Wynetka 16
Glencoe 19
Highland Park 23
Rockland 30
Waukegan 35
State Line 45
Kenosha 51
Racine 62
County Line 70
Oak Creek 75
Milwaukie 85

Milwaukie to Beaver Dam.

Milwaukie to
Schwartzburg 7
Granville 13
Germantown 18
Richfield 23
Cedar Creek 28
Schleisinger 30
Hartford 34
Rubicon 39
Woodland 43
Iron Ridge 45
Horicon 51
Junction 54
Oak Grove 56
Beaver Dam 61

Milwaukie to Madison.

Milwaukie to
Wauwautosa 5
Side Track 12
Junction 14
Forest House 17
Waukesha 20
Genesee 28
Eagle 36
Palmyra 42
Whitewater 50
Child's Station 55
Milton 62
Edgerton 72
Stoughton 82
Madison 98

Chicago to Fond du Lac.

Chicago to
Jefferson 9
Canfield 12
Des Plaines 16
Dunton 23
Palatine 27
Barrington 32
Cary 38
Crystal Lake 43
Ridgefield 45
Woodstock 51
Janesville 90
Fond du Lac 176

AMERICAN FRUIT CULTURIST,

WITH DIRECTIONS FOR

THE ORCHARD, NURSERY, AND GARDEN,

AND DESCRIPTIONS OF

AMERICAN AND FOREIGN VARIETIES.

BY J. J. THOMAS.

One Volume, 421 pp. 12mo., 300 Illustrations. Price 1 25.

NOTHING connected with practical agriculture is now attracting more attention than the cultivation of choice varieties of Fruit. Information of the best kinds, and how to obtain and successfully to cultivate them, is therefore sought by nearly every farm or lot owner. Hence, a complete, plain, and entirely reliable Fruit Book, has become a necessity to nearly every householder.

The author of THE AMERICAN FRUIT CULTURIST has been brought up in the Nursery business from boyhood, his father being a scientific and practical Nurseryman, and the author himself having had nearly fifty years experience as a practical Horticulturist, Nurseryman and Fruit Grower. Hence, his book is not a mere compilation of old ideas in a new dress, but is the result of a life experience in the Nursery, the Orchard, and the Garden, and is, therefore entirely worthy of the fullest confidence of the public.

The book undergoes periodic revisions, and is, therefore, always "up to the time."

NOTICES OF THE PRESS.

Among all the writers on fruits, we do not know of one who is Mr. Thomas' superior if his equal, in condensing important matter. Hence, we always look into his writings with the assurance that we shall find something new, or some improvements on the old; and we are seldom disappointed. This book is no exception. It is *full*. There is no vacant space in it. It is like a fresh egg—all good, and packed to the shell, full.—*Prairie Farmer.*

A cheaper, but equally valuable book with Downing's, was wanted by the great mass. Just such a work has Mr. Thomas given us. We consider it an invaluable addition to our agricultural libraries.—*Wool Grower.*

We can say with confidence to our readers, that if you need a book to instruct you in the modes of growing trees, &c., from the first start, the systems of pruning, etc., you will find the American Fruit Culturist an extremely valuable work.—*Cleve. Herald.*

MILLER, ORTON & MULLIGAN, *Publishers.*

Popular Biographies.

LIVES OF HENRY VIII. AND HIS SIX WIVES,
By H. W. HERBERT, 7 portraits, 441 pp. 12mo., ... $1 25

LIFE OF HENRY CLAY,
By HORACE GREELEY and EPES SARGEANT, steel portrait, 428 pp. 12mo., . 1 25

LIFE AND SPEECHES OF HENRY CLAY, being the above, to which is added his most able and popular Speeches, steel portrait, 633 pp. 8vo., . . 2 00

WEBSTER AND HIS MASTER-PIECES,
By B. F. TEFFT, D. D., LL. D., steel portrait, 2 vols., 1032 pp. 12mo., . . 2 50

LIFE OF GEO. WASHINGTON, by JARED SPARKS, LL. D., new and fine edition, steel portrait, 674 pp. 12mo., ... 1 25

LIFE OF WILLIAM H. SEWARD, with Selections from his Works, edited by GEO. E. BAKER, steel portrait, 410 pp. 12mo., ... 1 00

LIFE OF JOHN QUINCY ADAMS, by W. H. SEWARD, portrait, 404 pp. 12mo., 1 00

LIFE OF ANDREW JACKSON, by J. S. JENKINS, illustrated, 397 pp. 12mo., 1 00

LIFE OF WM. H. HARRISON, by H. MONTGOMERY, portrait, 465 pp. 12mo., 1 00

LIFE OF ZACHARY TAYLOR, by H. MONTGOMERY, illustrated, 463 pp. 8vo., 1 25

LIFE OF FRANKLIN PIERCE, by D. W. BARTLETT, portrait, 304 pp. 12mo., 75

LIFE OF BENJAMIN FRANKLIN, written by himself, with his Miscellaneous Essays, portrait, 375 pp. 12mo., ... 1 25

LIFE OF GEN. LAFAYETTE, by P. C. HEADLEY, portrait, 377 pp. 12mo., 1 25

LIFE OF LOUIS KOSSUTH, including Notices of the Men and Scenes of the Hungarian Revolution, and his Principal Speeches, by P. C. HEADLEY; with an Introduction by HORACE GREELEY; portrait, 461 pp. 12mo. . . 1 25

LIFE OF DANIEL BOONE, and the Hunters of Kentucky, by W. H. BOGART, illustrated, 464 pp. 12mo., ... 1 25

LIFE OF NAPOLEON BONAPARTE, LOCKHART, portrait, 392 pp. 12mo., 1 25

LIFE OF THE EMPRESS JOSEPHINE, P. C. HEADLEY, portrait, 383 pp., 1 25

LIFE OF MARY, QUEEN OF SCOTS, P. C. HEADLEY, portrait, 448 pp., 1 25

LIFE OF REV. A. JUDSON, by J. CLEMENT, portrait, 336 pp. 12mo., . 1 00

LIVES OF THE THREE MRS. JUDSONS, MRS. WILLSON, 2 portraits, 356 pp., 1 25

LIVES OF MARY AND MARTHA WASHINGTON, Mother and Wife of George Washington, by MARGARET C. CONKLING, portrait, 248 pp. 16mo., 75

LIFE OF LADY JANE GREY, by D. W. BARTLETT, portrait, 298 pp. 12mo. 75

LIFE OF JOAN OF ARC, by D. W. BARTLETT, portrait, 221 pp. 16mo., . 75

LIVES OF EMINENT METHODIST MINISTERS, containing Biographical Sketches, Incidents, Anecdotes, Records of Travel, &c., by Rev. P. DOUGLASS GORRIE, portraits, 408 pp. 12mo., ... 1 00

LIFE OF PATRICK HENRY, by S. G. ARNOLD, 270 pp. 16mo., . . 50

LIFE OF JOSEPH ADDISON, by LUCY AIKEN, 279 pp., 12mo., . . 50

☞ For sale by all Booksellers, or Single Copies sent by Mail, post paid, on receipt of price.

MILLER, ORTON & MULLIGAN, Publishers,

No. 25 Park Row, NEW YORK, and 107 Genesee-st., AUBURN

www.ingramcontent.com/pod-product-compliance
Lightning Source LLC
LaVergne TN
LVHW010144110826
845151LV00002B/419

* 9 7 8 1 4 2 5 5 3 8 3 2 3 *